CW00541684

*We Were Not Armed*

# PRAISE FOR
# We Were Not Armed

"The phrase 'folie a deux' describes the situation in which two people share a madness. 'We Were Not Armed' is the extraordinary account of a madness that takes hold, over a decade, of three generations of an entire family. Raw and undigested, Christine de Védrines' compelling account of how her family was destroyed by a confidence trickster is utterly gripping, disturbing and haunting. Time and again, I found myself thinking: is this a unique situation, one that could only have happened at this moment to these people, or is there something in all of us that is vulnerable, that means we too could succumb to this kind of madness?"

**Stephen Grosz,**
author of *The Examined Life*

# We Were Not Armed

## By Christine de Védrines

Translated by Angela Scholar

Appendix by Daniel Zagury

SKYSCRAPER

Published by Skyscraper Publications Limited
Talton Edge, Newbold on Stour,
Warwickshire CV37 8TR
www.skyscraperpublications.com

First published 2015

A CIP catalogue record for this book is available
from the British Library.

ISBN-13: 978-0-9926270-5-8

Designed and typeset by
Chandler Book Design

Printed in the United Kingdom by
Latitude Press Ltd

To the memory of my parents

To the memory of my cousin Bernard

To my husband and my children

To my family

To my husband's family

To Bobby, to our friends, and to those
friends of our children who have helped us
and still support us today

To our lawyers

*"Consider what your own part is in the disorder of which you complain."*

Sigmund Freud


*"…whose nature is so far from doing harms that he suspects none, on whose foolish honesty my practices ride easy."*

Edmund, in King Lear, Act 1, scene 2,
by William Shakespeare

# Contents

# Houses and People

## Houses:

Martel, château, home of Mamie and country home of Charles-Henri and Christine

Bordeneuve, country home of Ghislaine, 300m from Martel

Talade, close to Martel, home of Philippe

Fontenay-sous-Bois, location of Paris home of Ghislaine

Pyla, location of Christine's seaside apartment

Caudéran, location of the Bordeaux home of Charles-Henri and Christine de Védrines

## People

Guillemette ("Mamie") de Védrines, matriarch of de Védrines family

      Her daughter Anne, died 1997, married to Bertrand

      Her son Philippe de Védrines

            Brigitte, Philippe's partner

            Frédéric, Philippe's son

            Lucille, Philippe's daughter

Étienne, Philippe's son

Laurence, Philippe's daughter

Her daughter Ghislaine Marchand, née de Védrines

Jean Marchand, Ghislaine's husband

François, Ghislaine's son

Guillemette, Ghislaine's daughter

Her son Charles-Henri de Védrines, married
to Christine

Christine de Védrines, née de Cornette
de Laminière

Their son Guillaume

Their son Amaury

Their daughter Diane

Françoise, Christine's sister

Jean-Michel, Françoise's husband

Marie-Hélène Hessel, Christine's friend
since childhood

Thierry Tilly, conman

Maître Vincent David, mutual friend of Thierry
Tilly and Ghislaine

Jacques Gonzalez, co-conspirator with Tilly

Maître Picotin, lawyer specialising in victims of
cults and brainwashing

# Introduction

This afternoon, in the peace and quiet of the empty kitchen after the last-minute preparations that precede the lunchtime rush, I have reached my decision. I know the thought processes by which I have arrived here. The decisive moment was the conversation I had yesterday, with my boss Bobby – Robert Pouget de St-Victor. And now? It amazes me that after such a long time I should be taking an initiative on this scale and of this scope – and all alone too.

Charles-Henri meets me at the door. He accompanies me to work every morning and comes to collect me again at the end of the day. There are reasons for this. Affection is one. But this does not explain everything. We walk home together. In the busy streets of Oxford the lights are coming on in the pubs, students rush by on bicycles, in noisy groups. We pass several old half-timbered houses, then we go through a district of blocks of flats – pink, pale green, old and irregular, which soon give way to pretty little houses complete with tiny gardens, where bay windows project over perfectly tended lawns: the very image of the real world.

We make slow progress, because I limp badly, and my leg causes me pain. The passers-by we encounter pay no attention to this couple who walk with measured steps, and with a silent and somewhat detached air. They don't even glance at us. We're zombies. Each day we walk for almost an hour, going to and from work. We haven't enough money to take a bus, let alone run a car. Ninety percent of our pay is regularly taken from us.

Little blocks of flats have now replaced the houses, and there are hardly any more gardens. Early spring in England is not kind. On this particular evening a sharp wind lashes our faces, until in the Cowley Road we reach a decrepit concrete block of flats. We still have to climb the sixty steps of a steep and narrow staircase. After which, I will fling myself down on to the sofa. I will close my eyes. Exhaustion will overcome me, I will try to sleep. Charles-Henri will suggest we have a bite to eat, and will heat up a tin of soup.

But on this particular evening, exhausted though I am, nervousness and impatience rack my whole body. I don't know this yet, but it is a renewal of life that is coursing through my veins. I must say nothing to Charles-Henri; he must suspect nothing. We go to bed early, he falls asleep immediately, and I remain for hours in the dark, not moving, waiting for daylight. At one point, I get up and stuff into my bag all the papers I will need, all those I have been able to save. Proof. Evidence.

My story. Then I go back to bed, trembling for fear that he may have seen or even heard me. But no. He is asleep.

At six o'clock, I get up, take a shower and dress as quickly as possible. Nothing in my behaviour or appearance must be different from usual: I pull on my old jacket, my denim skirt, a sweater worn through at the elbows, my flat shoes, which could do with re-soling. In any case, I have nothing else to put on. We set out, Charles-Henri and I, repeating our walk of the previous evening, but in the opposite direction. He leaves me in front of Bobby's kitchen and goes off to his own work as a gardener.

I should like to behave as though everything really were just as it always is. I should like to begin cleaning and cutting up the organic vegetables, as I do every morning. But there is no question of that today. Bobby gives me my entire month's wages in cash. A car and a driver are waiting for me. Bobby embraces me, and wishes me luck. The car door slams shut. Throughout the whole journey to St. Pancras Station, I am incapable of uttering a single word; I am dumb with anxiety. The driver parks the car nearby, and we walk together towards the platform.

A mingled smell of hot fat, petrol and plastic fills my nostrils, and I am bathed in the white light that falls from the glass roof of the station. The smell and the light of my recovered freedom. I am oppressed by the crowds. My head spins, my blood throbs in my ears, my heart beats so fast that I can hardly breathe. But I go on. I walk towards the train, towards my cousin and my

best friend who are waiting for me. I walk towards my
true self, my life. I am ready for the fight. My name is
Christine de Védrines.

**Part One:** The spider spins her web

# 1

'Oh, of course! I knew all along he'd bring that woman!'

As I make my way across the lawn, these words meet me like a slap in the face. Charles-Henri, my husband, is a little way behind me, beside the car which he has just locked. Through the half-open French window I can see the silhouette of my sister-in-law Ghislaine – rigid, her arms folded – watching us without suspecting that I can both see and hear her. I am reminded immediately of her hostility towards me. Perhaps it has even increased with time. For some years now she has made no attempt to hide the antipathy she feels for me. But since childhood I have always known how to suppress my anger and resentment. I go into the drawing room smiling, as though nothing were the matter. There, seated on the sofa, my mother-in-law and Philippe, Charles-Henri's older brother, are waiting for us.

Ghislaine has converted Bordeneuve, an old farmhouse in Lot-et-Garonne, only three hundred metres

from Martel, our own country house, which is very close
to the fortified village of Monflanquin. She has restored
it with admirable good taste. The sitting room is vast, a
huge cathedral-like space, encircled by a mezzanine on to
which the bedrooms open. Martel itself was bequeathed
to Charles-Henri, the youngest of the family, according
to the express wish of his father, who died in 1995. It
is a property of fifty hectares, some of it farmland and
the rest wooded. My father-in-law, a practical man who
was anxious to keep the property in the family, gave it
to Charles-Henri because he knew that his youngest son
had the means to maintain it. It would be wrong to
conclude that this makes him the chief of the Védrines
tribe, which in fact is a matriarchy: Mamie, 89 years old,
is its reigning sovereign, and very close to Ghislaine, her
'minister'. Philippe, the eldest brother, and Charles-Henri,
the youngest, adore their mother, have infinite respect
for her and willingly submit to her iron rule. As for me,
the odd one out, I have done my best since my marriage
twenty-five years ago to be accepted, which, strange to
say, has become less and less easy, ever since the death of
my father-in-law, and then that of Anne, the oldest of the
family, in 1997.

What has brought us together late in this summer
of 2000 is a family matter. The affair is complicated:
some fifteen years ago, my mother-in-law and her sisters
sold Lacaze, a family house situated in the region. But
the purchaser, it seems, has discovered various recently
concealed faults in its construction, among them
problems with the water supply, and he is suing Mamie

and her sisters. Ghislaine immediately – and, as usual, very loudly – says a great deal, with the authority of a headmistress, which is what she is. Four years ago, the 'Femme Secrétaire', or the 'Femme Sec', as it is usually called, a secretarial college in Paris in the very chic seventh arrondissement, found itself in difficulties. The pupils' parents, of whom my sister-in-law was one – since her daughter Guillemette was studying there – got together with the aim of taking the college over and giving it a new direction. They appointed Ghislaine headmistress. She had not – perhaps – all the qualifications necessary for such a role, but she manages to execute her task admirably. Ghislaine is a paradoxical person. She has the reputation of having a strong personality. At a dinner party she readily takes over the direction of the conversation, which she cannot then let go. She imposes and disposes, especially where the family is concerned.

All the dreadful events that were to befall our family over the next ten years began with Ghislaine's introduction of a man called Thierry Tilly into our family circle. Jean Marchand, her husband, later said of her: 'Ghislaine has always had a truly natural authority, one that gave her power over her parents and her brother. I think it was this same power that allowed Tilly to infiltrate the rest of the family too. Annexing Ghislaine gave Tilly every opportunity to annex the others as well'. And yet, in spite of her dynamism and her ability to move mountains, Ghislaine often sees herself as a victim. She contrasts my comfortable existence in Bordeaux with her own: professionally exhausting, with two children to look after, and a husband she readily describes as unemployed, which is not entirely accurate. The problems she faces are never of her own making. There is always someone else around to blame. This is a weakness that Tilly knows from the very beginning how to exploit.

Not that things have been easy for my sister-in-law. First of all, she lost her fiancé. Next, she married and was then divorced, which caused her to have a nervous breakdown. She recovered and remarried, but she and her husband have been going through a difficult time recently, which explains her husband's absence that day. These disappointments following one upon another have embittered her. And the success of her little brother Charles-Henri, the united couple that he and I form, has perhaps exacerbated her sense of frustration. In addition to which, she greatly dislikes the idea that I may one day become mistress of Martel.

Martel is a small, eighteenth-century manor house, which a great-grandfather had restored in the style of Viollet-le-Duc, complete with turrets and pinnacles. It is not entirely to my taste, but, never mind, it's the family home and I like it there. It lies just outside Monflanquin, in the north of Lot-et-Garonne, less than two hours by car from Bordeaux. Monflanquin is a 'bastide', typical of south-west France, a sort of large village, of about two thousand inhabitants, perched on its own *pech* – its hill. In earlier times it had been fortified, and the Edict of Nantes had declared it a safe haven for Protestants, since we are here at the very heart of the Reformation in France. With the Revocation of the Edict, it lost its walls but kept the straight alleyways that climb up to a main square bordered by arcades and large houses of white stone. From the 'House of the Black Prince' you look out over an immense horizon of hills and fields. They call it the 'French Tuscany'. I can quite see why. I adore this region and especially Martel, with its woods and its fields, its lawns that surround the house and slope all the way down to the lake.

While my husband and his brother review the whole history of the sale of Lacaze from its beginnings, I go over in my mind recent summers spent at Martel. This annual family holiday means a great deal to me: I want my children to know their cousins, who don't live in Bordeaux. I want them to form friendships and family ties with one another. I want them to be close to the only grandmother that remains to them. I want them to create memories together. For a long time, while the children were growing up, Martel was a house filled with happiness. We were all of us reunited there; we organized endless impromptu parties; there was dancing, rushing around, and the sound of children laughing; there were bicycle rides in the surrounding countryside, bathing-parties, picnics, and lots of best friends. Childhood summers as they ought to be. Picture-book summers.

For me, by contrast, in spite of the good relations I managed to establish with Mamie, things became much more complicated once Charles-Henri had inherited the estate at Martel: not a day passed without my attracting sceptical remarks on the quality of the improvements I had introduced, my lack of taste, my poorly organized meals. But why, after all, should I complain? Criticism is common enough in families. And, recently, Ghislaine's character has hardened. She complains of the unpleasant atmosphere at school. People whisper behind her back. They try to catch her out. She feels constantly under threat. Her son François has even been attacked in the Metro. She takes it out on everyone except her mother.

And yet she is a dynamic woman, full of ideas, and with something of a magic touch. With her husband Jean, she has started a festival in Monflanquin called 'Music in Guyenne', which is proving very successful. It is attended by professionals and amateurs, who spend two weeks together, living in the neighbourhood and creating two works, which are then performed at Monflanquin, in local churches or large houses. It's charming. Responding to all this joyous activity, the village comes to life and resounds with orchestral rehearsals and singing.

The place is thronged. It is all Ghislaine's work, of which she is quite rightly very proud.

The problems with the water supply at Lacaze occupy us for quite some time that evening, and we find ourselves rather uncertain as to how to proceed. Philippe is a retired Shell senior executive, Charles-Henri a gynaecologist and obstetrician. None of us is a lawyer. There is a rule in both of our families: better a bad settlement than a good court case.

Ghislaine takes charge of the proceedings. She exchanges a brief glance with Philippe and Mamie, a glance I intercept and which astounds me: it is as though they are both of them aware of something we do not know. She goes on to say that she has in mind someone who might be able to help us. He is, it appears, a friend of M. Vincent David, himself a barrister with chambers in the Avenue Montaigne in Paris, and a colleague at the school: 'M. David introduced me to him when I had problems with the computers at the "Femme Sec", and he was amazingly competent! Besides, he has some quite highly-placed connections, and he's very intelligent…"

Philippe agrees: 'He's quite someone, he's been through Saint-Cyr' (the French military academy) 'and he's an official with the UN. I think he's been in the secret service, too, but he's very discreet about that. And besides he seems to know his way around the law. He owns several management companies…'

Mamie joins in too, adding: 'Yes, of course, what a good idea! He's extremely polite and very competent. I was struck by this when he came…'

Charles-Henri and I are a little startled: all three of them know him, he has been invited to Martel, but neither of us has ever heard any mention of him. He's discreet. That, we are to suppose, is the reason. Mamie and Philippe, still sitting side by side on a sofa, present a calm and composed front to any question we pose.

'Yes, he's very discreet', agrees Philippe. 'He's called Thierry Tilly. But I suspect that isn't his full name. He's from a very old family…'

In the view of the Védrines, a military man of good stock, well brought up, and recommended by a lawyer we are acquainted with, is amply qualified to undertake any problem of this sort. Ghislaine jumps to her feet, anxious to take charge again: 'I'll telephone him at once!' She lifts the receiver and dials his number from memory, a detail I note almost unconsciously: she must know him well, and telephone him often, if she knows his number by heart. Thierry Tilly answers at once, and Ghislaine hands the telephone to Charles-Henri, who explains the problem to him. The conversation continues for quite some time. My husband listens. I hear him repeat, several times: 'Ah, so you know all about that!… Yes, you've understood the situation perfectly… Very well, then? Good. Very good'. Charles-Henri replaces the receiver, apparently convinced that Tilly is the interlocutor we need, that he will intervene on our behalf at the highest level, and that there is nothing for us to worry about. He asks Tilly to ring back with any news, so we can be kept informed.

On the way home, I ask Charles-Henri what sort of impression this Tilly has made on him. He tells me the man is remarkably well-informed: he reminded Charles-Henri that, in 1995, the presence of his name on a list of supporters of Alain Juppé during the municipal elections in Bordeaux had provoked a certain hostility on the part of some of our neighbours. Since Juppé was, in any case, not electable, the affair had quickly subsided. Tilly has also told him that several people in the region are envious of the Védrines family, and that an attack of this sort (the threat, that is, of a court case over the Lacaze affair), although not serious in itself, is significant. We must be very careful. But he said nothing more specific, and Charles-Henri did not question him further: an omission that was to have consequences later. But, if this Tilly can help the Védrines family, why refuse? Charles-Henri, up to his eyes in work, has no desire to start running around lawyers' offices himself in order to get together some papers about an affair that clearly does not merit so much fuss.

I simply ask myself why Tilly should want to help us. He is a very busy man and has nothing to gain from such an involvement. Charles-Henri understood – or so he thought – that Tilly was in contact with networks of former members of the Resistance throughout Europe, thanks to the missions he undertakes for the UN. As it happens, during the war, while her husband was in a prisoner-of-war camp in Pomerania, my mother-in-law found herself alone at Martel with her two older children. Like everyone else, she practised self-sufficiency, living on the produce of the estate, and helping the local villagers whenever she could. She ran the household for her mother-in-law, her brother-in-law – with whom she did not get on – and her two young children. Her conduct during the war was in every respect admirable. And she won universal respect throughout the whole region.   Might she have participated, secretly, in the Resistance? She never spoke of it, but Charles-Henri reaches this conclusion from something Tilly has said, which corroborates a sibylline sentence that Mamie often repeats, recently, with a little smile: 'I will depart with my secrets!' Tilly himself, then, is perhaps responsible for helping and supporting these obscure and courageous heroes and heroines, when, later, they find themselves in difficulties.  This gratitude in high places for the courageous acts performed by his mother finds in Charles-Henri an echo that makes him prouder than ever of Mamie.  The love and respect he bears her are reinforced. He asks no further questions.  Besides, Philippe and Ghislaine, who were the first to make Tilly's acquaintance, seem very persuaded by him, which is yet another reason for him to feel reassured. We return to Bordeaux, our minds set at rest.

# 2

Charles-Henri and I met in 1969, outside the door of one of my friends whose birthday I was on my way to celebrate.  I remember finding myself face to face with a dark-haired young man with blue eyes, who was very amusing. I remember, too, entrusting to his arms and his care the cake I was carrying, so that I could ring the bell. We arrived together.

It was no *coup de foudre*, but rather a slow seduction. I was almost twenty. I had been going out for two years with a boy from whom, at that very moment, I was just beginning to distance myself a little. Meeting Charles-Henri precipitated the break. He was in his second year at medical school; I was in the faculty of arts. That evening, we talked a little, without anything further happening. Then we met again. We had friends in common and found plenty of opportunities for spending time together. We encountered each other at parties, then, gradually, we began to go to them together. He asked me to see a film with him, we discovered interests in common, such as lectures on travel or philosophy. Little by little I realized that I really liked him. He had a sense of humour, and at the same time he took his studies, his future, and life in general, very seriously. We were on the same wavelength.

Making a life for myself, being happy, these things inevitably implied marriage for me. I saw myself with a man both loving and loved, with children, and a profession. And, quite quickly, Charles-Henri began to appear to me as that very man, the future father of my children, the head of the family that was to be mine. His thoughts, meanwhile, were moving in the same direction. We had found one another.

The Védrines lived in Bordeaux, and owned an estate at Monflanquin. The father of the family, an agronomist, had been employed by the department of agriculture in Bordeaux, and had managed their land. Charles-Henri, the youngest of the family, had an older sister Anne, and a brother Philippe, both born before the war. Ghislaine and he were born afterwards, in 1946 and 1948. Their father liked to call the two older children 'the pre-war pair' and the two younger 'the post-war pair'.

Descended from an old line of Protestant country squires of Auvergnat origin, the Védrines had come to settle in the region more that four hundred years previously. I did not need to explain Charles-Henri's family to my parents. My mother and his had known each other ever since the time when my mother, much the younger of the two, had lived in Lot-et-Garonne; and both of them knew precisely who was who in the two families. Everything was just as it should be; we shared the same education, the same views, the same background. But when it became clear, after about eighteen months, that our relationship was really serious, the religious question became divisive: the Védrines were Protestants and we were Catholics. This greatly troubled my parents. They were neither bigots, nor fundamentalists, but practising Catholics, motivated by a single, firmly-held conviction: that one must marry within one's religion. Marriage is a difficult undertaking, and you don't agree on religion, this can cause all manner of problems. Especially when it comes to the education of the children.

At first, my mother was quite unhappy about the whole situation. The religious difference gave rise to interminable discussions; between my parents and me, but also between the two of them. For the first time ever, I saw them in serious disagreement: for, in spite of all she thought about Protestantism, Maman wanted me, above all else, to be happy; but father remained intransigent.

Fortunately, a cousin who was a priest and the principal of a large seminary in Bordeaux managed to smooth things over.

And the two families met. Our two mothers got on together very well. My father had more trouble with my future father-in-law. Not only were there religious differences between them, but their characters were almost wholly opposed. Protestants being in general more used to mixed marriages, this presented less of a problem to my parents-in-law than to my parents.

On the other hand, the religious education of any future children remained a thorny question. Conversations on the question with Charles-Henri became more and more turbulent, positions hardened, doors slammed. We got to the point of envisaging a separation, and so seriously, indeed, that we parted one spring, only to find one another again at the end of the following summer.

I remember this as a painful and difficult moment: for the first time ever, I was causing my parents real distress. But in opposing them I proved to them the strength of the love I felt for my fiancé. And it was this that, in the end, persuaded them to give in. Perhaps they could see, too, that we had given careful thought to our relationship: we intended marrying only after we had finished studying, and had begun to earn a little, so as not to be dependent on them. There was nothing to find fault with there. Taking all in all, they were happy with the marriage. Charles-Henri found his place very naturally in my family.

# 3

We were married in 1975, in the countryside in Lot-et-Garonne, at the home of my maternal grandmother, in a little Romanesque chapel on the edge of the estate. It was an ecumenical wedding, with a priest and a pastor. As was still the practice at that time, the Church asked me to sign a document undertaking to do everything in my power to bring up our children in the Catholic faith. What we did in fact, was to offer them both teachings, so that they could make their own choice later on.

Very conscious that Charles-Henri would remain a student much longer than I would, I did a diploma in archive studies so as to be able to earn a living wage as soon as possible. After our wedding, we moved into a little house we rented from my parents-in-law. Charles-Henri was a medical student at a teaching hospital, and I worked in the centre of Bordeaux. I was an archivist with the Institute for Business Administration, where I helped both students and university lecturers with their research there, work that I very much enjoyed.

I furnished our house with various items I was able to buy with money I had saved before my marriage. And we began a life as a young married couple who were, in effect, still students. Our life was not so very different from our previous one: we often saw friends, we went out together, spent weekends by the sea or in the country. In short, we were happy, carefree, and very busy.

Then, in order both to complete his training and to specialize in gynaecology and obstetrics, Charles-Henri decided to go to Tunisia. It was in 1977, the year in which our oldest son, Guillaume, was born. We spent two years there: four months in Bizerte, and then twenty months in Beja, in the grasslands of north-west Tunisia. I did not find this exile easy, especially at the beginning. Imagine how it felt to be a young woman of twenty-seven with a new-born baby, knowing almost nothing about the country, and having to set up house in a poorly-furnished apartment in the centre of a little town, and then left to her own devices all day long. Charles-Henri went off in the morning, and returned in the evening, tired-out. I met the families of other foreigners doing voluntary service – Germans, Poles, Czechs, Italians – most of whose wives worked. As I remember it, I felt lonely and alone for much of the time: I had no friends among the people of the country, apart from Sami, Charles-Henri's Tunisian boss, and Gaetane, his wife. And Beja's leisure and cultural facilities were non-existent.

But the positive side of all of this was that Charles-Henri was delighted with his work and got on very well with the team at the hospital. And he greatly liked and respected his boss, who had trained in one of the best universities in Paris.

But I had been used to an active social life, and I missed my friends and my family dreadfully. So I decided to turn this solitude to the advantage by reordering my priorities and by concentrating on my baby and my own intellectual and spiritual life. In this way I became less dependent on other people, and I took myself in hand. I reflected a good deal on my own position. I made friends with people who came from backgrounds very different from my own: Germans, Czechs, Poles, and members of the Italian community. The Italian women – each one a true Italian 'mamma' – were particularly warm and affectionate. They became fond of me, brought me little dishes, and gave me advice. The German women – extraordinarily good housewives – taught me how to look after my house. I also, little by little, formed friendships within the French community, friendships that have lasted, since we still see each other. Finally, I discovered the kindness of the Tunisians: towards the little baby that was Guillaume, but towards me too. I remember, going – as I did almost every day – to the market, passing one morning a little boutique that sold skirts. I liked the look of one of them, but there was nowhere to try it on. The shop-keeper said to me: 'I know you, you're the doctor's wife. Take the skirt home, try it on. If you like it, you can pay me tomorrow, if you don't, all you need do is to return it'. And that was all she asked of me. I liked this world where one could be generous and trusting towards a stranger. It struck a chord with me. I had never in my life encountered malice or wickedness. I couldn't even imagine such things. And the people I came across there were totally devoid of them. Better still, they encouraged me to adopt the same attitude. We had visitors too: Charles-Henri's parents came for a few days, as did my parents, and then my sister and her family.

Once we returned to Bordeaux, only too happy to rediscover my own little world, I never missed my time over there. Charles-Henri began to get work as a locum with better and more regular earnings, so that we were able to borrow enough money to buy a small house.

Amaury was born in 1980, and Diane in 1985. During that year, Charles-Henri decided to enter into a partnership with a colleague of whom he thought very well, a complex and likeable man. We were very enthusiastic about the project. Charles-Henri spent August in Bordeaux. Diane was not due to be born until September. So I went to Pyla on the Atlantic coast, where my parents owned an apartment on the waterfront. One evening – I remember that, at that very moment, I was watching the sunset – Charles-Henri telephoned me, distraught; the friend he was replacing during the holidays had just died, very suddenly. I returned to support him before going straight on to the clinic, where Diane arrived several weeks early: a moment of much-needed respite for Charles-Henri, who had the great joy of bringing his own daughter into the world.

I remember those days very well, when the happiness of having a girl after two boys was in stark contrast to the grief and despair of my husband, who was losing a friend and had to rebuild his professional future. Charles-Henri is not outgoing, but somewhat reserved, and his apparent authority disguises what is in reality a genuine shyness. During those days, perhaps for the first time ever, I thought he was even more fragile than he allowed himself to appear. The lost friendship and the abortive plan really hurt him, causing him such anguish that I wondered if my husband was capable of moving forward on his own in his professional life. Working closely with a friend was, for him, not simply a business arrangement, but had offered a life of close cooperation and mutual support. And he was not now going to have this. I was perhaps the only person to be aware of this weakness, since he was regarded by the outside world as a self-confident man who was well able to resist setbacks. I swore to myself that I would always be there, at his side.

In the end my husband found another colleague with whom to set up his practice. We no longer needed my salary, and I left my job as an archivist, on unpaid leave in order to devote myself to my children and my parents.

I do not like the word 'success' when it is applied to the material things of life. At the same time, it's true, we had arrived at a moment in our lives when everything had become easier. We bought an old and very pretty house of white stone with a garden, in Caudéran, a pleasant part of Bordeaux. It gave directly on to the park, the largest green space in the city. When we moved in, I was quite certain that we were entering what would always be our nest. It was to be the house where our children would grow up, and where our grandchildren would come. With this in mind, I arranged it all with great care. I wanted to create surroundings where everyone would be happy, where everyone would have his or her own little corner, and where we would enjoy coming together again every day. It was to be a house filled with happiness...

My parents came often. My mother was an exceptional person. She had had cancer in 1977, while we were in Tunisia, but, showing admirable courage, had won the fight. Although she was at the time still undergoing chemotherapy, she had not wanted to postpone her visit to us. So Charles-Henri had undertaken to administer her treatment. Our apartment, the climate, nothing was really right for her, exhausted as she was. But, she was only too happy to see Guillaume and to spend time with me, and showed us none of this. And her presence secured us a bright and joyful interlude during our time in Tunisia.

Her illness caught up with her soon after our move to Caudéran. I was thirty-eight years old. I adored my mother. She was an example to me. She had given me strength and energy, as well as love. Her death was the first real grief I had known, and a devastating blow. Nevertheless, I had had the happiness of seeing her with her grandchildren, in our new house, reassured about my own future. As for my father, who had never been expansive, he made no show of his grief. But what could have passed for indifference was nothing other than an insurmountable sorrow. Without my mother, he lost interest in everything, distancing himself ever further from life. I surrounded him with care and affection. I kept him as long as possible at home. He became ill and said to me then, several times, that he would rather go into a retirement home. I did not want this, but he insisted. We decided that he would go for a short time, a month at the most, to see how he liked it, and that we would decide afterwards. He went into a home that I had myself chosen, and which seemed to me entirely as it should be. He died several months later. He quite simply let himself die in order to rejoin my mother, two years after her own departure. At the age of forty-one, I felt myself, literally, orphaned. And so I reinforced my ties with my older sister, Françoise. The difference in age between us had sometimes given me the impression that she was taking over, as it were, the role of my mother. But now that we were able to speak more freely and I was able to confide in her without reservation, our mutual affection grew. We often spoke on the telephone. In the summer, she came to Pyla, or else we saw each other in Lot-et-Garonne where she owned a house.

My parents-in-law came to lunch with us every Sunday. I wanted them to see their grandchildren as often as possible. To my eyes, the extended family lay at the heart of all the affections, was a protection against all the misfortunes of life, and was a source of happiness. And this was especially so after the death of my parents. Perhaps I was naïve. I never considered, at the time, that the rest of my husband's family might resent this intimacy, which I had fostered with the best of intentions and in all innocence. No doubt my parents-in-law spoke too warmly of me. Ghislaine, during the Tilly episode, was to say to me: 'You stole my mother from me, Thierry gave her back to me'.

In 1992 my father-in-law gave the ownership of Martel to Charles-Henri, even though Philippe is the oldest of the family. From childhood onwards, Philippe had had a somewhat complicated relationship with his father, from whom he had been separated for three years, during the war, when his father was held in a prison-camp for officers in Pomerania. Given the family context, the gift of Martel disappointed him and caused him some bitterness. But, as it is not in his nature to harbour feelings of antagonism, he managed to overcome his resentment. And when he was able to buy Talade, an estate, very close to Martel, which the Védrines family had once owned, the affection he felt for this house soon dispelled all his earlier regrets.

But this was not so for everyone else. My husband and I were not really aware of any feelings of resentment, in the first place because the family was reunited only on special occasions and during the summer, and also because when Charles-Henri was there the atmosphere was different. When my father-in-law died in 1995, I of course supported my mother-in-law. When the opportunity presented itself, I took her with my friends to museums, the cinema, a conference. Delighted by all of this, she was always ready for another outing. And my friends liked her every bit as much as she did them. In the end, we often met at Martel, which she was legally entitled to use, because she preferred not to be there on her own.

After the death of my parents, I had made a point of getting involved in various activities, in order to forget my grief for a while, but also because I had inherited from my mother a taste for group contacts and group activities. Every Thursday, I had lunch with friends. I was a member of 'Bordeaux Accueille', an organization whose aim is to welcome new arrivals and introduce to them the town and its inhabitants. I was also a member of a book group – I adore reading – and I became very involved with my children's school, where I was the parent-representative for one of the classes. I was always rushing here and there, which was perhaps a mistake. Charles-Henri, too, for his part, found himself completely absorbed by his work as a gynaecologist and obstetrician. He practised in the largest clinic in Aquitaine, and his appointments diary was always overloaded. He had also taken on a role in the union. He left home at dawn and returned late in the evening. I was responsible for the day-to-day running of the house, and was often in sole charge of the upbringing of the children, since he could rarely take holidays with us. But we were a happy and a united couple; we understood one another. He relied on me for everything except his professional life, and I was very proud of his total confidence in me. In short, we were just like every other comfortably-off family, where the husband exercises his chosen profession by devoting himself to it and the wife is content to perform the tasks that fall to her lot. Classic, in a word, except for one small detail: were we not *too* preoccupied with our various interests and activities? Didn't we ignore opportunities for self-examination, for reflecting on what it was we really wanted to be? We never thought to ask ourselves questions about the family, about the latent disagreements within it, the dissensions that existed at its very core. They nevertheless loomed larger, every summer. But we didn't take the time...

# 4

Why would an overworked doctor from Bordeaux, up to his eyes in appointments and commitments, find time to pay a flying visit to Paris in order to spend two hours with a man, aged thirty-eight, about whom he knows next to nothing? It's a question worth asking, for so it was that a relationship was forged between Thierry Tilly and my husband, of such solidity that it lasted for nine years and almost destroyed us.

Towards the end of 2000, some months after their first contact over the Lacaze affair, Charles-Henri had had several telephone conversations with Tilly. Brief, but of such substance that, when required to do so, he jumped on to a TGV and made for the capital. At the Gare Montparnasse, a young man, slim, with small glasses, his demeanour extremely serious and sober, was waiting for him at the end of the platform. Tilly at once approached him, recognizing him, even though he had never seen him before. Could he have guessed that this man, not very tall and looking out for someone he doesn't know, is Charles-Henri de Védrines? Perhaps he remembered him from photographs he'd seen at Ghislaine's? They walked out together a little way on to the pavement in front of the station, exchanging the customary pleasantries, then went to warm up in one of the cafés that border the Place du 18-Juin.

Tilly sits down with his back to the light, opposite and facing Charles-Henri, whom he observes without him suspecting this. A relationship of equals is immediately established between them, Charles-Henri, fifty-two years old, and Tilly, thirty-eight. Tilly is discreet as to his own activities, but readily lets drop, in a roundabout way, names, places, and events in which he could have been involved, but always with an appropriate discretion, or at least one that he imposes on himself, giving it to be understood that he is not at liberty to say more. On the other hand, he seems to know a lot about Bordeaux, about what Charles-Henri has achieved in his work, and about how heavily his responsibilities weigh upon him. Charles-Henri responds to this, and reveals further aspects of his life, only too pleased to have an attentive audience. Their conversation soon takes a more personal turn. As is often the case between men of similar ability, status, and character, they speak the same language. But of what, exactly, do they speak? Of Charles-Henri's profession, of the everyday business of his practice, of his clientele, and of the difficulty of preserving a balance between one's family and one's professional life. Tilly, too, has known those moments when there is not enough time to watch your children growing up. He has two, of whom he sees rather little, not enough no doubt. 'We are all of us at the same point in our lives, when one has real responsibilities. Fortunately, there are our wives'. Charles-Henri has a wife too, who, as they say, provides.

This interlude in the café takes place in a bubble, outside space and time. Charles-Henri finds himself face to face with a man of whom he knows very little and who possesses a rare talent for listening. Without meaning to, and without, of course, realizing what is happening, my husband finds himself in a situation analogous to that of a patient who has come to consult a psychotherapist. One might think that the two situations have nothing in common. And yet, he unburdens himself easily enough. A good listener inspires confidence. Charles-Henri is not aware of this, and if anyone had suggested such a thing to him at the time, he would have shrugged his shoulders, or raised his eyes to heaven, perhaps, even, in exasperation.

In a subliminal way, and quite unconsciously, he reveals a comfortable way of life, holidays in Pyla, the large house in Bordeaux, and the guardianship of Martel – property and land he inherited from his father, and which is undergoing major modernization. They discuss the contentious sale of a house belonging to Mamie and her sister, and Ghislaine's problems. The other listens intently. And then he asks one question in particular – but is it a question? Or an observation, rather, one that might contain hints of a plot, or just of feelings of envy, of jealousy, of aggression even, on the part of certain people, which a family like the Védrines – comfortably-off, long-established, respected – might provoke.

By the time they part company, has Charles-Henri the feeling that he has acquired a friend, a protector, even? In the train that takes him back to Bordeaux, he goes over again, in his mind, Tilly's troubling words.

Historically speaking, there lies in the innermost depths of every Protestant – intact, and ready to reassert itself – the feeling of having to resist, to make a stand, the result of so many persecutions suffered long ago, so many wars waged, so many battles lost and won. And, after all, it was only some twenty years ago that Charles-Henri had had to fight to be able to marry the woman he loved. And then, there is another thing, more subtle still. His father liked to say, as he himself will later, that they are countrymen, that what is dearest to their hearts are the fields, the woods, and the stones of Martel, the gently undulating hills and pastures one glimpses from the windows, the smell of humus and of hay that, in the early morning, one breathes in. And for these things, too, they would fight to the end, as did their forebears. They have always had the feeling of belonging to a distinct and proud minority, of aristocratic, Protestant landowners. The Védrines, then, are not just a family but a clan, perhaps? You would not think so when we are in Bordeaux. But at Martel, yes. What I, his wife, would call 'the besieged citadel syndrome', my husband, is sometimes affected by. And all that is needed is for a stranger to reawaken it with sufficient skill for it to come to life all over again. Seen from that angle, Tilly proves himself to be very effective.

He is still at that moment an enigma, but this mystery itself represents a subtle form of seduction that my husband does not properly recognize. Charles-Henri looks after bodies, helps to bring new life into the world; but he does not ask himself often enough about the souls and the psychology of his family. He doesn't have time for this, it is not part of his work, nor of his way of thinking.

On his return home, that same evening, Charles-Henri tells me about his meeting with Tilly, a sensitive and lively person, apparently, and possessed of great charisma and intelligence. He mentions, too, Tilly's belief that our family is the object of some ill-defined attack, which we must confront. But that, thanks to him, we are no longer alone in our misfortune.

Then Charles-Henri introduces another subject, broached, so it seems, during the course of this first conversation: our financial investments. He suggests that I check what my adviser is doing, since the information available to Tilly indicates that we could very greatly increase the value of our capital. And it's true that I manage our affairs 'like a good family man', investing, for the most part, in life assurances and Treasury bonds. But, suddenly, I am amazed that a conversation that was supposed to be devoted solely to the best way of defending the interests of the Védrines family should have been diverted into the handling of our money, and of mine in particular. But Charles-Henri has something else in mind: how good are our advisers?

'Do you still trust them?' he asks me. 'You're never in any doubt about them?'

I remember that evening. We are in our bedroom. I had furnished it so that it would be as cosy as possible. I had bought two bedside lamps that give out a light strong enough to read by in bed and at the same time soft enough to create an atmosphere of serenity and repose. I like what I have done with this room, which is the image, it seems to me, of peace and tranquillity. But, at that precise moment, I have the fleeting impression that Charles-Henri is opening a window on to chaos. This lasts for no more than a second, but the unease it creates is to remain, hidden deep in my memory. Even now, more than ten years later, I find it there, intact, as I write these lines.

Confronted with what Tilly is suggesting, I react as anyone would: before taking any decision whatsoever, should we not find out more about him? My husband has political connections in Bordeaux, it would be easy enough to make a telephone call to one of them. And we could certainly get some advice from police intelligence sources. But Charles-Henri isn't taking in what I say. He does not oppose me, nor does he demand that I act in this way or in that. He simply says that yes, we could take some advice if that would reassure or please me, but leaves the question unresolved. Perhaps, simply, because it is late, he is tired, and a very full day awaits him early tomorrow morning. Perhaps he is persuaded, too, that I have decided to comply. I don't know. There will never again be any question of our seeking information about Tilly. I could have done it myself, but I let it go. Perhaps it was because I wanted Charles-Henri to take charge of the matter. Given that it was he who had been the instigator of this whole affair, it was his decision and not mine.

Life went on as before. I was busy with the children, with my work, and my various activities, Charles-Henri with his patients, with meetings of the doctors' union, and with his friends...

Then, two weeks later, Charles-Henri once again met Thierry Tilly, under the same circumstances as before, in Paris. But on this occasion, Mamie's problems were set aside in favour of the question of my investments.

Apparently, the sources of information available to my husband's new friend had reported back to him, to the effect that my investments were not secure, and that my adviser – who had looked after them, in my parents' bank, for years – was not, perhaps, as competent as I believed him to be. Nothing was put as clearly as this, it was simply implied...

That same evening, Charles-Henri had dinner with his sister at her house in Fontenay-sous-Bois, a suburb of Paris. The whole conversation turned, of course, upon that afternoon's meeting. Ghislaine got straight to the point, making a great deal of what Tilly had done during the past two years. At the very moment when the Femme Sec was performing really badly, Thierry had intervened and had helped her. And in a way, she went on, that was almost comical. He ran, at the time, a cleaning company, and it was in this way that, introduced by Maître Vincent David, he had come into Ghislaine's life. During the summer, his company had renewed and redecorated everything, which had been a real *coup* for the Femme Sec. And then, since he knew a great deal about information technology, he had helped her to install and to re-equip the whole place with computers, and at a conclusively competitive price too. Since when, indisputably, everything had gone much better at the school; so much better, indeed, that she had taken him on, and he was now her deputy. She could entrust him with any problem, however intractable, and he would deal with it. There were no two ways about it; he had become indispensable.

Charles-Henri, in general, believes what he hears. And so he is not at all surprised that an agent of the secret service – one who, moreover, whether former or not, is entrusted with missions for the UN, and is a director of several companies – should be ready to take orders from his sister. And to devote to her a significant part of his precious time. Even if this amounts to nothing more than lending a brief helping hand to a friend in the midst of his multiple responsibilities!

'Besides', Ghislaine says, 'Thierry is so intelligent, so intuitive, so receptive! I've known him for ten years'. She has no qualms about asking his advice on anything at all. They speak every day, and have lunch together several times a week. She has told him all about her family, of course, and its history, has described her brothers, her sister, who has since died of a brain tumour, and has spoken, above all, of Charles-Henri, of his professional success and of his wife, so immensely 'refined'... She has even told him how Charles-Henri and I met, about our time in Tunisia, the death of his friend and associate, the house in Cau,déran, and the apartment in Pyla. She has spoken of my family, too, of my grandfather, who was an industrialist. She has invited him to Lot-et-Garonne, and introduced him to Philippe and Mamie, who took to him at once. Their closeness might make one suspect a tawdry affair, but not a bit of it. He has introduced her to his wife Jessica, delightful and very elegant, and to her daughter Natacha.

According to Ghislaine, Tilly has the answer to every problem; and, above all, an extraordinary degree of trust has grown up between them. 'You'll see', she says, 'if you place your trust in him, he will repay it a hundred-fold! If you take the first nine steps, he will take the tenth'. Charles-Henri is already convinced. He prides himself on being a sound judge of people, and quick in weighing up any situation – a very necessary talent in a good obstetrician – and he has, besides, the sense that there is a very positive charge between himself and Tilly.

As the exercise of his profession demands, and as his character demonstrates, he is prudent and pragmatic. In spite of which, when it comes to this particular relationship, he invests more and more of himself in it, and does not notice the asymmetry that, thanks to Thierry Tilly's talent as a chameleon, this creates between them.

The next day, on his return to Bordeaux, he immediately raises with me the question of our investments. This time, it is the enthusiastic, spontaneous and somewhat naïve Charles-Henri who arrives home from Paris. He tries to persuade me that we should abandon the family financial adviser we have inherited. Only Tilly and his company, Presswell, can offer our property the protection it needs.

He is persuasive, seeming to have no doubts himself on the matter. As for me, I remain sceptical. I try to persuade him to think it over. I tell him we must take advice about this person and his company. He still won't listen to me, and even today, he has difficulty in remembering the warning noises I made.

The conversation becomes a little heated, but discreetly so, for we are not used to violent confrontations.

However a certain slight tension persists between us and gives rise the next day to a degree of distress, which our children more or less notice, without appearing to do so.

During subsequent weekends at Martel, the Védrines family, too, joins in the discussion, each of them in his or her own way, each of them both persuaded and persuasive, without listening to or hearing what any of the others are saying.

The idealized portrait of Thierry Tilly that Ghislaine and her son François always paint confirms Mamie, Charles-Henri, Philippe and his partner, Brigitte, in their favourable opinion of him. I try to introduce some rather more nuanced views on the matter, which no one listens to or wishes to hear… I feel myself isolated in the face of this firm family alliance, which, without excluding me, does not wholly accept me. Mamie has allowed herself to become totally infatuated with Tilly. She has lost all critical sense, worse still, she has elevated him, conferring upon him her own role as head of the family. We are caught in a trap, ensnared…

From that moment on, the daily exchanges between the absent Tilly and Ghislaine, his deputy, determine our everyday life. In the face of my sister-in-law's romantic and somewhat paranoid flights of fancy, which can become contagious, I try to keep my distance. Nevertheless, cut off from all my friends and my close family, I end up by giving in, so as not to make the situation even more difficult.

Confronted by a situation so extraordinary and so unlike anything I have ever known, I crack. And I agree to everything, to the point of not even asking my bank what it knows of a company called Presswell, in whose favour I sign cheques for quite considerable sums.  I add my signature with death in my heart, and with a powerful feeling that I am committing an enormous folly, but motivated always by this decisive argument: that the affection of my family is beyond price.  Henceforward, there are for us two worlds: the external world, and us, cut off, but together.  Tilly would often say: 'We are all in the same boat and I am the captain'.

Thus it was that I handed over my money to a perfect stranger.  I had, in fact, already met him twice, but was not aware of this.  In May, before his first meeting with my husband, I had gone to Paris for three days with my daughter Diane, who was at the time fifteen years old.  We stayed with Ghislaine, at Fontenay-sous-Bois, in her large house surrounded by trees.  At lunchtime her son, François, had arrived with a man quite considerably older than himself, somewhat dishevelled in appearance, wearing sneakers, baggy shorts, and a faded sweatshirt.  He was not tall, quite thin, with a stoop, and tow-coloured hair: a nobody, or so it seemed.  My sister-in-law did not introduce him to me.  She indicated briefly that he was a teacher and was helping her son, who at the time was working for his diploma at the Femme Sec.  The individual in question offered me his hand.  A limp and feeble handshake.  He at once struck me as detestable, and I even wondered how it was that my sister-in-law could let François go around with such a person.  It was Tilly.  When I recall this meeting, I still do not know why

Ghislaine did not pronounce his name. I have never asked her, but I feel certain that he had, for reasons of his own, told her not to do so.

I often say that Thierry Tilly was lucky in his dealings with us. That is certainly the case here. If, when Tilly came to see us in Bordeaux in order to pocket our first cheques, I had been able to identify him as the individual I had met in Fontenay-sous-Bois, nothing of all this would ever have happened.

Similarly, the following July, when the 'Music in Guyenne Festival' was at its height, Ghislaine had passed through Martel accompanied by quite an elegant couple: he, fair-haired and thin with little spectacles, an ordinary type, unremarkable, and she large, dark-haired, and athletic. Without introducing them to me, she had shown them around Martel, from top to bottom, room by room, clearly taking great pleasure in it. The house was full of friends and cousins, I was relaxed, and at home. I paid no attention, nor did I recognize the teacher I had met in Fontenay.

When he arrives at our house in Bordeaux, in order to collect our cheques, he is no longer the same person, but a dashing business-man, sporty, and in good shape. With his small spectacles, well-cut hair, and side parting, he is the very image of the ideal son-in-law, well-spoken, and who displays, as well as an imposing presence, an impressive self-confidence. His handshake, which is enough to break your fingers, displeases me, since I see it as a manifestation of a will to power. And this new version of his person does not convince me any more than did the previous ones.

At first, he behaves in a way that ought to calm my fears: everything has been registered with the tax office, which has issued a signed acknowledgement of its receipt of cheques payable to Presswell Ltd. I remain no less anxious, however, and I say to him: 'Up until now I have always entrusted my money to high-street enterprises, whereas I know nothing about your company. If anything happens to you, I will have no idea who I should turn to in order to find out where my money is and eventually to recover it. I should like to have a bit more information, in order to be easy in my mind'. At which, he throws back his head, as though offended, and assumes an air both furious and wounded. Almost theatrically, he allows a moment of silence to elapse, while fixing me with an icy stare, and then he retorts, brusquely: 'Listen, Christine, no one talks about trust to me. Either you trust me, or you don't. None of the people I work with ask themselves questions of that sort, they believe in me. I won't tolerate doubts about me being raised, it's a question of quality of work!' Charles-Henri, already anaesthetized, shows no reaction, while I, promptly – and foolishly – beat a retreat.

Oddly enough, it was at the very time that we were first getting to know Thierry Tilly and he was beginning to interfere in our family affairs, that we experienced a series of misfortunes. I remain persuaded that this was pure coincidence. But at the time they seemed to lend substance and credibility to the lies Tilly was telling about a conspiracy of which our family was the object. This run of bad luck began with a series of car thefts. We each of us have a car, both of which were stolen on several occasions. Then my car, which had just been serviced, caught fire at the toll-booth in Marmande, while Charles-Henri was at the wheel and on his way to Monflanquin. The following summer, two cows died on the farm, an unprecedented event. The vet thought they must have swallowed some barbed wire – which surprised even him. And then someone stole a farm trailer and some seed from one of our sheds. I reported it to the police. And – a bright spot in this run of bad luck – the trailer reappeared the following week, as Tilly had said it would, and my smallholder's account was credited with a reimbursement of the cost of the stolen seed, without any intervention on my part. Charles-Henri, who, since the beginning of the New Year, often talked on the phone to Thierry, told him of our various set-backs. Thierry responded with ever more detailed explanations as to why the Védrines family was being targeted. No, he couldn't, as yet, say exactly who was behind these machinations. But he mentioned the Freemasons: – 'It's well known that they are very numerous in the South-West', but, in any case, his informants were working on it. (We have since learned that Tilly had been expelled from the Masons for embezzlement). And, as to the reimbursement for the theft of the seed, it was he who intervened in the matter: we really were having too many problems to deal with all at the same time!

Moreover, when, at about the same time, our estate was threatened by a plan for a reservoir, designed for the irrigation of crops but which would cover two thirds of our land, he promised us he was in control of the situation, and assured us that the plan would come to nothing. And indeed, several months later the idea – fiercely contested throughout the region – was abandoned.

Confronted by a succession of such incidents, some people would blame the stars. The Védrines see it as a plot hatched against them, whose origin is explained to them by Thierry Tilly. This may seem risible and stupid. But chance, when it combines with ill-will, becomes a powerful tool. And if someone in whom you have placed your trust not only does not disabuse you but on the contrary confirms your anxieties, what was only a vague notion becomes a certainty. A certainty that also makes gullible people – us – extremely distrustful of any stranger; so that everyone who does not belong to the immediate family becomes suspect. In my case too, therefore, all of those around me need reassurance, to be certain that I have not gone over to the 'enemy clan'.

I love my husband. And my husband is a Védrines. At the time, this is enough to make me ready, quite quickly, to accept anything at all, so long as he continues to love me, and his family to receive me with affection. I tell him the extent to which their attitude worries me. I am distressed, but the moment I try to explain my distress, I become distraught. Soon afterwards Tilly tells Charles-Henri that I am depressed, that I must be prescribed Tranxene, that this will restore my equilibrium. As a result of this treatment, my reactions become dulled and I am soon marginalized. I have always wondered what it was that in the depths of my being created this desperate desire to be loved and accepted, a weakness that has led

me, time after time, to go along with any course of action
or decision that my closest family imposed on me, even
if it was contrary to my most vital interests. I might do
battle for a long time, but it almost always ended in my
giving way.

# 5

When I am asked to describe my childhood, three words
come immediately to mind: happy, loving, solitary.

My parents met during the war in Lot-et-Garonne.
My father, demobilized in 1940, had returned to his
profession as an insurance loss-adjustor, and was
practising it in this region. My mother had retreated
to her parents' estate with my sister Françoise. When
my parents were married, my father was forty years old
and an incendiary bomb had left him deaf in one ear.
He was a handsome man, blond, with grey-blue eyes,
whose appearance and very British sense of humour
were no doubt inherited from his English mother. He
was reserved, perhaps because of his poor hearing, but
also by temperament. With little taste for small talk or
the social round, he read a great deal, and above all else
liked being with his family. My mother, by contrast, was
gay, lively, warm-hearted, and very fond of society. They
were a close-knit and loyal couple.

My paternal grandfather had been a colonial
administrator in Africa. He died very young, at scarcely
forty years of age, probably from malaria. My father,
then, was orphaned very early and had taken charge of

his own upbringing. Somewhat reclusive, he was very attached to his family and its history. Among other things, he often spoke to me of an ancestor guillotined during the Revolution and buried in a common grave in the cemetery at Picpus.

His political convictions tended towards the right, but he was capable of changing with the times. He was always responsive to other people, a quality he displayed in the course of his work as an insurance loss-adjustor, where he acquired a reputation as a man of integrity and great humanity.

My sister was 16 when I was born. The difference in our ages has never come between us, but the fact is that I therefore grew up as an only child. I have always regretted not belonging to a bigger family. Always, from a very early age, I looked out for her coming home from work. I adored watching her get ready to go out in the evening with her friends. I thought she was perfectly beautiful, and I admired her very much. When, as was only to be expected, she wanted to be more independent and left home to set up house with a cousin, her departure left a great void in my life. Was this, perhaps, the first time I had known what it was to be abandoned? I was seven years old.

My maternal grandparents lived in Bordeaux, in the same street as we did. My grandfather was co-manager of a family and regional firm, founded in 1783, which specialized in metallurgy. Above the offices belonging to this business, there was an apartment, which my parents had taken.

My father's work as a loss-adjustor took him, from Monday to Friday each week, all over the south-west region. Left alone with my mother, I trembled at the thought that he might have an accident. Was it because he sometimes recounted the accidents and the dramas he became involved in? Or was it because he always travelled by car? A cloud of secret anxiety enveloped me during the week. My happiness returned when he did. Once I was old enough, my parents took me out with them every weekend. They adored the cinema and took me, still very young, to see films such as *Ben-Hur* or *Michel Strogoff*. I cannot have been more than eight or nine years old. I still remember it: across the cherry-red curtains of my little bedroom, as though on a screen, Roman chariots dashed, Mongols galloped in pursuit of Strogoff, and I called out to my mother. These nightmares haunted me for a long time.

I must have been a hypersensitive little girl: throughout the second year of my primary school, Mademoiselle Charlotte, my teacher, terrorized me. I can only suppose she was particularly strict. But it made me so unhappy that I dreamt about it every night, and every morning went to school as though to a torture-chamber. My mother wanted to send me to another school. I refused, determined to face and to overcome the fear that haunted me. By the time June came, I was no longer afraid (which is to say almost never afraid) of Mlle Charlotte; but it had been, for me, a year of real torment.

My grandfather came to see us almost every day on the way to his office. One morning, he suffered a heart attack. His staff, at a loss as to what to do, brought him to our house. He remained there, paralyzed, for more than six months. My grandmother came to see him regularly. My mother was immensely busy looking after her father during the whole of this time, and I felt abandoned, since I could not begin to understand why my grandfather did not return to his own house with my grandmother. At last, he did return to their apartment, where he died soon afterwards.

Although I was lonely, I never wanted to leave the house. I refused to join the Brownies. The thought of going to camp at Easter and in the summer, and of leaving my mother, terrified me. I preferred to stay at home all day, either close to her or alone in my bedroom, reading. I lapped up the Famous Five, the *Signe de Piste* series, and then, as I grew older, English novels. We all liked reading. My father preferred works of history that had some connection with the War, as well as biographies of politicians or of personalities he admired: French kings, Churchill, de Gaulle. He was a regular reader of *Le Figaro* and *Sud-Ouest,* and always did the crossword, after he had studied the literary pages and decided which books to buy for himself, my mother and me. She devoured novels and biographies, and especially those that were about women. The family unit was snug, a cocoon, where I found everything I needed: love, intellectual stimulation, culture. Why would I have gone anywhere else?

As I grew older, of course, I changed. In the first place, when I was thirteen years old, I met Marie-Hélène. Opposites attract. She arrived in my school at the start of a new year, knowing no one: her family had just returned from Algeria, where they owned a vineyard. We bonded at once: one brown-haired, the other dark, one shy, the other bold, one secretive, the other extrovert, one who spoke softly, the other loudly, one who smiled, the other who laughed... We were made for each other. Fifty years later, she is still my best friend, one of the people who have saved my life.

With the arrival of Marie-Hélène my life was transformed: I was always at her house, or she was at mine. Her parents and her whole family, so numerous, a real tribe, were all of them like Marie-Hélène absurdly generous, noisy, and funny. Her friendship changed everything; it transformed me. Thanks to her, I emerged from my cocoon and, from being a shy little girl, became an adolescent who was a member of the college volley-ball team, loved rock and roll, fashion, and interminable conversations about everything and nothing, but especially, I think, about boys. Girls' talk, in short. I also discovered that she had a little brother with Down's Syndrome. Up until then I had never encountered anyone with a handicap. I admired and respected Marie-Hélène and her family for teaching me to accept, with love, disability and the handicapped.

We had always spent our summer holidays with relatives, first with an aunt in Guérande, and then with my grandparents who owned an estate at Laugnac, near Agen. It dated from the eighteenth-century, and was very pretty, crossed by an avenue of lime-trees more than a century old, whose perfume has remained with me to this very day. As a small child, I followed my cousins everywhere. We made dens, bathed in the stream, joined in the harvesting of the wheat and the picking of the plums, and finally, at the end of the summer, the gathering of the chasselas grapes. Maman never dreamt that anyone could be, even for a moment, idle. Having been, at first, a simple spectator in all this, I soon became, as an adolescent, 'a seasoned agricultural worker'. There lingers still, in my nostrils, the scent of the plums we picked. Next, we placed them in rows on grids; they cooked gently; we turned them over one by one. Then, once they were cooked and cold, we put them into packets and went to sell them in all the local markets. This amused me no end, I liked playing at being 'a plum merchant', but I also took it very seriously. Afterwards, there was the harvesting of the chasselas grape, which one had to snip off and place, very carefully, on special paper. I still remember how sticky my fingers became with the juice of the grapes, and how sweet they tasted… Later, I even looked after a flock of sheep. When Charles-Henri inherited Martel, a somewhat similar estate, everything was familiar to me. And I took on, without hesitation, the task of running it as a farm.

Once I was fifteen or sixteen, I began going to parties, dancing to Procol Harum and the Shadows, flirting while listening to Françoise Hardy, wearing Cacharel shirts and ballet-pumps with mini-skirts or jeans: never were girls more normal, more cherished, or more pampered, than my friends and I. My only real problem was in deciding what dress to wear for next Saturday's party, what boy had or had not noticed me, and would he be telephoning me to ask me out to the cinema? When the holidays at Guérande came to an end, my aunt having died, we rented a house at Pontaillac and I went boating. Then, one summer, I took a language course and, the following year, went to Ireland on an exchange with a girl of my own age. It was a happy time, a time when I had not a care in the world, but of which I'm told a leader-writer in *Le Monde*, Pierre Viansson-Ponté, had written: 'France is bored'. As for me, I was not bored for a single moment.

Always a diligent pupil, I passed my final exams at school with quite a good grade. I chose, as the subject of my philosophy essay, 'Love and passion'. Could there be any subject more interesting to a girl of eighteen? I have no idea what mark I received. My pen simply flew across the paper; and I had swotted up the subject well enough to be able to deploy some well-placed quotations.

I remember very well the events of May '68, which I saw on television, as well as the demonstrations in Bordeaux. Our college was closed, and so, with great sagacity, we refashioned the world as we thought it ought to be. At home, the subject was scarcely mentioned. In my opinion, the students were meddling in matters that were no concern of theirs. I have always been an obedient child. My mother used to say: 'You grumble, you fly into a rage, but you always do as you're told!' Besides, there were never any serious differences at home; I had no brothers or sisters sufficiently close to me in age for me to squabble with. It's as though I have never learned how to pick quarrels: I prefer to avoid them. It may seem paradoxical on the part of someone so quick-tempered, but so it is: my opposition to anything at all has only ever been a façade. When I wanted to study law and go to the École Nationale de la Magistrature, Papa decided in favour of the faculty of letters, and marriage. And so I took a degree in literature and English. The surprising thing is that, within the literature department, the consequences of May '68 were still a live issue, so that I felt at the start completely at a loss. But then everything returned to normal...

At the age of eighteen, just before going to university, I went off in the summer to Bristol to work as an au pair. I looked after two young children while doing a course in English. We got on so well that later the whole family came to my wedding. Then, on my return, I began my degree course, and at the beginning of the following year, I met Charles-Henri.

**Part Two:** We are taken captive

# 6

The first real move that Tilly makes against our family is in November 2000, when he stage-manages a fantastical scenario at Bordeneuve, Ghislaine and Jean Marchand's second home. The cast includes Ghislaine, her husband Jean, Mamie, Philippe, and Charles-Henri.

One fine autumn afternoon Charles-Henri, at work in his consulting-room, receives a telephone call from Ghislaine:

'I'm very worried. Jean is deeply depressed and in danger of breaking down completely. He's at Bordeneuve. Fortunately, Maman and Philippe are with him and doing everything they can to prevent him from leaving the house and doing something stupid. It's absolutely essential we get him seen to and into hospital'.

'Why? Is it so very serious? Are you sure?'

'Absolutely certain. It's essential we find a psychiatrist'.

He has no sooner put down the phone than Charles-Henri receives a second call: it's Tilly...

'This is a very serious matter, Charles-Henri, it
really is urgent', he declares. 'You must get hold of a
psychiatrist. Ghislaine needs you. She's afraid Jean will
do something stupid. We're all counting on you!'

Extremely concerned, Charles-Henri telephones one of
his psychiatrist friends, who agrees to come to Bordeneuve
at once. He himself leaves his office immediately and joins
his colleague. But Jean is very opposed to any attempt
to detain him against his will, and very displeased at this
interference on the part of his in-laws. Alone in his room,
he rejects their offers of help. By the end of this day, most
unfortunately, Tilly will have discovered for the first time
how to sow dissension between the brothers-in-law. He
will also have succeeded in introducing a degree of disarray
into the family, thus taking a first decisive step towards his
total control of my husband and of Philippe.

Not long afterwards, I receive a telephone call from
a cousin whose daughter is a student at the Femme
Sec. He's very concerned: it appears that the school
is in financial difficulties, that the staff are threatened
with dismissal, and that the heating has broken down.
Knowing nothing of what's going on there, I can't offer
him any reassurance. That evening, I tell Charles-Henri
about it. He says that both he and Mamie have written
quite substantial cheques for Ghislaine, in order to help
her out. But they are both of them persuaded that this
is a purely temporary measure...

It is at this same time, too, that Thierry Tilly gets
us to set up with our children two property companies,
as he does also Philippe and his partner Brigitte, as well

as Mamie, and Ghislaine. Guillaume, our oldest son, is completing his degree in business studies at Marseilles and, as a boy of twenty-two should, he is enjoying the busy and carefree life of a student. He has already encountered Tilly, the previous August, at dinner in Ghislaine and Jean Marchand's house in Bordeaux. He came away impressed by his expertise on 'smart cards,' an activity Guillaume knows well, having worked for Gemplus, who are specialists in this area. As far as he is concerned, this was a casual encounter. But when Charles-Henri telephones him and asks him to come to Bordeaux for the weekend to talk about 'important matters he cannot discuss over the telephone', Guillaume at once obeys. What he is asked to do, along with his brother, Amaury and his sister, Diane, is to sign documents setting up a registered company. These documents are to be filed, at Tilly's insistence, with the tax office in Villeneuve-sur-Lot, because he knows that this official procedure will reassure us and relieve us of any suspicions we might have.

The whole diabolical mechanism is in place, and we are drawing our children into it.

But I have another and much more pressing concern: at the age of nineteen, Amaury is supposed to be completing his second year of study at commercial college. He has absolutely no interest in this. He skips class, hangs around with friends whose influence on him worries me, and smokes pot. We are always arguing, our relationship is deteriorating, and we no longer find the right words with which to communicate. I talk to Guillaume about this. I've got into the habit of regarding my older son as the second head of the family. He is about the place more often than is his father, and sometimes assists me in decisions I have to make. Hoping to help his brother, he has a quiet word with him, but to no avail. Charles-Henri and I are at our wits' end. We consult various professionals, but without them offering any real help. Ghislaine, who is Amaury's godmother, wants to help him too, and passes on to me the ready-made solution her mentor has offered: Amaury must be removed from his friends, from his whole environment, and sent to the UK. At once, seeing the good sense of this solution, we adopt it. The Oxford International School of English – OISE – organizes courses that are highly regarded. Tilly, however, has already enrolled him. Why did I not take matters into my own hands, knowing OISE well, as I do? It has offices in Bordeaux, and several children of friends have already gone off to language courses in Europe. But no, everything has been arranged before I even know what is happening. So Amaury finds himself in Oxford, and we send money to Tilly so that he can pass it on to him.

It is in this way that Tilly takes possession of Amaury and begins to manage his day-to-day life for him, down to the very last detail. Little by little, he succeeds in establishing a real bond with him. Amaury has at last found someone who speaks his own language... A real friend...

Amaury is living with a family and following a course that involves, or so it appears, total immersion; so that, when I ask for my son's address and telephone number, I am not given them. When I so much as make this request, I am told, with an air of authority worthy of a chief of police that, for reasons of safety but also for his own good, it is better he remain in isolation, cut off from his family. No details are given, but the obscure danger that hangs over us all is invoked, with such conviction that I end by believing it. Then, when I find myself alone, logic and reason return and with them a whole host of unanswered questions: if we are indeed in danger, why is nothing done to protect us? When a citizen is under attack, he can appeal to the police, to a lawyer. But in this case, it appears no such thing is possible. When I raise the matter, Charles-Henri replies by invoking only one thing: secrecy. The whole subject is too serious for us to discuss it casually. We do not know yet who is involved. It would be dangerous to have recourse to the conventional arsenal I am suggesting. Ghislaine, for her part, is voluble on the matter: surely I can see that for two years now, a whole series of events, all of them damaging to us, have followed one upon the other? Tilly has discussed this at length with her. In Thierry's view, Amaury's behaviour is the perfect illustration of what we are threatened with: if he had not been sent to England, he would, at some point, have been persuaded to take hard drugs. Thanks to Tilly, the operation mounted against Amaury – and therefore against the whole family – has been successfully frustrated. But we must remain on our guard. What mother has not seen an enemy, in the suppliers to her children of marijuana and other substances? I must be very careful: such is the burden of this and many other such conversations.

As far as external appearances go, everything seems
normal. We pretend: Charles-Henri goes on working
immensely hard, I continue with my usual activities;
whereas we are, if the truth were told, no longer as we were.

My husband, when faced with such a threat, seems
able to lead a normal life. I am not. I fear for my family,
I imagine I am being watched. Rather than going out, I
prefer to stay at home. When my friends phone me, I cut
short the conversation. In time, however, I reflect, and
I react. My daughter is still at home, and I do not want
her to suffer from this situation. She is following a course
at the Collège de l'Assomption, where I am a parent
governor. I am also involved in various sporting activities
she has signed up for. Some time later, I am asked to take
on the presidency of Bordeaux Accueille. I am about to
accept, when I receive a call from Thierry Tilly. He argues
that there is at present too much insecurity surrounding
my family for me to take on so prominent a role. So,
after talking it over with Charles-Henri I decline the offer.
It is as though, every time I begin to emerge from under
the weight of this threat, it catches up with me again.
And so, to the astonishment of my friends, I withdraw
my application for the presidency of Bordeaux Accueille.
My life, that year, continues in this same way, with high
points and low, all of which I keep to myself.

But the threat I'm constantly told is hanging over me
affects me less than the strong feeling that my husband,
his mother, his sister, and Philippe are hatching plans with
Tilly which they are keeping from me, and of which I see
only the results.

I have no part in any decision that is taken, whether this concerns our own safety, that of our children, or of our property. There is scarcely any real discussion between Charles-Henri and me. I am simply presented with a *fait accompli*, which I am obliged to accept. I know that this is all Tilly's work, but I never see him, nor do I hear from him. Absent though he is, he oppresses me. I fear him much more than if I were constantly in his presence. Besides which, on each of the three occasions when I did meet him, he put on a different face for me, so that I have no very clear idea of him as a person. I know only one thing: I do not like him.

An impression of total emptiness takes possession of me. I feel a great sadness, a crushing sense of helplessness. Normally, I would have discussed this with Marie-Hélène or my sister. I would have shared my worries with them, we would have talked it all over, they would have supported me. But on this occasion I retreat into myself, I cancel, abruptly, my Thursday lunches, I see my friends less often, all of whom notice, when I run into them, the change in my behaviour. They cannot understand it, but suspect, perhaps, marital difficulties I prefer to keep to myself...

Why do I not seek help? Why do I say nothing?... Because of my husband? My total trust in him never wavers. If there were the merest grain of truth, even, in what he tells me, I should never forgive myself for having betrayed him. Everything about him – his profession, his moral rectitude, his unfailing decency where I am concerned – has always, up until now, spoken in his favour. How could I dissociate myself from him? As I see it, Ghislaine is a manic-depressive who needs to control everything; Philippe does not like conflict, and lets himself all too readily be dominated by his mother and his sister; but I have complete confidence in Charles-Henri. He loves his mother and his sister, but he knows their failings and especially their need to dominate. From whatever angle I try to view the problem, I cannot disentangle myself from the blind attachment that ties me to my husband and children. I even accept the extraordinary relationship that has grown up between Tilly and him. My husband appears to have established a relationship that is based on friendship, trust, and mutual compatibility. How could I deprive him of that?

Had I known what was happening in Charles-Henri's practice, I might perhaps have acted very differently. From the start of this year, his professional bank account is peppered with urgent credit transfers in favour of Tilly, transactions that are listed in ways that can only excite bafflement and concern: 'Reorganization of the Profession', 'Establishment of a Company for the Reprocessing of Medical Waste', 'Child Welfare'. As for the sums involved, they vary between 2,000 and 10,000 euros, sometimes more. Every time Tilly makes such a demand, Charles-Henri is obliged to perform the transaction himself: he leaves his consulting-room, even though the waiting-room is full, and, whatever the time of day, crosses the whole of Bordeaux in order to visit his bank, which, however, offers no reaction to this radical change in the behaviour of a long-established client. And all of this without saying a word to me.

In the summer of 2001, the whole family goes to Martel. Ghislaine arrives in a state of terrible anxiety. I attribute this to the preparations that are under way for the wedding in September of her daughter Guillemette; but then, by chance, I learn that, in June, the Femme Sec has in effect dismissed the whole staff, and I understand better the state my sister-in-law is in. 'Musique en Guyenne' takes place in July. It is to be the last such festival. Moreover, it goes quite badly: Ghislaine has an angry verbal exchange with the conductor of the orchestra, of whom she thinks nothing. The unfortunate father of one of the guests, afflicted by Alzheimer's, forgets himself to the extent of relieving himself in public during an open-air dinner, at which point Ghislaine makes a scene, claiming that someone is trying to ruin her festival. Next, apparently, a young participant in the festival informs her of an instance of sexual misconduct, so that the general atmosphere of the whole event is suddenly under suspicion. My sister-in-law becomes paranoid, but her brothers pretend not to be anxious about the state she is in, and her mother makes excuses for her on the grounds that she 'has had so much to put up with'. I must, then, be kind and patient with her, I who have known – and it's true – only happiness. In other words, we hear, but do not listen to her. Nevertheless, what she is saying to us gradually pervades, invades even, our minds and our thoughts. The brain-washing has begun.

Throughout the whole of this festival, moreover, the general atmosphere is very different from anything we have known in previous years. In addition to the squabbles

between the performers and Ghislaine, relations, even at
Martel, are not good.    My sister and her husband, and
my cousins Bertrand and Anne, all of them regularly
invited to this occasion, are disagreeably surprised by the
reception they are given by Mamie, who, unlike in the
past, hardly addresses a single word to them, even when
she is not being frankly cantankerous.

'What's wrong with your mother-in-law?' asks
Bernard, who has never known Mamie to be other than
charming to him.

'I haven't the least idea, but I should very much
like to know!' I reply, troubled by this atmosphere, and
distressed at seeing my closest relatives badly treated.

Françoise comforts me, attributing all of this to the
old lady's agitation over her grand-daughter's forthcoming
wedding.    Mamie has always taken on Ghislaine's worries
as though they were her own.    Watching her daughter
struggle with problems she herself does not understand
must cause her great distress.    But then, Charles-Henri,
of all people, has a violent and damaging altercation with
my brother-in-law, Michel.    It concerns the organization
of the festival, and is wholly, if remotely, controlled by
Tilly.    My cousins, my sister and her husband, all of
them very uneasy, leave quite soon afterwards.    As for
me, when I come to hear of the incident and ask Charles-
Henri the reasons for the position he has taken, he tells
me that Thierry had asked him to act in this way 'so that
everyone will be obliged to make a stance'. Certain people
are not welcome, for reasons he cannot yet explain.    My
sister and her husband feature, apparently, on his list.

'Françoise and her husband? My closest relatives?' I display more than mere scepticism. 'What could anyone have against them?'

'We don't know everything', Charles-Henri retorts.

'Then tell me what we do know'.

But Charles-Henri won't be drawn: 'I don't want to worry you. Besides, I don't know the whole of it myself'.

Trying hard to suppress my irritation in the face of all these mysteries, I reply, calmly: 'Up until now there have never been any secrets between us. It seems to me that I am sufficiently grown up to be able to take bad news. Ever since you met Tilly it's been obvious to me that you're hiding things from me'.

'I'll explain everything later. I promise you,' says Charles-Henri quietly. 'Everything will be all right'.

He says this with obvious sincerity, which is all I am asking for. But in spite of this, my anxiety is not dispelled.

On September 1st the marriage between Guillemette, the daughter of Ghislaine and Jean Marchand, takes place in Bordeneuve and Martel. It is a lovely occasion: she is marrying a young pianist from Nice, and all the bridegroom's friends come to sing and to put on a concert for us. Seeing Guillemette on her father's arm and surrounded by all our friends going up the nave of the church at Monflanquin, filled with flowers, who could imagine us to be a family in distress? From the church in Martel, the bride and groom cross the village in a barouche. There are aperitifs, cocktails, dinner; and the party goes on late into the night. The young perform

Provençal dances in the park, while Mamie, in her role as grandmother, and mistress of the occasion, reigns queen in our midst. A perfect moment. But more illusory than real. The list of guests has been vetted by Thierry Tilly and Ghislaine. Some of them are given to understand that they are not welcome; the parents of Jean Marchand, for example, to whom we have been asked not to say a word, which is, to say the very least of it, awkward... Out of politeness, I try even so to look welcoming. As for Mamie, she does not even greet them. At lunch the next day, attended by family and close friends, she will choose to remain in her little sitting-room.

There is never again to be a Védrines family celebration at Martel. When Ghislaine leaves again for Paris, Charles-Henri and I stay on for two days, in order to tidy up, before returning to Bordeaux; while Mamie decides to extend her visit so as to enjoy the autumn weather, and Jean goes back to Bordeneuve.

But, one week later, on 7th September, a strange quarrel, very like that of November 2000, breaks out. While I am at Martel with Philippe and Charles-Henri, Ghislaine bursts in and insists that her brothers accompany her to Bordeneuve, where Jean is. They fall into line. Ghislaine, curiously, given the occasion, is wearing a cocktail dress. She is also wearing gardening gloves, and carries a bouquet of dried flowers which, on arrival, she throws into Jean's astonished face, while shrieking hysterically: 'Here it is, all the proof that is needed of your vile machinations! I found it in our garden in Fontenay. You have forty mistresses. You are a monster!' Utterly dumbfounded, my brother-in-law argues with his wife for over three hours, without being able to make her see reason. Philippe and Charles-Henri wait outside. Tilly, on the telephone, follows the progress of the whole operation. Then, abruptly, he orders the two brothers to bring the interview to a close and announces precisely the manner in which things will proceed: they must tell Jean to leave. He will calm down and agree to leave again for Paris. And indeed, exactly as Tilly has predicted, Jean packs his suitcase and agrees to get into the car, escorted by his two brothers-in-law and by Ghislaine, who accompany him as far as the station in Agen. And so Jean returns to Paris. Arriving at the family home in Fontenay, he discovers that the locks have been changed. He spends the night going through Ghislaine's computer, where he finds Tilly's emails, one of which spells out, down to the very last detail almost, the performance he has just taken part in. He tries to contact Ghislaine, who bangs the phone down and can't be contacted again. When he finds that their joint account is completely empty, he takes fright and decides to cut off all ties with the Védrines family while trying to save his children, François and Guillemette. This he will be unable to do.

Tilly had persuaded Ghislaine that sending Jean away was the only way to save her marriage.

Why did Jean not come to tell me about it? What exactly happened that day? Why did he not help me to recognize Tilly's powers of manipulation, which he had been experiencing at close quarters for a long time now, for what they were? Another lost opportunity…

On the other hand, Jean does get in touch with my friend Marie-Hélène whom he knows well. He tells her the whole story. She becomes anxious. She comes to see me to find out what is happening. But first of all she tells me about Jean. He has, it appears, been vilified for several months now by Ghislaine and her children, and is already talking about a divorce. In spite of my friendship for Marie-Hélène, this immediately inhibits any frank exchange of views. She tries to get me to talk. I put an end to the conversation with the desperate feeling of there being no way back. I tell Charles-Henri about it that same evening. He remains very calm but assumes an air of gravity such as I have never seen in him before: he has discovered dreadful things about Jean. He does not want to shock me by going into details, but I must trust him. This man is not worthy to be the husband of Ghislaine. My husband displays enough conviction to persuade me. All the more since it was Ghislaine and her children who gave him the evidence. Jean was planning, apparently, to leave home and to start a new life in the United States with another woman. They are all three devastated. Jean is henceforward excluded from the Védrines family.

On September 11th, two airplanes piloted by terrorists strike the twin towers of the World Trade Centre in New York. Guillaume, who was working in the United States and had a plane ticket for the twelfth, has to delay his departure. We discuss this terrible event. He could never have been a passenger in either of these planes since his reservation wasn't for that date... but Thierry knew that something serious was going to happen. Hearing this, we are all persuaded that Tilly advised him not to leave until the 12th.

The autumn advances slowly. Diane has returned to school, Amaury to Oxford, Guillaume to the United States, so that during the day the house feels very empty to me. At Ghislaine's suggestion, my mother-in-law has decided to remain longer this year at Martel: she adores that house. She loves harvest-time; and the freshness of the October air in the country does her good. At the end of November she is still there. Charles-Henri suggests I go and join her. I can see no good reason for this, and have no wish to leave him, nor to abandon Diane who is still going back and forward to school every day. I do not like to think of them on their own. But he insists. I refuse all the more vehemently in that I sense the influence of Tilly on this decision. Whereupon the same old tale is revived on the danger the family faces, and the threat to Martel. Then Diane who, at sixteen years, likes the idea of enjoying a little independence while remaining within the comfort of the family home, joins in. She can get by on her own very well, whereas Mamie, at eighty-eight years old, ought not to be alone. But, why, I wonder, does Mamie choose not to come back to Bordeaux, where she would be just as well looked after? It's a mystery. It's she who has decided to remain in Martel, where she feels 'better and more protected', as she herself puts it. As usual, I resist and then give in, and, on the 2nd of December, I arrive in Monflanquin. In my own mind, everything is quite straightforward: I am happy to keep Mamie company until Christmas. Afterwards, after the holidays, we will return to Bordeaux.

The next day, on her birthday, I telephone my sister and she tells me she is selling her house in Lot-et-Garonne. Why? 'Oh, well, you know, we will see the Védrines less and less. So what is the point of keeping a house so close to Martel?' I am greatly distressed, both by this news and by the sorrow I hear in her voice. Françoise is persuaded that we are estranged because of the differences that arose between our husbands at the time of the music festival, even though it is clear that she is not withdrawing her affection from me. I do not attempt to dissuade her. I say nothing to her of my problems. Slowly, the poison instilled by Tilly into the Védrines has infected me too. Could it be that my sister has become one of my enemies?

The weeks that remain before Christmas pass quickly. My mother-in-law, delighted at being no longer on her own, very much wants Christmas to be a happy and memorable one. She finds me a ready accomplice in any such project: we both of us like special occasions. Martel, with its spacious rooms, its immense drawing room where even the tallest Christmas tree has all the room it needs, its monumental fireplace, and the immense oak table in the dining room which has seen so many happy family reunions, lends itself perfectly to this. We spend our time choosing presents and having them delivered, buying Christmas decorations, setting up and decorating the Christmas tree, getting in food, checking that there is as much wine in the cellar as we will need, and then adding more. I make grand expeditions into the woods, collecting mistletoe and armfuls of green boughs. I speak regularly on the telephone to Diane and Charles-Henri to make sure that everything is all right. When life suddenly becomes normal again in this way – when I manage to forget what has happened – I have the impression of emerging from a nightmare and I persuade myself that everything will soon be as it used to be. I manage to tell myself, too, that, even if we have lost money (and I remain very anxious as to Tilly's amazing investments), we are all together as a family, and that this is all that matters. It is for this reason no doubt that I throw myself so whole-heartedly into the preparations for Christmas, in a way that delights my mother-in-law. Our relationship is excellent. We enjoy many happy moments together. In the evenings, she recalls her past life, recounts stories from the time when her children were little, her husband's return from the war, and summers in Martel... During these days before Christmas the atmosphere between us is very good.

But when Ghislaine and her son François, as well as Philippe and his partner, Brigitte, join us a few days before the 24th, all of this changes: the house becomes charged, immediately, with electricity...

Philippe is a true Gascon: a gourmand, sociable, high-spirited. He enjoys life, and his generous dimensions bear witness to this. My brother-in-law is a kind and courteous man, who dreads conflict and quarrels. He generally avoids them, by protesting loudly and vociferously, until peace is restored. Brigitte is discreet, and very easy to get on with. So I am astonished to see Philippe on edge, tight-lipped, and barely friendly towards me. His proper upbringing and natural warmth prevent him from being disagreeable, but I sense a change in him. He is just back from Paris where he camped out in the offices of the Femme Sec in order to lend help and support to Ghislaine.

Little by little the atmosphere becomes tense. Ghislaine tells us about her interview with Tilly's boss, who goes by the name of Jacques, but whose surname remains a secret. She made a trip to England especially in order to meet him. She seems completely captivated by him, presenting him to us as a man of a certain age, and immensely kind and good. He said a most extraordinary thing to her: that if she wants to save her children, she must effect a total separation from Jean until he undergoes treatment for his depressive tendencies. But Tilly will help her. Obviously this will be very hard for her and her children, but he has convinced them of the truth of the accusations made against Jean

Ghislaine's daughter, Guillemette, joins us for the New Year celebrations, leaving her husband in Nice. She, too, does not leave, but stays on. Tilly has managed to persuade her that her husband is just like her father, and that she must divorce him...

Charles-Henri arrives with Diane and with Amaury, who has completed his course in Oxford. My son is in good spirits and on excellent form, has given up smoking anything at all and is making good progress in English. I am delighted that his time there has been so successful. As for Guillaume, he is still in the United States. The Femme Sec is in the process of declaring itself bankrupt, Ghislaine is separated from Jean, while Guillemette, every bit as tense and strained as her mother, is in the process of divorcing her husband Sebastien. I am deeply perplexed as to what has gone wrong in this marriage, which has lasted scarcely three months. But she gives no explanation, other than that she has made 'a tragic mistake'.

Nevertheless, on Christmas Eve, we make a communal decision to celebrate it appropriately. We prepare dinner all together, and we dress for the occasion. Ghislaine doesn't like the Christmas tree decorations, takes them all down, puts too many of them back, abandons the whole thing, then returns and starts all over again. It's exasperating, but we manage to remain calm. The telephone rings several times. I'm prevented from jumping up to reply, on the grounds that 'We've already had enough interruptions'. And so as not to spoil the festive mood, I let it ring. We exchange presents, drink enough champagne for the world to appear in a better light, and end up going to bed quite early, but without any upset or drama.

Christmas Day does not go quite so well. Ghislaine stirs up trouble for me with my mother-in-law. Behind my back, she lets drop the most stupefying lies about me: I am a liar, a thief, I am deceiving Charles-Henri. In my ignorance, I cannot understand Mamie's change in attitude towards me, her unpleasant remarks, her veiled reproaches. We've just had such a happy time together. When I complain of this to Charles-Henri, he shrugs his shoulders: his mother has always been volatile and moody, she'll get over it...

On the afternoon of the 25<sup>th</sup>, the Monflanquin police ring at the door. They have been contacted because we are not answering the telephone. It's my sister. She's anxious about me. They are 'very sorry', the police say, 'to disturb Mme de Védrines, but they must do their job'. Ghislaine replies, in acid tones, that we are all of us very well, but that we take the telephone off the hook when it rings and we do not wish to answer it. They know, do they not, that the house is big, and that it takes quite some time to answer the phone? They sense that they have done the wrong thing, and before leaving the house they apologize.

Ghislaine returns to the drawing-room and rounds on me. 'I've told you again and again that you should have nothing to do with certain members of your family! The police! At Martel! That's proof enough, if we needed it, that we're being watched! This visit by the police is highly significant and you are to blame!'

When Ghislaine is in a state like this, there is no point in trying to talk to her.

I should like to have said to her that, if we had answered the telephone in the usual way, none of this would have happened; but she won't listen, so that is where the matter rests. Her reaction brings me to the verge of tears and, at the same time, irritates me.

The atmosphere at the dinner-table is dreadful. I have prepared the whole meal, and am again the object of unpleasant remarks on the part of Ghislaine. She claims that Christmas is a very sad time for her, alone as she is, abandoned, and burdened with so many problems. I retort that Christmas is the children's festival and that for them at least, one might make an effort. What is it that, at this moment, provokes an outburst of anger on the part of my mother-in-law, presiding in the place of honour at the head of the table? To what degree of irritation has she been driven that she allows herself to act in this way? She seizes her plate, which fortunately is empty, and throws it at my face. The missile just misses me and crashes on to the floor. For a few seconds, a terrified silence prevails in the room. The children exchange stupefied glances. Normally, I would have got up and protested, made a scene, even. But on this occasion, when nobody takes my side, when nobody asks my mother-in-law the reason for such behaviour, I am rooted to the spot, unable to utter a word. We have entered hell.

Much later, I will try to understand, with the help of a therapist, why it was that, on this occasion, I remained quite uncharacteristically incapable of reacting. I began to see things more clearly after she had explained to me the syndrome of the battered wife. When you have reached a certain stage, you feel guilty, and so you believe that any effort to resolve the situation must come from yourself.

# 7

After Christmas, Charles-Henri and Diane return to Bordeaux. Ghislaine, by contrast, settles at Martel with her children. Mother and daughter are parted from their respective husbands. This double separation plunges them into an indescribably depressive state. Amaury, too, remains at Martel, and I confess that I find his presence and his affection a great support. For there is no longer any question of my returning to Bordeaux. I remain incapable of explaining why and how I have been persuaded to remain in this quaint old house, charming in summer, uncomfortable in winter in spite of the improvements we have effected, and above all in an unbearable atmosphere. I stay on, no doubt, because of the continued presence of Mamie, who does not want to return to Bordeaux either. Philippe too, newly retired, settles down at Martel with Brigitte, much as they would like to return to Talade. But why do Philippe and Ghislaine, each of whom owns a house nearby, choose not to return to their own hearth and home? It would be ungracious of me to pose such a question, I who am their hostess. They would doubtless give a reasonable reply: that they wish to keep Mamie and me company, for example. In short, the tribe that has regrouped around the 'matriarch' spends the winter at Monflanquin. Which does not fail to surprise the villagers, but they do not risk asking questions as to 'what's going on at the château?'.

Several weeks later, Ghislaine and Guillemette decide to go to Nice in order to end the young woman's marriage. My sister-in-law, in the threatening tone of voice she will always use with me from now on, orders me before her departure to leave an answerphone message, and never under any circumstances to answer the phone or to ring back. No one will from then on be able to reach me by telephone. Mother and daughter spend very little time in Nice: only long enough to destroy Guillemette's marriage. Thierry Tilly has given the order. Ghislaine, automaton-like, obeys, to the point of registering with the police a further charge, to the effect that her son-in-law had threatened her with a knife. This 'will make their divorce simpler'.

During all this time, Tilly has remained invisible, but always very present. In the end Ghislaine admits it: this regrouping of the family is all his doing. They exchange emails and phone calls every day, and he issues his orders to her: not to communicate with the outside world, not to answer the telephone, not to let anyone in, whether postman, police, or relatives, and above all to intercept my mail. So that very many letters will never reach me. It is for this reason too, that we have no cleaner, no help in this vast barracks where I am responsible for supplying the needs of eight to ten people: cooking, housework, laundry. I am the maid. Nor am I well treated. Ghislaine tells me that we must all stay together in order to confront a threat that remains vague and yet paramount. At the present moment, we have no precise information, but Tilly will soon find out. In Ghislaine's eyes, as in Philippe's, we are experiencing a kind of call to arms. Philippe, who likes to say he is a soldier at heart, is quite happy about this. And Tilly knows just how to humour him: 'Philippe! You were in Algeria. You've been under fire. You're the only one who understands what I'm talking about'.

Philippe passes the time playing computer games. Brigitte devotes herself to endless knitting. Ghislaine is to be found sitting in the salon with Mamie, who is embroidering a tablecloth for Tilly. A favour reserved up until then for her children, and an indication – oh, so revealing! – of the place he now occupies in her eyes. As for Amaury, he helps me and keeps me company. With him, I can relax. But he is as I am, or almost, in that he doesn't understand much of what is going on all around us, whereas I can see very well that some unspoken preoccupation is agitating my sister-in-law and her brother, particularly Ghislaine, but we hardly ever exchange a word. Sometimes I try to approach her. I take my book into the drawing-room and read by the fire. My mother-in-law belongs to a generation whose hands are never idle: she embroiders, she knits, she sews. Reading, in her eyes, is a sign of sheer laziness, and she lets me know it. And so I desert the family and shut myself up in my own room. This is frowned on. What am I up to? Nothing. Except that I brood on the absurdity of my situation and the behaviour of the Védrines.

As the weeks go by, Mamie finds it more and more difficult to embroider. She is developing cataracts. She complains of seeing everything 'through wire netting'. Ghislaine replies that she herself has seen beams of light in the trees at night. Thierry has apparently explained to her that our enemies are trying to unnerve us by directing laser beams at us. Who could on earth could subscribe to such nonsense? But her mother believes her, is distressed, and it soon becomes an obsession with her. As for me, I say nothing. At the weekend I tell Charles-Henri about it. He tries, in vain, to reassure his mother and his sister, but without success.

'Surely you're not going to believe any such nonsense! Do stop imagining things!' 'It's not as easy as that! Just you watch out!' is their answer. 'You're completely naive! You don't understand a thing!'

At which point Charles-Henri gets me to sign documents agreeing to sell all my financial assets. I'm reluctant to do this, but he insists. And I sense that he, too, is under pressure. I beg him to tell me what is wrong: on my own here with Ghislaine and her mother who aren't at all nice to me, it is I am who am beginning to imagine things. If, in addition, I feel him to be under pressure, then nothing is right. He assures me that everything is fine, but that he is overwhelmed with work, and is facing various financial problems in his practice, which, however, will sort themselves out. That my husband should have problems with money, for the first time in years, alarms me much more than do the laser beams in the garden. He says that he and his colleague must make some further investment in order to modernize the practice, and I accept this explanation. Why, in spite of the confidence I have always had in my husband, do I still feel a certain doubt, a real unease?

That evening, after he has left, I go over everything in my mind, trying to reconcile the erratic behaviour of Ghislaine, her daughter, and Mamie, who are now imposing on us a virtual incarceration, with Philippe and Brigitte's very evident anxiety about the whole situation, and with Charles-Henri's whole manner, which I find more and more enigmatic and tense. Everything leads me to believe that they, all of them, have some very serious concern. Something of which I know nothing.

Thierry Tilly's orders are a form of harassment: one day we are obliged to close all the shutters and live by electric light. Several days go by. Ghislaine gets an email: the state of emergency is lifted. We may reopen the shutters, but not go out into the garden. All the same, we must, of course, stock up with food. Philippe and Ghislaine take charge of this. I'm allowed to do it from time to time, but never on my own. Ghislaine decides when and how. She is also in charge of the telephone, which no one else may answer. It's true it doesn't ring very often. The people who live in the village see us pass by, always in pairs, distant, unfriendly, quite unlike what they are used to from the Védrines; and they do not understand what is going on. As for the postman, he's under orders too. I often write to Guillaume but have no address for him, once again 'for reasons of security'. When one of our number goes to Paris he hands my letter on to a messenger. But I never receive a reply. I'm astonished. 'No', they say, 'nothing's come for you'.

Sometimes I fly into a real rage and declare that the whole situation is completely crazy, and will end in disaster. At which point I experience a total reversal of the usual situation: everyone is kind, and speaks gently to me: 'Poor Christine, it's really hard for you! It's no wonder that you fly off the handle!' Amaury is commissioned to administer some 'conversation and comfort'. Diane and Guillaume receive emails from Tilly telling them to write some soothing things to me in order to calm me down.

And so I find in my email in-box nice little notes: 'Cheer up, Maman we love you, we're proud of you. We're going to come and see you. Everything is going very well here'. This comforts me, brings tears to my eyes. And everything goes on exactly as before.

Not quite, however... One day, I notice an email describing the loan of my apartment in Pyla to Tilly's parents. I almost choke with anger: whose idea was this? Maître Vincent David's? Ghislaine's? No, Tilly's, without a doubt... I am furious, but, in the interests of the common good, I agree to go along with it. My husband makes nothing of it.

As for Ghislaine, she simply shrugs her shoulders. The implication is that, while I may be the owner of Martel, I'm not in charge there, even of my own personal possessions. Tilly's parents visit Martel to thank me. They seem like nice, ordinary people. Not at all the child bride and the armed diver, member of the secret service, that Tilly had described to us. But I'm not fooled by this. I still have the impression that Tilly's presence is becoming more and more invasive. And a word comes to mind: cancer. It turns out to be accurate. Tilly's undermining work was done insidiously like an infiltrating tumour which, by the time it is discovered, has already done irreparable damage.

Charles-Henri and Diane come every weekend. My daughter is affectionate, happy, amusing. She tells me what is happening at school. And she is anxious to reassure me: she is, so she says, very sensible, eats properly and doesn't go out too much. For me this is a real breath of fresh air. Charles-Henri asks me how things are going at Martel, and confirms that everything is proceeding as usual at Bordeaux. I mention the matter of the post. He tells me that he too no longer receives any mail at home. It's normal. 'No' I reply, 'it's not at all normal'. From then on, important letters travel by other routes.

In June, Diane passes her baccalaureate in French with very high marks. Immensely proud and reassured by this, I imagine that with this behind her she will face next year's final baccalaureate with confidence and calm. And then a surprise: Tilly invites us to London. I press Charles-Henri to accept: not only do I want to leave Martel, but I should like to know a little more about our investments. Besides, I have another idea in my head, of which I say nothing to my husband: it was Tilly who first spoke of a plot, a threat, and it is he who seems to know everything there is to be known. I go to London, then, determined to ascertain what this whole affair is about, and what we can expect to happen next.

Tilly has booked rooms for us in a very pleasant hotel in Chelsea; and it's there that he comes to find us. With his well-cut dark blue suit, his tie worn under a pullover of fine wool, which I guess to be cashmere, and his Burberry raincoat, Tilly could pass for an Englishman working in the City. Jessica, a brunette, both bigger and younger than him, is very pretty and lively. They are the very image of a happy couple, vivacious, and full of energy. Thierry comes across as communicative, cultivated, keen on history; and he regales us with all manner of anecdotes. He speaks of his childhood, of his very youthful mother, and of his absent father. He says he went to Saint-Cyr because he comes from a long line of military men, but that later he preferred to specialize in commercial law... He is charming, and very different from the representative of the Presswell Association who came to Bordeaux to collect our first cheques. A friend, in short, who dazzles us with his conversation and his suggestions as to the artistic and cultural opportunities that London has to offer, before leaving us abruptly. He is up to his eyes in work. But Jessica puts herself at our disposal. She would like to show us London, take us to the Vermeer exhibition. There is talk of their children, their move to London, their new life there, quite as if we were old friends. That evening, we meet up with Thierry again and have dinner together. Our visit is short: only two days. Not for a moment are there any questions about our safety: we move about freely, no one seems to be on our tail. And so I say to Charles-Henri that I should like to have some details about this plot, and that I'm going to ask Thierry about it: and that, this time, I want something more than vague remarks of the 'I can't tell you anything!' kind. At which Charles-Henri says, in a tone of weary solemnity such as I have never heard him use before: 'Up until now I have done everything possible to protect you, to preserve your peace of mind, and not to cause you any greater anxiety than you are already suffering. Do you really need to know the details? Have you not seen the results? Everything that has happened these past two years in Bordeaux and Martel? The truth is that there are, most certainly, people who have us in their sights. As things are we are not managing too badly. I have heard of other much worse cases. The essential thing is to hold firm. And the less you know, the better you will manage'.

I insist that I am quite grown-up enough to understand: 'Tilly is always talking about the Freemasons. You must have some idea who is behind that!'

He looks at me, exhausted. Then he says: 'No more than you have. Tilly's people are looking into it. On the one hand, there is an investigation going on; on the other, we are protected, which is why it's best not to talk about it'.

I can see that this is only a half-truth. Charles-Henri's exhaustion and his air of tension lead me to suspect something much more serious. But I don't want to worry him. I tell him that I love him, and that it grieves me to see him looking so tired. And he smiles. 'As you know, my being able to count on you is already crucial as far as I'm concerned. The important thing is that we're together!'

I'm shaken to the core by this, and deeply moved. So I decide that when I get back to France I will be circumspect. But the very notion of circumspection troubles me. Does that mean shutting myself away at Martel, not saying anything to anyone? Try as I might, this question haunts me.

Neither of us even hints at the question of our investments. Well brought up people, no doubt, don't discuss money. But the Tillys accept invitations from us every evening, and our taxi fares are always settled by Charles-Henri. In a word, we are invited to pay for everything. When, at the end of our visit, I mention this to Charles-Henri, he dismisses any such reflection by criticizing my ill-will. Surely I am not beginning to be obsessed by money? At which, feeling mean, I stifle my prejudices. Besides, Jessica is kind, and very nice, and this speaks in favour of her husband, and, in part, reassures me. After our return home, Philippe and Brigitte go to London for a visit very similar to ours. Thierry showers them with presents for everyone, including Mamie.

At the end of August. Thierry suggests to Charles-Henri that Diane be sent to boarding school in Poitiers. There's an excellent private boarding school there, run by the Christian Union of Saint-Chaumond. His people have made enquiries: on the one hand he himself is afraid that some violence may be done to her if she remains in Bordeaux, especially by those bent on retaliation against us, while on the other, this institution is wholly respectable. He says that Diane cannot remain alone in Bordeaux, which is logical enough, but doesn't for a moment entertain the idea that we could, all of us, return to the family home. Diane, although she doesn't at all welcome this move, is obliged to obey. I take my daughter to Poitiers and leave her in tears in a place I would not perhaps have chosen but which, I must admit, maintains the highest standards. It isn't going to be easy for her to adapt to life in a boarding school, even if, today, I believe she has very good memories of her time there.

On my way home, I take stock of the situation: my daughter and I are separated, she is a long way from home, and I resent this; Amaury has gone back to London and I know nothing of his circumstances there, nor of what his stay involves; my letters to Guillaume remain unanswered, unless Ghislaine passes on some message or other to me; Charles-Henri looks exhausted and I still have to find out the precise nature of the pressure he is under. As for Philippe, every time he appears to question Tilly's orders or Ghislaine's criticisms (which happens rarely), Brigitte reproves him. We are a family riven by disagreements, but we suppress them because the Védrines clan has always been stronger when united. Every time some threat or other is brandished in front of us, we close ranks. The necessity of living together, as a clan and a pack, has even allowed some of us to hope that these threats had disappeared. Suspecting Ghislaine to be in difficulties will, for example, have led Charles-Henri to pay his sister's share in the cost of the cocktails for Guillemette's wedding: Philippe and Guillaume will help her to settle part of her tax bill.

At the end of September, Jean Marchand lodges a complaint against his ex-wife, accusing her of misuse of public funds: 180,000 francs had disappeared from the account of the 'Music in Guyenne' festival of 2001, while Ghislaine was treasurer. When she hears of this, she bellows in anger: 'That bastard, who was always cheating on me and wanted to abandon us, is ruining us now. He won't stop until he's destroyed everything'. Apparently Ghislaine never imagined that Jean would go to such lengths. She seems surprised: 'I'll tell Thierry about this, he'll sort it out'. As for the rest of us, who know nothing about the financial affairs of the festival, we are stunned. What on earth happened?

The year 2002 draws to a close without any change to our way of life at Martel.

# 8

After finishing college in 2001, Guillaume went to work for Rhodia, a plastics manufacturer, in their marketing department near New York, and was delighted with his job. Tilly, who had gone to New York and made contact with him, had persuaded him it would be better for him to move into his apartment, with two rooms and an office, very close to the UN, an apartment that was also Tilly's workplace. It's true that Guillaume would therefore have to make long and tiresome daily journeys between Rhodia and the centre of Manhattan, but through Tilly he would meet various very important people, one in particular, for example, a millionaire, who was also a generous donor to many humanitarian foundations. Like us, on his behalf, Guillaume felt full of self-confidence. And, at the age of 23, he thought such contacts promised well for the future of his professional life. Tilly made regular journeys between London and New York. Once or twice during this time, he sent Amaury, too, to New York to deliver a package to his office, procedures that gave my sons the impression, not only that he was an important man, but that he had considerable means at his disposal. All this made them more impressed, and hence more ready to oblige.

Early in 2002, Guillaume's voluntary civil service came to an end. We knew that he wanted to remain and work in the United States for some time yet. This was his dream. But Tilly intervened: the family situation had become, to say the least of it, fragile. We needed our son. He must put his dreams and his future on hold in order to come to our aid. He was persuaded: Guillaume, shouldering a new responsibility, landed from New York in a state of some anxiety, and became first of all his father's chauffeur. And indeed, Charles-Henri, under constant pressure, had lost all the points on his licence and been unable to do what he had to to regain them. Then, with spring just on the way, Tilly summoned our son to London, where he remained.

Maître Vincent David, who had arranged the very first meeting between Ghislaine and Tilly, had also launched with him a plan for investing in some new building in Albiez, a village in the Maurienne, which was being developed as a little ski resort. Tilly suggested several times to Ghislaine, Philippe, Brigitte and the children that they stay there. He invited them in his usual way: without himself paying anything. I nevertheless appreciated these invitations, in which I was never included: in the absence of the others, peace and calm were restored to Martel. And why Albiez? Because Tilly's parents owned a boutique there, which sold sports clothing, and where Ghislaine was invited to show herself a good customer and Guillaume to pay for this with his credit card, to the point where he spent there everything that he had saved.

On their return to Martel, the atmosphere began once again to become oppressive; whereupon Thierry took on the task of organizing our activities. Besides the 'closed shutter' alerts, he told us to do various more or less pointless things, such as washing the walls and floors thoroughly, cleaning out the cupboards, dusting the pictures. This pleased only one person, Mamie, who thought that there was nothing more important than taking good care of the house. She surveyed the work, wanted more done, exclaiming all the while: what a good idea! When Ghislaine told her it had come from Thierry, her face lit up. 'Now there's a man who knows what's what!' Frankly, she was the only one who welcomed the task. Everyone else balked at it, especially me.

The atmosphere was always tense. Mamie criticized the meals I made, just as she was to criticize the ones Brigitte later provided at Talade. Ghislaine, very unhappy about her separation from Jean, complained of the cold, of the poor quality of the linen that was supplied, of everything, indeed. Sometimes I despaired of ever finding anything at all that we could agree on. As for Mamie, she sided with her daughter on everything, completely disregarding our past collusion. In response to their moaning, I checked the astronomical fuel bills, the equally staggering cost of food, and suggested to them that they share the costs, since it was Charles-Henri who was supporting everyone. At this, they would contain their recriminations for a day or two, then it would start all over again. One day, François and Guillemette declared that they could no longer bear this atmosphere, nor their mother, nor anyone else, and asked to be able to have their meals in their room in order to avoid being at table with the rest of us. Only Amaury helped me to put up with it all of this. He was the only person I could have a 'normal' conversation with. I had believed that, by making concessions, one could succeed in maintaining a modicum of peace, an idea that was, time after time, proved to be mistaken...

This difficult situation was being managed, skilfully and from a distance, by Tilly.

One day, Tilly sent me a computer from London, and asked me to email him a list of our activities every day, what my view of them was, how my relationship with the others was going, and any curious or exceptional incidents I observed. In short, to keep a diary, in which I would record everything that happened. I think I obeyed once or twice but then protested that I found it tedious and no longer wanted to do it. Tilly's presence – even in his absence – was, in itself, quite oppressive enough, without my undertaking to send him daily reports. Almost immediately after my rejection of his request, the computer disappeared back to London with Ghislaine or one of the children. The latter were often sent on missions to Paris or London, always as a matter of urgency and always at Charles-Henri's expense. These orders, these unforeseen and frequent comings and goings, ensured a constant atmosphere of tension and made regular outbursts of anger on the part of one or other of us only too likely. After all, we believed ourselves to be under attack, whereas no such thing was really happening. Reality and time, for us, no longer existed.

And then – one day – the cataclysm...

It is Saturday. Charles-Henri has told me he will not be coming, because one of our friends is having a baby that day, which he is due to deliver. The telephone rings and for once Ghislaine does not immediately seize

it, so that I am able to take the call. At the other end of
the line, I hear the voice – very anxious, moreover – of
the young woman in question: Charles-Henri is neither
at home, nor in his consulting-room. He has been out
of reach for twenty-four hours now, and her labour has
begun... I don't know what to say to her, and I hang up,
desperately worried. Charles-Henri would never abandon
his work, nor a patient. He's a totally reliable doctor,
well known for that. Something serious has happened
to him. I decide to return to Bordeaux. But, while I am
getting into my car, Philippe and Ghislaine move theirs
in such a way as to block my passage. I am consumed
by rage and fury. Only Amaury manages to calm me, by
pointing out that it won't help matters if I let myself get
into this state. Charles-Henri will certainly telephone
us and explain everything. He reminds me how entirely
reliable his father is; he would never leave a patient on
her own. In fact, the whole thing is certainly a complete
misunderstanding, and my pregnant friend has panicked
for no good reason. I nevertheless spend a sleepless night,
consumed with anxiety. Everyone except me knows
where my husband is: he is in London with Tilly.

Sure enough, it is indeed Tilly who has asked him
to join him this weekend, by car and with Guillaume,
to discuss with him various important matters, but on
no account to tell anyone about this. This weekend
follows a long period of stress for my husband, arising
from the audit, required by Tilly, that Charles-Henri has
made of his practice. The distinguished lawyer Maître
Vincent David has been appointed to give credibility

to the process. I now know that Tilly is in debt to
Vincent David and has found in this way the means to
discharge this debt, by off-loading it on to Charles-Henri,
who manages to persuade his partner of the necessity of
such a proceeding. The latter nevertheless is much less
persuaded of the need for him to pay for it, and for good
reason: the document arising from the audit, which
itself amounts to no more than two pages is invoiced at
90,000 francs, of which 70,000 represent the lawyer's fee.
The partner has had it examined by an accountant, who
has sought legal advice, and has ended by issuing fifteen
legal proceedings, several of them against my husband.
Charles-Henri is at the end of his tether: for more than
two years now he has followed the advice, consented to
the demands, withstood the pressure put on him by Tilly,
and he now feels himself caught in a trap. But Tilly is at
this point the only person he can call on to help him out.
The solution the latter advocates is radical. My husband
no longer has any choice: Tilly has persuaded him to give
up his consulting room and to abandon all professional
activity. The plot has become so threatening that Charles-
Henri must have some protection.

The next day, having prevented me from returning to
Bordeaux, Philippe and Ghislaine disappear for the whole
day. I don't complain, nor do I ask for an explanation:
my sister-in-law's absence opens up an oasis of calm and
tranquility. The reason for their absence, which I will
discover later, makes my blood run cold: during the course
of a single night, helped by his sister and his brother,
Charles-Henri, having entrusted his patients to two

colleagues whom he respects, moves his consulting-room into our house, takes down his plaque, and disappears from view. Not from ours, however: he arrives in Martel. It is a broken man, who, suffering from nervous exhaustion, having turned his back on a profession he loves, his position in Bordeaux, his friends, his whole world in fact, comes to join me in Monflanquin. He tells me, quite simply, that it is no longer possible for him to pursue his profession under normal conditions, and that he is throwing in the sponge. I am devastated by this news. But I like to think that I have grasped something that will help explain all of this: Charles-Henri is at the end of his strength, he is no doubt depressed, he needs to stop. I think he's going to be on leave for a long time.

As for me, my brain teems with questions. How are we going to live? How are we going to meet our obligations? How are we going to help our children?

Tilly has the answer: given Charles-Henri's qualifications and his expertise, he has no hesitation in promising him a professional future beyond anything he might imagine.

The very presence of Charles-Henri at Martel, in spite of his state of physical and moral exhaustion, altered the atmosphere: there was as it were, a rebalancing of power. At least, I thought so for a moment. But there was always, in fact, the tightly-knit Védrines clan – the two brothers and the sister – following Tilly's orders, obeying, and imposing obedience. And me, the odd one out. Much as I wanted to be part of the group, I could nevertheless never manage to follow blindly everything that was asked of me without asking questions and without objecting. Between loyalty and rebellion, I always felt myself torn in two.

In April, Tilly decided we did not need to declare our tax liability, arguing that given the financial problems of the practice we were in considerable deficit, and that it was the inland revenue that owed us money.

'Paying doesn't solve everything', he was fond of saying. 'Not paying solves nothing at all' would have been my reply, if I had been able to speak to him.   But he always did everything through Ghislaine and Charles-Henri.   I, who up until then had always managed our affairs, was punctilious on this matter.   I preferred paying too much to making some mistake. The burden of Tilly's new directive was perfectly straightforward: the tax man extorted in order to bleed us dry. 'Extortion or not', I said to my husband 'We will be prosecuted'. He made the expected reply: Tilly would see to it. He knew someone in Bercy who... I didn't believe a word of it.  But I had arrived at a point where fatalism had become my way of life.  The infernal machine had been set in motion and as expected, penalties and confiscations multiplied. The amounts to be paid out soon became astronomical...

The year went by without there being any change in our status as 'voluntary prisoners'.  As to the word 'voluntary', that remains arguable.   I did not know it, of course, but our friends, my family, and even the inhabitants of Monflanquin were beginning to ask serious questions as to what was happening to us. We were the object of unhealthy curiosity on the part of some, and of great anxiety on the part of others, who loved us.

Some of our friends did manage to keep in touch; and we allayed their fears and suspicions. Others made attempts to visit us, but were coolly received in the courtyard of the house. Realizing they had committed some sort of faux pas, they retreated, in a state of very great perplexity.

But the disappearance of a well-known doctor and his wife – both of them descended from long-established families in the region – not to mention their children, was bound to arouse some interest and concern. In September a journalist from *Sud-Ouest* appeared, prowled around the whole place, and tried to speak to us, before being, of course, ushered off the premises.

These visits contributed to an increase in the tense atmosphere inside the house: it was only too clear that 'our enemies' were ready to try anything. Among our number, it was Ghislaine and Philippe who were the most alarmed by this. A few days later, an article appeared in the *Sud-Ouest* under the headline 'The Monflanquin Recluses'. The Védrines lodged a complaint, alleging violation of family privacy. That calmed things down: we wanted to be left in peace; and, soon, a total silence fell.

In spite of this, as the months went by other people became concerned about our fate. My friend Marie-Hélène wrote to the public prosecutor in Agen to register her disquiet about my disappearance. On several occasions, she hired a private detective. Mamie's other grandchildren, those, that is, who had not fallen into Tilly's clutches, lodged a request for legal protection, in order to help their grandmother, and alerted the Association for the Defence of the Family and the Individual in Lot-et-Garonne. Jean lodged several complaints and denounced Tilly's manipulations. Brigitte's nearest relatives, both in Rouen and in Lot-et-Garonne, began to take action. My first cousin, too, communicated his concern to the state procurator in Agen, but was reminded of the legal aspects of the situation: if adults chose to live in seclusion in their own home, if they decline to answer any questions and let it be known that they were acting according to their own volition, no action against them could be contemplated. The police station in Monflanquin, which was in constant communication with us, themselves filed a number of reports. But none of them had any effect.

In June, Mamie, Ghislaine and Guillemette left us and went to join Philippe and Brigitte in Talade. I don't remember the reason for this but I do remember, very clearly, the relief I felt at their departure. I told myself that the plot that was threatening us had already succeeded, since the family was breaking up. Our enemies outside the family were perhaps also inside it, but this was not an idea that I shared with anyone else.

Summer came, and with it, once again, the comforting hope of being able to go to Pyla with Diane and Charles-Henri, and perhaps also with Amaury. But I was deluding myself. Tilly had already embarked upon the sale of my apartment there. While Diane spent the summer with us, Ghislaine's son, François, and Amaury left to rejoin Tilly in London. François came back for a short visit in order to tell us of the splendid scheme he was about to enter upon with Tilly. This was the first I had heard of the Blue Light Foundation. It had been dreamed up by Tilly and a man of whom I vaguely remembered having heard: Jacques Gonzalez, the famous Jacques whom Ghislaine had described to us as being Tilly's boss. According to Philippe, this assumed name concealed a Spanish grandee – a philanthropist – who led a very discreet existence in Paris. His Blue Light Foundation had funded various philanthropic organizations in China and elsewhere. Ghislaine's son François invited us, moreover, to go and look on the Internet at the photograph of a certain Louis de La Poëze, a personal friend of Thierry's boss. We saw him handing over a large cheque for the construction of a hospital. In other words, Charles-Henri could play a part in the creation of such hospitals, and in the training of obstetricians in the developing world where they were cruelly lacking. Philippe would manage the relations with China. Obviously, this whole idea seemed to me fanciful to say the least, but the plot against the Védrines appearing to have been forgotten and Charles-Henri seeming to believe in this new scheme so firmly, I had not the heart to discourage him.

After all these years spent at Martel, something, quietly, insidiously, gave way inside me. When Charles-Henri outlined his plan, I could find nothing to say either for or against it. I acquiesced without discussing it further. A voice deep within me still protested, but more and more feebly, that we were mad, that we had lost our bearings... What I felt, rather, was a sort of intoxication, of vertigo: a turning in on myself, a loss of any sense of duration, an ever more pervasive inability to react. I saw us as incapable of reaching back up again towards the real world, and I could no longer do anything to prevent this.

During that year, we were stripped, progressively, of everything, or almost everything, we owned. We sold the apartment in Pyla, then our family house in Bordeaux. As to this last, I tried to oppose it with what I believed to be an unanswerable argument: 'Where will we go when we leave Martel? When we want to go back to Bordeaux?' But I ended up, as always, by giving my husband power of attorney to go to the solicitor's and sign the relevant documents. I was not allowed out of the house, being, according to Tilly, particularly under threat. I was never able to be present at the sale of any of my properties, nor at the removal of their contents. The truth of the matter was that Tilly saw me as the weak link. He took, then, every possible precaution against me. Charles-Henri does not remember our talks on the subject, nor his sister's decisive role in the matter. From the sale of our property, we had to set aside 200,000 euros to placate the taxman, and then 150,000 euros to buy back some land at Martel. Now, when I received by fax the breakdown of the amount derived from the sale, I saw that the 150,000 euros were going to Tilly. More anger, more fighting on my part. I did not want to sign this fax but Ghislaine got on her high horse, as did my mother-in-law. I felt trapped and alone. I was cornered. Nothing very new there: I am afraid of conflict, once my initial anger has abated, and I give way. The principal beneficiary of this whole affair, Thierry Tilly, as always completely invisible, remained in London. My sister-in-law continued to be his factotum, his subaltern, her master's voice. Tilly dispatched everything – all our furniture, all the objects that were in the house at Caudéran and the apartment in Pyla – to London, where they were sold, piece by piece, for his benefit and without our knowledge. Every time the sale of one or other of our properties took place, the taxman took one part of the proceeds, Thierry another. We had less and less money to meet our everyday expenses, and the assistance we gave our children, not to mention all the demands – penalties and taxes – that descended on us like an avalanche. We learnt later that the money we sent our children was diverted, for his own use, by Tilly. They lived in a state of near-deprivation, in spite of the ingenuity shown by Guillemette and Diane in making sure they at least had something to eat.

During the autumn, the idea began to take shape in my head that it was not perhaps fanciful to suppose that people were beginning to be concerned about us. As a farmer from Martel, I was a member of a cooperative for the use of agricultural equipment, CUMA, which my father-in-law had helped set up. This meant that I had the use, for a specific period and in specific quantities, of the equipment needed for harvest, and that I settled invoices for its use. From the very beginning, all the agricultural works on the estate had been carried out with the help of CUMA. We had opened an account with Crédit Agricole in Monflanquin specifically for this purpose. In good years we broke even, in bad years we fell back on our resources. Now, Tilly had 'borrowed' money from us, and from this account, 'for six weeks, just to get over a difficult moment', as he put it. But this 'loan from a lady farmer', as he had called it, had not been repaid by the autumn of 2003, and I therefore owed 7,000 euros, or thereabouts, to the farmers' cooperative, which, for a business of 50 hectares, is not excessive. I know other members who have owed much more and for much longer. I, however, who had never fallen behind with a payment, no more than had the Védrines before me, found myself on this occasion short.    Normally, the president of the cooperative would have telephoned me to remind me of my obligations – indeed, perhaps he had done this without being able to reach me – and I would have written the cheque on the spot. I had given no reason for the delay, nor asked for more time in which to repay what I owed. I could have done so. I could even have asked the CUMA for a loan, but 'it was Tilly who was seeing to it'. The creditors greatly dislike debtors who don't keep in touch, but pursue them the more insistently and rigorously.

We are deeply attached to the land. My whole life, including my childhood and adolescence, is bound up with harvest-time, with the dry smell of the ripening wheat, with the noise of the machines, with the little animals that take flight at the approach of the reaper. I not only have a sentimental, and a sensuous, perception of all of this, it is also a part of my active life. The pleasure of weighing out the seed, and then of seeing the bales of hay piled up for the winter, has always offered me a sense of stability: I have always felt, while managing the estate at Martel, that I was playing my part in the continuing life of this family.

So that the arrival of the gendarmes, escorting lorries and bailiffs come to seize our harvest, was for me a very violent trauma, and even – and I have no hesitation in writing this – a physical blow. I was alone at Martel: Charles-Henri was in Bordeaux, the others elsewhere too, in Talade, in London. I can still see myself running between the gendarmes and the bailiffs, trying to prevent them from taking my harvest, shouting that this must not happen, that I could write a cheque. But no. I had no cheque-book; and, anyway, so the gendarmes said, 'it was too late'. I phoned Ghislaine. She maintained an Olympian calm, which I saw as indifference. She had no notion that this confiscation of the harvest was a wound inflicted on Martel, on the land itself, and a disgrace: never in the whole history of the Védrines had such a thing been known. She adopted the business-like, slightly superior tone of a person with authority: 'It's only what Thierry was expecting. Everything will be all right'. I hung up no less concerned: if someone was attacking the harvest in Martel, and thus the whole estate, there was a real danger. Once again, and unlike other people, we were never behind with our payments. Why such a radical measure against us?

We had entered an administrative and financial labyrinth: not paying our taxes or our largest bills had unleashed an avalanche of refusals on the part of the bank, as well as of formal demands, notices to third-party holders, estimations of taxes. We ourselves were desperate never to shirk, nor even avoid, our fiscal obligations, but, according to Tilly, this was merely a 'strategic and temporary' procedure. Although I had previously known how to manage my inheritance, I was now out of my depth. Neither Charles-Henri nor I had the ability or the strength, to face all these legal procedures and legal disputes. It was the first time in our lives such a thing had happened, and nothing had prepared us for it.

But in accepting our own shortcomings, we were at the same time consenting to Tilly's handling of our affairs: he was, he said, 'used to this kind of problem'. It was 'nothing at all out of the ordinary'. His intention, as he explained to Charles-Henri was to 'entrust the future supervision of our affairs to Guillaume, which would be an invaluable experience for him. And besides, he would of course have Tilly's own team as a back-up in this!' We went along with this, persuaded, even, that this experience could be useful to him in his career, and an opportunity such as we ourselves were unable to give our children. So Guillaume ended up carrying out Tilly's orders in his handling of every legal matter or contentious issue that the family faced. Little by little all the adults in the family – Ghislaine, Philippe and Brigitte – unloaded their administrative and legal problems on to a young man. Tilly prevented the adults from fulfilling their proper role. I broke down in tears when I discovered that Tilly had ordered Guillaume to take on Jean's solicitor, and to represent Ghislaine in her divorce proceedings against him. I greatly feared that, as a result of this, Jean would harbour a personal resentment against my son, even though the dossier had been prepared by Ghislaine, who did not wish to be present herself at this meeting. I could not bear the thought that one of my children should be sent to the front in this way, in the place of an adult. Exhausted by all of this, and subject to constant pressure, Guillaume obeyed out of fear, believing he had a legal obligation. Mamie, very worried about her daughter's problems, both encouraged Guillaume, and thanked him for the help he gave his aunt in her hour of need.

Guillaume, meanwhile, was turning increasingly towards Thierry Tilly, whom, like us, he saw as a confidant, a supporter, and even a mentor – a man who always had an answer to any question, a solution to any problem, even if this solution consisted of dropping everything he had been doing. Tilly knew everything. He was always ahead of the game, always had some bright idea. He had wanted to persuade us, his parents, that Guillaume had a future and a privileged place in his own considerable empire.

At this time, in spite of the anxiety on our behalf that some of our friends continued to feel, we were regarded as madmen, people upon whom there was no relying, since we had so visibly lost our reason. Such was the witness borne by the people who passed to and fro in front of this great shack of a place, with its shutters closed even though it was known that eleven people lived there. One sees such people sometimes in the countryside, on the fringe of society, who no longer want to leave the house, who watch out for the least intruder, ready to shout at them, to warn them off, to throw a few stones at them, or to brandish a peashooter as a deterrent. But we, who were not on the fringe, who had previously enjoyed an excellent reputation in Bordeaux, had become the local 'crackpots'.

# 9

The year 2003 ended momentously: the tax office sent their bailiffs to Martel to seize all the furniture and fittings.

Once again I was forced to relive the humiliation of watching the bailiffs at work, this time in my own house. Stunned and appalled, I watched, powerless, the destruction of all my memories and those of preceding generations. I felt humiliated, 'violated', destroyed. Ghislaine reassured me by saying that nothing would be sold. But not a bit of it. All of our furniture, everything, was, in the end, auctioned.

It was impossible for us to remain in this empty house: we had to fall back on Philippe in Talade, which is quite close to Monflanquin. Talade is a little manor house, which had belonged to the Védrines family three centuries earlier. It had been lost to the family, but Philippe had managed quite recently to buy it back again.

With Mamie and Ghislaine, Philippe and Brigitte, we found ourselves with even less space than at Martel, even though the children were not there: Charles-Henri and I slept in a tiny child's bedroom on two mattresses on the floor. It went without saying, for everyone – and especially for me – that this would only be for a few days, a few weeks at the very most. But afterwards, what? Where would we go?

In point of fact, we lived from day to day. We no longer had ways to tell the time. Our situation was such that our lack of money meant we had to postpone certain purchases. Batteries for our watches came into this category. There were certainly still some clocks in the house – although here perhaps my memory begins to fail me. When you no longer know what time it is you very soon lose all notion of the passage of time and even of days. Even with television news and current affairs programmes, I completely lost my temporal reference point; which was no longer of any importance.

This moment looked as though it would go on for ever. But, curiously, our life as a couple was in a sense restored: having Charles-Henri with me the whole time was a situation we had never experienced, except during holidays; it added to the unreality of this period. He was in charge of the vegetable garden, and he took up sketching. We spent a lot of time together, which helped us to get by, but also prevented us from taking any action. When I worried about the future, he would reassure me; 'It is a very bad time, but if we just keep going, everything will be all right'. Taking Tranxene calmed my anxiety but kept me in a state of apathy.

The *deus ex machina*, Thierry Tilly, had his own special catchphrase, which I have already quoted, and which was adopted by my sister-in-law as a mantra: 'If you take the first nine steps, the tenth will be achieved by the services I provide'. What steps? What services? No one dared even to ask the question. My impression was that we were heading straight for a brick wall. We were living on the pensions of Mamie and Philippe. Tilly, of course, was always busy: it was he who was in charge of our money, which in fact had become his. Soon, so he reassured us, we would recover it all, and even more.

Ghislaine had commandeered one particular corner of the house, which allowed her sole charge of the telephone, the fax and the internet. She was in daily contact with Tilly. They were extremely close, intimate even. She was the only one of us to use with him the familiar form of address 'tu'. It was at this time that, under the direction of Tilly, she was preoccupied with concluding the divorce of her daughter Guillemette. We later recovered the emails she sent to my niece: all of them spoke of 'an unfaithful husband, ready to abandon her, a man with no respect for any legal or moral authority, a hypocrite'. And so on. The same language, in other words, that had been used to vilify Jean. Anything would do, so long as it distanced Guillemette from her husband, who could understand neither what was happening to his marriage, nor the aggressive behaviour of his young wife.

I sometimes wondered why Tilly did not put pressure on Charles-Henri, too, to seek a divorce. I can see only one possible explanation: he needed first to strip me of everything I possessed. And besides, he had perhaps calculated that Charles-Henri would stick to me, and that a divorce might even be against his own interests. He left me, then, in the bosom of the family, but strictly supervised, and thanks to the Tranxene, sedated.

We were allowed out of the house only with permission, which was granted by Tilly and communicated to us by Ghislaine. To do the shopping, which was reduced to the minimum, we used my car, the last that remained to us. Until the day, that is, that Tilly needed it, when it departed for Great Britain, never to be seen again. We lived five kilometers from the village. We took a taxi or, sometimes, Philippe's neighbour, a charming Englishman, gave us a lift in his car. If the truth were told, the only outing that required my presence would have involved some banking transaction. But having nothing left in my account, I was spared this. Sometimes, I would say to myself: 'If anything happens to me, who, apart from the Védrines family, will know anything about it?' It must have been telepathy, because it was at this very time that Marie-Hélène, missing me and deeply concerned, launched an official enquiry with two of my friends into the whereabouts of missing family members. This enquiry ended up in the police station in Monflanquin. I was summoned. I went, accompanied by Ghislaine, who, with authority and conviction, and without allowing me to utter a word, indicated that I was very well and that this enquiry was entirely improper: 'Since when has a citizen been forbidden to live with his or her family in the country? Is one obliged to write to one's friends and to inform them of one's every movement?' The gendarmes decided, once again, that, in spite of our strange behaviour, nothing was amiss. Yet another opportunity missed.

Everything I possessed was gone, or so we all thought. But Tilly was nothing if not thorough: I still owned some professional premises, which I shared with my sister.

They must be sold. My sister took a lot of persuading.
She wanted to know, naturally enough, the reason for this
decision, and she wanted to meet me. I understood all of
this and, privately, willed her to resist. I should so much
have liked her not to give way. But Tilly told me to write
a formal letter, addressing her as 'Madame'. My sister,
unable to understand this unexpected coldness, was hurt.
Although she could hardly believe what was happening,
she signed, with the feeling that between her and me the
break was final. This sale, too, was concluded without my
having to go to the solicitor. It was Ghislaine, authorized
to act for me, who conducted all the transactions with
the purchasers. On the day that the papers were signed,
finding that only Ghislaine and her son were present in
the office, my sister and brother-in-law became anxious.
But they could only conclude, once again, that I had
definitively turned my back on them.

This whole episode, of course, as well as my sister's
reluctance to do what I was asking of her, revived all the
usual tensions within the family: my mother-in-law's
acrimony, and Ghislaine's threats along the lines that
'Christine must be made to understand that her animosity
and her selfishness are nothing short of treachery. First a
missing person inquiry by her friends, now this sale that
her sister is objecting to... She's trying to hold things up,
she's conspiring against us...' Without specifying with
whom precisely she suspected me of being in league, she
took on a knowing air, threw a complicit glance at her
brother, Philippe, and said no more. The silence that
followed, heavy with innuendo, increased the feeling

I already had of being reduced to nothing. Of being rejected. Useless.

As if my 'treachery' were not enough, a veritable cascade of troubles descended on us, one after the other. Ever since Charles-Henri had resigned from his position, his professional account with the Société Générale, emptied to satisfy Tilly's needs, had registered an overdraft, authorized but never made good, of 70,000 Euros. It was not a joint account, but the bank declared me jointly responsible for it. We were both of us, therefore, liable, and I found myself in the end being taxed on my own property.

At the same moment, the agricultural cooperative in Monflanquin, which had never recovered the 7000 euros we owed it, took possession of our wood, and of an iron shed we owned; and it was during this time, too, that Charles-Henri was subjected to a whole series of legal proceedings arising from Tilly's intervention in the management of his medical practice and his interference in our family life.

At this moment, we were not only ruined, but heavily in debt and wholly discredited.

When I look back, I still wonder how it was that we were reduced to this. Not that we had ever had money to spare, but, the moment it no longer comes in, and that the assets which guarantee it have disappeared, the creditors pounce on the victim. Worse still, they burden him with penalties, with bailiffs' fees, and with legal proceedings, so that the debt increases exponentially. We had, frankly, no idea how to protect ourselves. And even if we had, we would have needed to break out of our psychological imprisonment, to reawaken our intelligence, which was 'lying fallow', and to resuscitate our determination and willpower. On every level – psychological, moral, material – we were totally denuded. Caught in a spider's web, our every movement imprisoned us just a little bit more. And because all of us, to different degrees, felt ourselves trapped, we resented each other: we each of us held the others responsible for our plight.

But when confronted by the enemy, we acted as one. Thus, when Tilly told us that there were journalists snooping about the place, that we must immediately retreat into the house and close the shutters, we obeyed. When he asserted that his informants had spotted suspicious characters in the woods that surrounded the house, listening in to headphones, we believed him. And for several hours, united by a collective fear, our mutual antagonisms disappeared, only to reappear again later.

The constant state of alert we lived under, the very real threat to us that our creditors represented, the daily problems caused by the lack of the means to feed ourselves and to furnish the necessities of life – we had to ask Ghislaine to buy even such simple things as soap or toothpaste – finished by exhausting us, both mentally and physically. We stopped looking after ourselves: Brigitte suffered intolerable headaches, Philippe complained of pains in his legs, I had lost several teeth, as had Ghislaine, and the children too. Only Mamie was allowed the care that her great age demanded. But the rest of us gradually became weaker, including Ghislaine, in spite of her being appointed head of the household by Tilly. We were becoming more and more vulnerable.

Tilly kept me in his sights, without relaxing his hold on me. During his conversations with Ghislaine, I was the object of slander that grew ever more specific, ever more unpleasant, and which she communicated afterwards, drop by drop, to everyone, with the exception of Charles-Henri. She began with vague allusions, mysterious remarks, to the effect that what I had done was so serious that she would prefer not to speak of it, hoping to spare the family pain. In spite of this, she then described me to Mamie as 'a drawing-room tart', a name that was well chosen to carry weight with a mother-in-law born in 1913. According to Tilly, I had 'taken full advantage' of Charles-Henri's absence; this was well known in Bordeaux, everyone enjoyed joking about, it was the talk of the town. Those 'so-called Thursday lunches'... But, no, she would not say another word about them. Mamie had enough imagination to cross the 't's and to dot the 'i's, and openly pitied Charles-Henri. To Philippe and Brigitte she said: 'Be careful, she's a kleptomaniac!' Objects, keys, books, trinkets, did indeed disappear, sometimes reappearing in unexpected places, or not at all. I well remember a passport belonging to one of the children that we had been seeking for a long time, and which I was finally accused of having pinched. Trinkets are one thing, but a passport is important. The passport could not be found until the day it reappeared, miraculously, among the things repatriated from Oxford...

Needless to say, the general atmosphere in Talade became atrocious. But the objective had been achieved: I no longer knew what to do – denials were pointless, and only implicated me more and more. I became depressed and visibly thinner. Underneath it all, I was waiting for something to happen. Although he knew nothing of these machinations, Charles-Henri could see that things were not well, and listened to me when I recounted the unpleasant goings-on I discovered. And then he would ask me to be patient, to make allowances: 'You know how she is', he said. 'Thierry tells me she could attempt suicide at any moment. We must try to understand'. It was not my fault. Nor Ghislaine's. He too, at that moment, was submerged in a hell of his own.

We had, by now, spent almost three years in Talade. Could this be possible? Doing what? Gardening, odd jobs, obeying various orders: 'All shutters to be closed', 'Cleaning', 'Writing the daily report on the household', 'Preparation of judicial documents'. Always as a matter of urgency, so as to leave no time for reflection or analysis. We obeyed in various ways. A difficult daily life, and the measures we took to try to salvage what we could, occupied us fully. But, more than all of this, we had lost all sense of time. It fades when one simply drags oneself from one day to the next. Months and years slip by, shadowy, unreal.

Brigitte, Philippe's partner, experienced the same difficulties as I did over the management of the household. Ghislaine was responsible for all the relevant documents, and the two of them did not get on. Brigitte, unused to an arrangement of this sort, often went off in tears to shut herself up in her room.  Alone, like me, in the midst of this family, she rarely had the opportunity to confide her sorrows in anyone.  I should have liked to support her more.  But as soon as she approached me or we spent too much time together, Tilly was informed, and we were prevented from continuing our conversations.

Then, one day, our children returned from Great Britain: Ghislaine's children – François and Guillemette – and my children – Amaury and Diane. Guillaume had stayed on in England.

# 10

Our children returned in August 2005, without offering any explanation as to why they came. Thierry Tilly had moved to Oxford.  He had not paid the rent on their lodgings, and so they had been evicted.  But they were told to say nothing, and to continue to obey Tilly's orders. When I saw them, I was deeply shocked.  All four of them were gaunt and haggard, very wasted, very thin.  Amaury's hair was down to his shoulders.  Ghislaine took me to one side and warned me: 'You're depressed.  Amaury is too. Whatever you do don't talk to him. You'll only make him worse'. Philippe and Brigitte received the same warning. That such a thing should be said to me! The way my son looked... Every time I think of it I am reduced to tears.

In spite of this, having my two little ones back with me again did me good.  For years I had felt myself deprived of them, dispossessed, unable, except on rare occasions, to talk to them. They had assured me, while they were in London, that everything was going well for them. They were, both of them, studying: Diane had applied for a place at Edinburgh University, Amaury was doing an English language course that would allow him, too, to take up a place at a Scottish university, although his plans were less clearly defined than Diane's.

At first, all I was concerned about was getting them back into good shape. I talked a little to Amaury. He was nervous, and always on the verge of tears. His two cousins treated him badly, talked to him as though he were a dog, to the point where I complained about it to them. I had never seen them like this before. 'It's for his own good' was their only explanation. Amaury, then, withdrew from the family and organized his time in his own way. He was, with me, the first to get up in the morning, had breakfast, then took some exercise. Afterwards he worked for a while with his father, either in the garden or in the workshop where Charles-Henri made model boats. This new collaboration with his father allowed him to discover his artistic capabilities and to discover a real talent. He began to carve in wood, and produced some truly beautiful objects. This work soothed and calmed him. When I asked him what had happened in London, his reply could be summed up in a sentence: 'My cousins prevented me from being'. This was all he would say, and, above all, he was unwilling for me to interfere in any way. It was only very much later that I discovered the full truth of the matter. For the time being, I wanted only one thing: to rebuild a good relationship with my children. I devoted all my energies to this.

My children had decided to remain silent because they wanted to spare their parents and because they were too afraid of Tilly to disobey him. This was unfortunate, since what they had to say would have opened our eyes. Mine, at any rate. For my part, I only later learnt what Amaury had been through. I cannot express what I felt about it: the grief, the horror, and guilt... I had failed in my task as a mother; I had been unable to protect my children.

When they first arrived in London, Amaury stayed with François and Guillemette, and then with Diane, who had been evicted from her apartment. For some reason or other, relations between my son and his cousins quickly became difficult and he complained of this to Tilly, whom he thought of as a friend. The latter settled the matter in his usual way. In a very elegant building in Regent Street, there was an office belonging to the Blue Light Foundation, or so Tilly claimed. Amaury could move in there if he agreed to respect certain rules. No one must know that he lived there: so that there was to be no noise, no coming and going during office hours. No strangers were to be allowed in. He was to wash in the toilets on his own before the staff arrived, and sleep on the floor in a sleeping bag. His sister or his cousins would bring him one meal a day, which would be quite enough for him. Tilly set other rules for him too, on the grounds that the disagreeable behaviour of his cousins towards him did not come from them but, on the contrary, from his own behaviour. He must undergo some self-examination, if he was to make progress.

Amaury stopped going to his classes. He never left this empty place in which Tilly had left a few books, some satanic horror films, and a note-pad on which he was to record, day by day, his thoughts and his progress. Forbidden to go out, condemned to wash in ice-cold water, he stopped looking after himself. It became more and more difficult for him to hold out against this psychological imprisonment. François and Diane brought him his meals, while becoming increasingly distressed to see him wasting away. He was dying of hunger. Tilly called in regularly, upbraided him, and insisted that he spend more time writing: a necessary exercise, so he said, if he was to succeed in becoming himself. He endured this hell for nine months, during which time we believed him to be in a decent English establishment.

Until one particular morning, when there was a knock on his door. Amaury, believing it to be his sister or his cousin, answered it and found himself face to face with a bailiff. Not only had he no right whatsoever to be living in this office, but also, for months now, no rent had been paid. He was forcibly ejected and moved in with his cousins, with the result that their flat was now overcrowded and Amaury was given a very frosty reception. He was blamed for having lost a perfectly good apartment through sheer stupidity. He was treated as a complete idiot, and as such, was allotted the entrance hall, and was forbidden to go any further into the apartment, to have his meals with the others, or to watch the television. Tilly, the author of this treatment, called in from time to time to discuss it with Amaury's cousins.

Added to which, they didn't have a penny between them, in spite of the considerable amounts of money we were sending them, since Tilly appropriated the greater part of this for his own personal use. They had discovered shops that sell products each day whose use-by date has already passed or soon will, and which are therefore reduced to something between thirty and seventy per cent of the original price; Diane, who went to the canteen at lunch-time, brought back fruit. They had neither heating nor hot water. They only just managed to survive. It was fortunate, in a way, that when the rent was in arrears, the children were forced to leave their lodgings and return to France.

I got back my second son quite quickly. But with Diane, things were very different. She was nice to me, attentive even, but, hearing her talk, I discovered that she had fallen completely under some outside influence. For example, when recalling her childhood, she gave an account of it that bore no resemblance at all to what had actually happened. She presented herself, when compared with her cousin, in an unflattering light: she was more spoiled, had always had nicer toys, prettier dresses than Guillemette. I was the more astonished by this in that Guillemette was almost ten years older than she was, and they had not grown up together. But Diane was convinced of the view she put forward: that she had been privileged in comparison with her cousin, who had suffered as a result of this. Since her return, moreover, Ghislaine and Guillemette had managed to win her affection and her confidence. Nothing unusual in this, except that it distanced her from her father and from me.

There were, from that moment onwards, two clans in Talade: Ghislaine, her children and Diane on the one hand, Charles-Henri, Amaury and me on the other. Mamie maintained a little distance from this situation, but followed Ghislaine. As for Philippe and Brigitte, they were trying to find just a little bit of space for themselves in their own house, and suffered dreadfully over their separation from their children. When their birthdays came round, this caused the parents a genuine and deep distress. The scene at breakfast time provided a caricature of the situation we found ourselves in. Ghislaine and her children rose late and were thus the last to have breakfast. They remained at the table for an hour, sometimes more, deep in discussion. I had the impression that a daily briefing was in progress, from which the rest of the house was excluded. They fell silent whenever we entered the room. What was Ghislaine saying to them? She was, no doubt, relaying Tilly's orders. She was also, no doubt, passing comments on their relatives. I was very reluctant to believe I had lost Diane. I told myself it would pass, that she was only twenty years old. When the situation became normal again, everything would be all right. But what grieved me even more was that she showed nothing of this. She was relaxed with me, irreproachable, but without inviting a single real conversation or affectionate exchange. It was as though she had something against me, but preferred to leave me in ignorance as to her true state of mind. The more I tried to approach her, the more she distanced herself.

It was six years now since Tilly had entered our lives and, except for our three meetings in Bordeaux and London, one telephone conversation, and a few e-mails, I hardly knew him. Which is why when, in August 2006, Ghislaine announced that Tilly was expecting us – Charles-Henri and me – in Oxford, I was very surprised. I was even more surprised to learn that he wanted, quite specifically, to see me. He wanted to discuss the progress of our investments. 'At last!' I said to myself. During all these years, and in spite of my state of mental exhaustion, I had collected and preserved all the documents concerning any sale we had made, our legal fees, and any other action we had had to face. The total was in the region of four and a half million euros. As far as I was concerned, there was no doubt at all that all the money we had let go was going to reappear, at least in part, thanks to IOUs of debts we held, supported by proofs. We could expect to see, at last, the end of our nightmare.

Escaping the pernicious atmosphere at Talade and no longer having to listen to my sister-in-law's diatribes gave me a new energy. I packed our suitcases with a light heart. We took very little with us: our stay was to last no longer than three or four days. We took the train, the bus, the boat, and then the bus again from London to Oxford. When we arrived, Thierry and Guillaume were waiting for us.

**Part Three:** At the centre
of the web

# 11

The impression that Thierry Tilly makes on us when we arrive – his appearance and general demeanour – in no way resembles what his dictatorial rules of conduct or his orders might have led us to expect. We find again, instead, the lively and friendly young man who had invited us to London. Elegantly attired in navy-blue flannel trousers, a white shirt, and a navy blue pullover, slim, almost sporty in appearance, and very eloquent, he apologizes several times for the accommodation he has arranged for us: a little house, undergoing restoration and festooned with electric wires, several rooms of which are still barely habitable. The kitchen is unusable but the garden is full of flowers and, in the corner, there is a very pretty arbour. 'When it's finished, this is where Guillaume will live', he says, producing the desired effect on parents, delighted by the prospect of where their oldest son will live. In our own room, the furnishings are limited to a table, a single chair, and a mattress on the floor covered with a flowery eiderdown.   I don't know why this should be so, but I really like the flowery cover.   Charles-Henri says nothing.   He is looking out of the window at Thierry's large and comfortable house opposite, where Jessica, their children and Guillaume live. Is he thinking of Caudéran?  As for me, I prefer not to remember Caudéran, our lovingly furnished Bordeaux home, with its beautiful and well-appointed kitchen, its sitting-room, its bedrooms, including our own, with its large and comfortable bed and intimate atmosphere. That's all gone now.   And I reflect upon what we are reduced to:  a mattress with a flowery eiderdown laid on bare floorboards.

Jessica receives us warmly, and invites us to stay with them for as long as we wish.  I would rather spend my days with her than in the cold and miserable little house. Thierry immediately sets the tone for the whole visit: 'I'm aware that your stay in Talade was no picnic, so please now take advantage of the English summer and of our home'. In the days that follow, we establish a rhythm: breakfast with the Tillys, conversations on everything and nothing with Jessica. I help her with the housework. I do the ironing.  Charles-Henri grumbles: 'You're not the maid, you know!' But I don't mind at all: Jessica is charming and, with two adorable children, has as much to do as she can cope with.  Thierry and Guillaume share the task of taking them to and from school.  One day, they ask me to do it.  I've quite lost the habit of being in town, and especially of walking on my own through the streets, or taking the bus.  I have to make an effort.  I am now having to rediscover all of those customs and habits we acquire when we live our daily lives in a city, and to which we normally give no thought. And I have hardly any money, except for a little loose change...

As a consequence of having only one meal a day, in the evening at Thierry's, my husband is beginning to suffer. Disrupting our eating habits is a weapon that Tilly will use several times to disorientate and confuse us. And since we have so little money, Charles-Henri cannot simply go out and buy something to supplement his diet. He manages to get a little oatmeal at lunchtime. And, in the end, he becomes used to this more frugal diet.

Thierry spends most of his time up in the attic, in his office, except when he disappears for the whole afternoon. He has long discussions with Charles-Henri, who becomes evasive when I ask him what they talk about: 'This and that, our plans for the Blue Light Foundation'. They have not even broached the matter of our financial investments. And Thierry's only remark on this this topic is limited to a somewhat strange piece of advice: 'Don't talk to Jessica about money. She's a bit fragile at the moment, I'm afraid; she's having trouble with her mother. To tell you the truth, I'm counting on you to look after her a little: she needs it!' Which is an order I obey gladly enough. And we get on well together: I could even say we live in perfect harmony, which is a very pleasant change from how things were in Talade.

As for Guillaume, he keeps me company when the chores that Tilly imposes on him allow him to do so. Tilly speaks to him as to a very junior employee, whether he wants him to fetch the children from school, to take mail to the post, or to look something up on the Internet. I have the impression that at times my son fills the role of a young male *au pair*, at others of a messenger or a trainee. This corresponds neither to his abilities nor to his education. But Tilly declares himself extremely pleased with Guillaume. Just a little more training and he will be ready for a position either with the UN, or with the foundation... 'He has a future, that boy', he assures us. One might ask oneself how the thousand and one little tasks reserved for Guillaume would qualify him for a position with the UN. Guillaume seems tired, but he is so motivated that I do not even ask myself this question. I knew that everything he endured was out of love for his family.

After two weeks of this rather agreeable existence, I rediscover my fighting spirit, and one morning, as we are finishing breakfast, I say to Thierry that I should like to know how our investments stand. Diane is about to go to Edinburgh University; it is, in fact, high time that she enrolled. I wonder how we are going to finance her studies, as well as all the costs she will incur there. He rises, puts down his table napkin: 'You are quite right, Christine, we must get to work! Come with me'.

I follow him. Charles-Henri does not move. I am not entirely surprised at this: after all, it is I who have made the greater investment in Tilly's company and in the family trust. We cross the road, in the direction of our own garden, and go to sit in the summer-house. Thierry likes one-on-one conversations: it is there that his powers of persuasion are at their most effective.

'Well now', he begins, 'I must tell you, first of all, about the "transmission"'.

'The transmission...' This was the first time I was to hear the word that was to be at the centre of the most bizarre episode of all in Thierry's takeover of our family. 'Like Charles-Henri,' he went on, 'you are descended from a very old family. Do you know what your maiden name, de Cornette de Laminière, means? It means 'the guardian of the mine. And this definition acquires its full meaning in the context of the inheritance. Does that mean nothing to you?'

Such is my stupefaction that I remain speechless. I shake my head, dumbfounded. What on earth is he talking about? At this he adopts a reverential tone, as though he were entering a quasi-sacred domain: 'There exist in France a few very ancient families who are guardians of treasure entrusted to them, over the centuries, by kings, so that they may come to the aid of the most impoverished and guarantee a certain equilibrium. These families pass on the secret from generation to generation. Yours, in other words, possesses considerable hidden riches. You must certainly have some knowledge of it. The place, and the way to retrieve it must have been given to you'.

For a moment, I think it's all a joke, but he is deadly serious. All the same, I do not for a moment give any credence whatsoever to what he is telling me, and I retort: 'But this is completely and utterly surreal!'

He glares at me, his blue eyes now icy cold, and retorts in a menacing tone: 'Christine! I forbid you to use that word!'

'There has never been anything, in the whole history of my family, to suggest even remotely the existence of such a treasure! You must be mistaken!'

He sighs. This time, I infer from his expression that I am a simpleton.

'Such a thing is never, of course, entrusted to lawyers. It's much too important. I know for a fact that this transmission was made. My boss witnessed it. We are its most immediate guardians, its protectors. Your reaction proves only one thing: that the immense burden it represents was too heavy for you, and you have lost all memory of it. That sometimes happens. My boss has already seen several similar cases'.

It is at this moment that I realize just how deeply rooted his certainty is. He will not give up until I rediscover it, this memory. I try once more to disabuse him: 'Listen, my parents did not keep any secrets from me. They never spoke of one, never even hinted, that there might be one to keep. The family papers contain no trace of any transmission of this kind. You are quite mistaken about it'.

But he stands his ground: I am the guardian of a secret, that of a fabulous hoard of gold and jewels. By now we are walking around the garden, and in spite of my denials he persists: I can certainly recover it, this secret. The conversation is going round and round in circles, seems to me quite mad, and finally, provoked, I put a question to him: 'Since you know all about it, why don't you tell me? If your boss is already in the know, then everything is completely straightforward!'

'Unfortunately, Christine, this is not so! There are procedures we cannot ignore. We cannot change the rules just for you'. And then he changes his tone, adopting one of almost fraternal kindness: 'Don't worry! I will help you; you will recover this memory that is eluding you!'

We go back to his house. My astonishment has been replaced by disquiet. He is driven by such conviction that I do not see how I can disabuse him. I go at once and report all of this to my husband. He adheres, without hesitation, to this incredible story. The antiquity of our two families, and their complete respectability, are enough in themselves to lend perfect credence to this theory. It is only fair to add, at this point, that it is now six years since Tilly began to manipulate us. Exhausted by it all, we are wholly in his power...

My parents, and I after them, have never made anything of our possessing an aristocratic name, nor of the origins it implies. Nor have the Védrines. As far as we are concerned, the antiquity of our families imposes on us, quite simply, the duty to maintain the name with dignity. Thierry Tilly, in his dealings with my husband, exploited this, and used it to win his support.

But Tilly himself will go further. Our enemies know that we are in possession of this secret. They are prepared to do anything to get hold of it. And the first person under threat from this is my oldest son, Guillaume. Thierry warns Charles-Henri: if we do not do something, there will be 'dead meat', to adopt his own colourful way of putting it. It is, he goes on, in order to protect him that he has always kept a close eye on Guillaume.

So here I am, sitting on my flowery counterpane, devastated by the enormity of what I have just discovered. This whole plot, of which so much has been made for several years now, and of which I knew nothing at all, turns out to be nothing other than a treasure that is hidden and coveted by others! Tilly tells me, moreover, that Bertrand, my nearest cousin, is among those other people, people 'who know'.

I do not believe it. The truth of the matter – but there again, I will discover this only later – is that Bertrand, very anxious about me and my children, and learning that Diane is in London, has made some discreet inquiries. I do not know how Thierry discovered this. He is now convinced that he owes his eviction from the apartment in London (for unpaid rent) to my cousin. So he has obviously had him in his sights for some time now, since he knows how fond I am of him.

'The more serious the matter, the more easily it slips the mind', as Thierry remarked to me one day, when in a confidential mood. I have forgotten what it was he was referring to at the time. But, in the present case, the saying acquires its full force: Charles-Henri is begging me to do all I can to remember this 'transmission' and so save the family. I reply that I have no memory of it, nor, if it does exist, do I see how to recover it. Charles-Henri throws me a sceptical glance: no one would forget such a thing, unless they chose to. After two weeks of respite, I have the impression of descending, once again, into hell.

After this, I 'work' every day with Thierry. 'The memory', he tells me, ' is a sort of computer. It contains millions of files; one cannot have access to all of them simply by clicking. Some require logical and disciplined investigation, through the association of ideas. We function in the same way'. Docile as I am, I make an effort to concentrate, and he gets me to talk about my family. In this strange context, I go off, as it were, in search of my ancestors of whom I know very little: my grandfather died when he was forty and my father was a man of few words. I never questioned him as to our origins. And so I raise more questions than I provide answers. How and where did my grandfather meet my English grandmother? Why is he buried in Dieppe when the family vault is at Montmorillon? What, at the end of an extraordinary life, happened to my father's older brother? I know that, very anglophile, he lived in Great Britain, married there, and had a son. Then he embarked with his family for Australia. On the boat, on their way there, my cousin died of some illness, I don't know what. Immediately on landing, my uncle wrote a letter to his brother, to the effect that, in spite of the death of their son, he and his wife were relieved to have arrived in this country, which they were discovering with pleasure, certain that they would be happy there. After which, total silence. My father tried every possible line of enquiry but, in spite of all his efforts, he never again had news of his brother, nor heard anything more about him. This disappearance delights Tilly, feeding, as it does, his obsession about a 'transmission': my uncle, clearly, knew the secret and so they got rid of him. As always, it is the unidentifiable 'they' that are evoked.

In order to secure Charles-Henri's complete collaboration, Tilly has an idea: he sends him off to Paris, in order to visit what Tilly calls his 'services'. Charles-Henri goes off one morning, by car, with Guillaume. Since they're going, they are given computers to deliver to his 'boss', Jacques Gonzalez. Tilly has warned them not to take any security risks: 'Make sure you're always on the look-out!' A rendezvous has been arranged for them, in a café at the Porte Champerret. There, a tall thin fellow, by the name of Pascal, nicknamed 'the Great', seeks them out, borrows their car to deliver the equipment they've brought, then disappears. He reappears several hours later, returns the keys and vanishes. There is no mention of any visit to Charles-Henri's 'services'. On the other hand, Charles-Henri and Guillaume cannot leave again without Tilly giving the green light. They are obliged to wait from five o'clock in the afternoon until three o'clock in the morning before they can leave again for England. Using safety as an excuse, Tilly imposes his own timescale on them, thus keeping up the pressure on them: a tried and tested technique for preventing any initiative on their part.

On their return, Thierry takes Charles-Henri to one side: 'So sorry you had a wasted journey, but it was inevitable for reasons I can't tell you. You must nevertheless help Christine by pretending you have seen my offices, and assuring her that you have been shown the proofs of the existence of the 'transmission'. This will help her to recover her memory'.

Obediently, Charles-Henri says to me: 'Listen, Christine, I have seen the offices. And I am very happy about it all. Guillaume is valued there. And, above all I was shown reliable documents, which prove, beyond any doubt, the existence of the transmission. The transmission certainly took place…'

He himself is so persuaded of what he has been told to say that I take what he tells me at face value. I must recover this memory! And this time, it is no longer Tilly who is pushing me, but Charles-Henri.

# 12

One morning, Tilly waves under my nose a copy of my parents' family tree. He had found it among the contents of our house in Bordeaux, which were supposed to be locked up and stored in a container in London. 'You will need this document in order to sign the legal papers confirming your donation of the 'transmission' to Guillaume'.

There's no respite for me, I must recover it, this 'transmission'. I do not reply. My memory still refuses to release it, this famous secret, while my self-appointed 'confessor' is always there, his ears pricked. I am under ever greater stress. I cannot buy Tranxene in London. My supply is exhausted, leaving me with all the side-effects you might expect to follow such a sudden and brutal deprivation of the benefits it brought.

One afternoon a sudden decision is made to go to Brussels. To celebrate my eighteenth birthday, one of my father's sisters, who had married a Belgian, took me to a 'coming-out' ball in Brussels. It's another version of the one in Paris, but the principle is the same: young girls dressed in haute couture dresses are introduced, formally, into Belgian high society. This has given Tilly a new idea: 'You're going to Brussels with Guillaume! The end is in sight!'

Charles-Henri is to remain in Oxford, because this trip is just between our oldest son and me. We are to go to a bank with my identity card and ask to see the safe deposit box that bears my name. But, how am I to recognize the building? 'By seeing it!' Tilly assures me, suddenly excited. And he goes off for a briefing session with Guillaume. 'As soon as you've regained possession of the transmission, you must go to a lawyer'. I object to this, pointing out that according to him, lawyers should never be invited to get involved in this affair. He sweeps away this objection with a shrug of his shoulders.

We leave that evening by coach and travel all night: Guillaume has just been to Paris by car, and is tired, so Tilly declares, using this as a justification for making us take this form of transport. Next morning, we tidy ourselves up as best we can in the toilets at the bus station, and begin our tour of the banks in the centre of Brussels. I don't know the town: I have never been back since the famous ball. Guillaume has a town plan and leads the way.

The first bank is a branch of HSBC. I show my identity card and explain that I have an account there, quite an old account. The bank official, without further questioning, taps away at his computer and shakes his head: there's no account, no safe deposit box, under that name. The same thing happens at the second bank, at the third, and the fourth. We go from one bank to another and from one failure to the next. Tilly, on the end of the telephone, is getting anxious. He rings us every quarter of an hour, and harries Guillaume. We hardly stop even to swallow a sandwich. As the afternoon progresses, we suffer, alternately, negative replies from banks and explosions of rage from Tilly. The tension between him and Guillaume becomes more marked. At five o'clock everything closes, the metal shutters come down, our pointless quest is finished. We have so little money that we find beds in a youth hostel. Overcome with weariness, I am not even hungry. I am a puppet on a string, vainly seeking something that does not exist. The temptation to be done with it all is constantly present. I am assailed by ringing in my ears, by bouts of vertigo.

The next day, Guillaume says to me, sadly: 'Do try harder, Maman. This is ridiculous!' We resume our pilgrimage. I would never have believed there could be so many banks in Brussels. And as we once again cross and recross the city on foot, I begin to fail. Tilly, always at the end of the line, changes his tactics: 'Go to the Place Royale!', where – or so it appears – my body language will prompt me into remembering something. But, not a bit of it, my body language tells me nothing. Confronted by this void, Tilly goes on the attack: 'Your mother knows very well, but will not say'. We go back to the youth hostel. Tilly orders my son to interrogate me and not to let me sleep. Guillaume takes no notice. As for me, worn out by these two days of walking, I fall into a deep sleep.

On the third day, eavesdropping on conversations between Guillaume and Tilly, I hear the latter assert, yet again, that I have in my possession all the relevant information and am keeping it to myself. Once again I consider suicide. Rothschild's, the last bank we visit, provokes, on my part, an explosion of tears and misery. I reflect that, after the war, Jews dispossessed of their total inheritance have gone through the same procedures as I have, but with justice on their side, whereas I am ashamed of what Tilly is making me do, and of my weakness.

We have just experienced the worst week of our lives, and our return journey is no less wretched. I arrive home, where Tilly and Charles-Henri are waiting for us, and I hear myself saying to Tilly: 'Thierry, am I still one of the eleven?' The eleven are the family. I do not want to be thought a traitor; I have done nothing wrong. And I have become, once again, a little girl lost, terrified at the idea of being rejected. I see myself imploring Tilly not to scold me, but to let me still be one of the group. When I look back on this episode, I remember quite clearly that, somewhere inside me, a minute part of my mind remained alert. But no more than alert: incapable, in other words, of prompting any action on my part, a state of mind that shows Tilly that he has regained his influence over me. That he has me in his grip. And he therefore displays an unwonted degree of kindness towards me.

My husband, by contrast, cold-shoulders me. He speaks to me as little as possible, and avoids me when he can. He busies himself doing jobs in the house, where the work has not advanced by one iota, and spends long periods of time with Tilly who consolidates his power over us by destroying me in Charles-Henri's eyes: on the one hand, so it seems, I lie, and I betray my family, on the other, I have seriously damaged my children. For example, when Amaury began to smoke hashish, not only did I do nothing about it, I actually increased the amount of money I gave him. Charles-Henri is very sad indeed to see his whole world disintegrating in this way. He listens to the false accusations, and reports them to me; but in fact they strike no chord in him, nor do they carry any real conviction. On the other hand, he does not defend me, but does everything Tilly tells him to do, a situation that is, as I see it today, completely paradoxical.

At the end of October, we celebrate Guillaume's birthday, while, throughout November, the leaden atmosphere is unrelieved: I am supposed to be reflecting. But upon what? And how?

With the onset of winter the house is bitterly cold. The heating works on a time switch that is activated by coins. Tilly supplies them – when he chooses to. He's using Charles-Henri to renovate an office, but he almost never, or hardly ever, speaks to me.

And then, on November 20th, we witness a quarrel between Jessica and him: she had gone to do some shopping, and their joint credit card has been refused. Tilly arrives, beside himself with rage, and, turning to me, says: ' We've all of us had just about enough of you, Christine! You have impoverished, stripped bare, and virtually ruined my family, and your own! And all because you refuse to give the transmission! It's all your fault!

Now, go to your room, at once, and think it over'.

And so begins a physical and psychological sequestration, not unlike that which Amaury experienced the previous year in London. Confined to my unheated bedroom, seated at my table, I am compelled to apply myself to such written work as will activate my memory and deliver this so-called transmission to my son. I am not permitted to leave the house, but I am not locked in, and I am allowed to use the bathroom. Every night Charles-Henri comes and sleeps beside me. Tilly has persuaded him that this confinement will be good for me. It will allow me to get my bearings, to find the cause of the mental blockage that is obscuring my memory, and so solve our problem. Charles-Henri is in no doubt about this, Tilly's fairy-tale having become a reality for him.

Tilly has confiscated not only my identity card but also my watch, my engagement ring, and a necklace given me by my father on my fortieth birthday. These items, it appears, contained tracers, which would allow our enemies to keep track of me. He also confiscated my flowery eiderdown. I had said how much I liked it, this eiderdown. A detail, perhaps, but none the less destructive for that.

So as not to give way to despair, I spend my days reliving childhood memories, reciting poems to myself, retelling the stories of books and films I have enjoyed. I have to confess that I also, at that time, considered suicide. Three things deterred me: my faith in God, my children, and my determination to bring the truth to light one day.

Tilly had chosen to use psychological harassment against me: and so Guillaume, who is under threat too because of me, must always be within Tilly's reach, must never be at a distance of more than ten yards from him. My eldest son has become invisible to me. And I am a bad and unworthy mother. And since I persist in remaining silent, Tilly's boss is going to send me to 'a cell he has the use of, which is underneath Les Invalides'. Jacques is used to recalcitrants like me, and he has a team that specializes in physical interrogation. When the inmates are allowed to leave, they are released at night into the streets of Paris. 'They are good for nothing now except being interned: they have been driven mad'. I am filled with guilt, and with fear. But deep inside me, an instinct for survival, this streak of obstinate common sense, perhaps, that I've already mentioned, tells me not to think, not to believe Tilly's assertions. I retain, almost without thinking about it, the hope that this nightmare will, some day or other, come to an end.

In his dealings with me, Tilly alternates between threats and exercises in persuasion. I am therefore obliged to copy down, from his dictation, phrases and formulae designed to enlighten me:

I want to, therefore I can.

I know what I must do.

ACT. Otherwise DANGER.

Keep to the essentials.

A transmission has taken place within my family. It contains references to my family name.

This transmission has been properly administered.

I have some recollection of this. Traces of it remain in my memory. I *must*, and I *can* recover them.

This is possible. This transmission represents an astonishing opportunity for us all...

All its constituents are positive ones:

- Love of my family.
- Love for my family.
- Thierry's friendship and the support of his patron.
- No judgment on my part.
- Very positive plans.
- The possibility of being able, with this transmission, to help others (thus continuing the work of the Laminières).
- It is all *very easy*.  It is within *my reach*.

I am obliged, too, to make a list, along the following lines: I must

- Reflect.
- Look myself in the face.
- Have complete confidence in myself, twenty-four hours out of twenty-four.
- Show humility.
- Begin at once.
- I am capable of this.
- Concentrate on the desired goal.
- Do not lie to myself.
- If I do not do this, I endanger the lives of Guillaume, Amaury, Diane.
- I will be a bad mother.
- I must be able to look myself in the face.

Christmas 2006 comes and goes. Then New Year's Day. Without my situation changing in any way: someone brings me breakfast and dinner. No one speaks to me except Charles-Henri, but his remarks are all of them variations on the same theme: the transmission. Tilly comes to look at what I have written, shouts, gets worked up, bellows with rage sometimes, because I am making no progress, then leaves, claiming to be going to work. Months go by in this way. I have no clear notion of the passing of time, and, above all, I can no longer imagine any sort of future.

One day, I have had enough. I'm cold, I'm consumed with anxiety. On a sudden impulse, I leave my room, and go down into the street. On the house opposite, there is a camera. Tilly appears almost immediately and, pointing at it, bellows: 'Are you crazy? Go in at once, you're endangering your children's lives!' And he pushes me back into the house.

In my previous life, and at Martel too, I read a great deal. My favourite antidote to stress was reading detective novels. Here I haven't a single book. Tilly, via Charles-Henri, sends me Molière's *L'Avare,* along with a message, to the effect that 'she will get the point!' He brings me, too, a biography of Napoleon's first wife, Josephine de Beauharnais. He lays it down, with great solemnity, in front of me: 'Take very great care you do not suffer the same fate!'

An allusion, of course, to her repudiation by Napoleon. He now knows all my weaknesses: as with my children, losing my husband would destroy me. But he remarks: 'As you must have understood by now, all your family have left you. You're on your own'. I don't know if he means by this my near relatives – my sister, my cousin, or even Marie-Hélène – or my children. As to the former, I will discover that they have never stopped trying to save me, even if it turned out to be in vain. But at least they never abandoned me. As for my children, they did not abandon me either, they were quite simply prevailed upon in the most disgraceful way to distance themselves from me.

In the spring of 2007, suddenly, and without any apparent reason, my imprisonment is at an end. Charles-Henri informs me of this in an oblique way: he leads me to a place some five hundred meters away, points out a dilapidated house, and says: 'There is our new house'. It's a street where the buildings, all of them of the same design, are lined up in a row: bow-window, single storey, a patch of lawn in front. Once again, everything needs doing. Tilly has negotiated, with the owner, a substantial reduction in rent in exchange for certain improvements: ceilings, soundproofing, redecoration. And we start upon a new existence as building workers. The owner sometimes comes to give us a hand. Thierry is in charge, and deals with him. The rest of the time, we are, the two of us, Charles-Henri and I, alone together. Needless to say, Tilly pays us nothing, but gives us a little money for our daily expenses. A minimal amount.

Having been confined for four months and subjected to unremitting psychological tension, the manual work and the peace and quiet do me good. A sort of routine emerges, consisting of work, meals, walks along the Thames. Summer has come. We walk a great deal, discovering with pleasure an agreeable English custom: the owners of fruit trees leave boxes of fruit in front of their gardens and invite the passers-by to help themselves. As a means of improving our everyday diet, we take endless advantage of this.

François, Ghislaine's son, whom we believed to be in Talade, calls on us one day. He has just arrived and wants to say hello to us. In point of fact, he has been in Oxford for several months now, but we knew nothing of this. This explains why Charles-Henri and I have not been allowed to go into the centre of the town, but are restricted to walks along the river banks. Why this visit? Why this lie? It is, of course, another of Tilly's orders, another of his unfathomable ideas. A few days later it is Diane and Amaury's turn to visit us, accompanied by Tilly, a visit that is very much harder for me. They voice only one question: 'Maman! Why don't you make this transmission?' Thierry has persuaded them that I am refusing to give it. Because of me, Diane must give up all thought of going to Edinburgh, and Amaury cannot continue with his education. They are both of them working, and working in somewhat precarious circumstances. They cannot understand my obstinacy. How could I be so hard? How could I deprive them of any assistance when a single word from me would enable us to resume our former life? Charles-Henri does not correct them. Worse, they absolutely refuse to believe me when I assert that I am totally devoid of any such memory. I had hoped that, in spite of Thierry's visits and his endless aspersions, in the end this whole affair would simply peter out; but I now see, only too well, that no one, apart from me, has any intention of letting it go. I sense that my children, in the face of this surreal situation, are up in arms. They depart again, leaving me with an even greater weight of grief on my shoulders.

Why am I burdened with this story, this alleged transmission? I now know the reason: I asked too many questions, even if I always ended by giving in. I was a sceptical and disruptive element. Tilly did not like me and wanted to destroy me once and for all.

Summer and autumn pass by without anything in particular happening. My husband reminds me regularly of my responsibilities, and I implore him to believe me when I declare that I have, really and truly, no such memory. But he persists in disbelieving everything I say. Up until now, I have always given way in the face of any more or less sustained demand or request he has made of me. My resistance surprises him. But he continues to believe that what I lack is not memory, but the time to recover it

Throughout this whole period, Tilly has continued to pursue his plan of destroying me in Charles-Henri's eyes: he has proof of my infidelity, of my frivolity, of the rackety life I was leading in Bordeaux while he was working so hard. My husband says nothing to me of these slanderous lies, asks no explanation of me. Rather, he accepts Tilly's stories, but forgives me everything.

The winter of 2007 arrives and, in January 2008, Diane and François come to see us. Charles-Henri is not there. Doubtless he has gone to buy building materials.

They invite me – in a tone that brooks no denial or delay – to go with them: Tilly is waiting for us.   We walk for quite some time, leaving the residential quarter for one that is less pleasant.   My daughter and my nephew say nothing and walk just ahead of me, looking grave. I ask no questions, knowing that they will not reply. My children and I have reached a point of almost total rupture, orchestrated by Tilly.

We arrive at a modest little house, narrow and very tall.   We go into the entrance hall and, at the bottom of the stairs, Tilly greets me with a broad smile: 'Christine! I have good news for you.   We are going, at last, to solve the problem of the transmission!'

# 13

We go up the stairs to the next floor.  Thierry opens the door of a room.  To my great surprise I find, seated around a table, Charles-Henri, together with Philippe and Ghislaine, whom I had believed to be at Talade.  I should like to ask for some explanation, but am not given time to speak.  Diane and François join us and shut the door again behind them.  Thierry is the first to speak:

'This is a very important moment, Christine!  We are about to resolve the problem of the transmission.  Besides which, we must do so: my boss is starting to become seriously impatient.  I have questioned Charles-Henri, Philippe and Ghislaine at length.  We have come to the conclusion that you are in possession, not only of the Laminière transmission but the Védrines transmission too!'

It is perfectly clear to me what has happened: the three Védrines have sworn they know nothing but that I, perhaps, have the information they're looking for.  My denials are in vain, they have all of them been conditioned by Thierry.  I object: 'Why me, when Grandpa had two sons?  You have always said that this transmission was handed on to the oldest son!'  I defend myself at every step.  A discussion then arises, during the course of which Ghislaine attacks me on the matter of my relationship with my father-in-law who, according to her, indulged my every whim and talked to me in very intimate terms.  The proof of this?  When Charles-Henri went to Tunisia, ahead of me, in order to find an apartment, I dined with him, tête à tête, while my mother-in-law was away from Bordeaux. I seduced him, and he entrusted the transmission to me. Ghislaine is vehement on the matter. With Tilly's encouragement, she exposes this imaginary complicity between her father and me, using it as an argument in support of his theory. During the whole of the discussion, she plays the role of the unrelenting public prosecutor. She deploys, one by one, her allegations: the dinner before the departure to Bizerta, and the visit my parents-in-law made there. Her father must certainly have confirmed the transmission during that trip.

I gaze at my brothers- and sister-in-law. I no longer recognize them. Today, her eyes narrowed and dark, her mouth pinched, all her features tensed, Ghislaine is the very image of severity and suspicion. Philippe is unbending, impassive, and even if it is an effort for him, registers only grim determination. If I take my cue from them, I have no choice but to yield. It is twenty-five years now since I joined their family. Twenty-five years of memories destroyed by Tilly.

Then, Guillaume arrives. He is the only one of them to defend me. Without questioning the idea of the transmission, he says: 'But, when it comes down to it, why would it be Maman?' They ignore this question, since, as far as the others are concerned, it does not even arise. Later on, Tilly asks Guillaume to go back to Lot-et-Garonne. He will not then, thank God, have to witness the trial behind closed doors – the trial in camera, the *huis clos* – that is to follow.

Of those present, Charles-Henri takes the least part in the proceedings. As the youngest of the three, he

has always been more or less under the influence of
Ghislaine.   Caught between his wife and his sister, loyal
to his family, he is very unhappy, distraught even, by the
situation we find ourselves in.   But he tries to establish
a calm and reasonable atmosphere in which to conduct
our discussion.   This always results in the same demand:
it is I who must speak.   Tilly is present, but says very
little, leaving it to my brother- and sister-in law to lead
the discussion.   But he is quite clearly expecting me to be
so affected by what I hear that I will be persuaded into
taking some action.

Three quarters of an hour later he closes the meeting
and we go down to the ground floor.   I notice that
Ghislaine leads the way down the staircase and positions
herself just inside the front door, as if she were trying
to prevent me from escaping, in case, that is, I had any
thought of doing so.   I feel trapped.   We reassemble
in a sort of small sitting-room, which looks on to the
street through a bow-window veiled in net curtains and
in dark and heavy curtains.   Furnished with a sofa,
two armchairs, a single upright chair, and a little table,
it is perfectly neutral and shabby.   The fabric on the
armchairs is almost threadbare, the wall-paper faded.
The bottoms of the walls ooze with damp.   I am struck,
momentarily, by one detail: there is not a single picture,
a single object, it is a completely impersonal room.
The children leave us.

Some of us sit down, others do not.   I remain
standing, as does Tilly who, furious with rage, comes in
noisily, accusing me of betraying my family by my silence.

He returns, yet again, to the theme of the threat that my children face, and berates me for my selfishness, my stupid obstinacy. Faced as I am with all the adults of the family, this is all too much for me. In tones of great gravity, and with her eyes on Thierry, Ghislaine intervenes: 'I have to tell you, Christine, that I have never seen Thierry so angry. You must have done something badly wrong, something very serious!'

Tilly tells me to sit down. I go towards the sofa where Charles-Henri is sitting in order to place myself next to him. And, seeing him move along to give me room, Ghislaine continues: 'You see! Even your husband moves away from you. It must be obvious to you by now that you will never again have him at your side! It's finished! You've destroyed everything! You're on your own'.

So keenly do I feel this remark that I, who up until then have been standing up to Tilly, am all at once defeated, psychologically and morally. From now on, I will give in to everything without resistance, as if I inhabited some parallel world. The Stalinesque trial can begin.

This remark of Ghislaine's is, or so it seems, the signal for a real attack on me to be launched, an indictment intended, as I almost immediately understand, to cut me off from my husband, and to deprive me definitively of his support. I do not remember everything I was accused of. One thing, however, perhaps the most ridiculous of all, is asserted by Ghislaine: 'You had Guillaume baptized in the church of Saint-Seurin, behind the altar, and without telling anyone, even Charles-Henri'. Ghislaine paces up and down the room, waving her hands, speaking loudly, articulating each word, emphasizing it, as though she were an inquisitor revealing damning proofs against the accused. 'We all know it. Maman was told early on. She has kept it to herself in spite of her distress. She wanted to spare you, Charles-Henri,' she adds more gently, turning towards her brother.

An absurd accusation, since the two churches – the Reformed and the Catholic – recognize the same baptism.

Charles-Henri says nothing. It is a charge, which, if it were true, would indeed be serious: I would have lied to my husband on a delicate matter. He is a committed Protestant; and such an action would have been a betrayal. At the beginning of the indictment, I had tried to defend myself, but, in the face of this last attack, I give in and say nothing. And I, who am very emotional, will never once cry during the whole of the fortnight that is to come.

Thierry, now aggressive, now kindness itself, renews the attack on me. I content myself with simply listening to him. At which point he decides to rehearse our life as a married couple, demonstrating, indeed, how remarkably well informed he is about our life together, from the moment we met until the present. But what interests him is the journey that my parents-in-law and my own parents made to Tunisia. The transmission would surely have been confirmed around Guillaume's cradle. If my mother, undergoing chemotherapy at the time and, therefore, most unwell, came too, this must have been in order that she might reassure herself that everything had been correctly done.

Then he announces an amnesty, whereby 'everyone may declare, without fear of punishment, what is on his mind, and what errors have been committed'.

But the only person who is expected to speak is me. Tilly disappears from time to time. He has installed a mattress in a neighbouring room. He no doubt goes off there to have a rest. This session of Stalinist self-criticism, in which I am the only player, and during which all the others vent their own frustrations by attacking me, lasts until the following day. We are forbidden to sleep or to eat during more than twenty-four hours. Only Philippe, on account of his age, is to be allowed to rest for a while. Ghislaine for her part reports on the situation to Tilly. At last we are given permission to have tea and biscuits, a permission that is not extended to me for as long as I refuse to co-operate. I persist, nevertheless, in repeating that this story of a transmission is absurd and lacks any foundation. This reinforces Tilly's aggression and animosity towards me. Very soon, silence is imposed on me.

Late in the afternoon Tilly appears and declares: 'Christine, you are not worthy to look your family in the face'. Grabbing me roughly by the arm, he forces me to sit on the chair in front of a little table that faces the wall, so that I have my back turned towards the rest of the room and therefore to the others.

I am forced to remain seated on this chair, except to go to the toilet. Eventually, I am given tea and biscuits. After the closing speech for the prosecution, we return to a veritable interrogation, to which I reply sometimes orally, sometimes in writing, with a pencil, on little pieces of paper.    If this were a police station, Thierry and Ghislaine would be the two 'sadistic' cops, and Charles-Henri and Philippe two observers, who intervene very little.    I am assailed by a torrent of questions.    First of all, where is the transmission?    In which bank?    I draw up, from memory, a list of banks in London, in Brussels, in Germany.    I venture various incoherent bits of information.    I who have never studied finance, pronounce on cashflows, transactions, transfers from one bank to another.    In truth, I have nothing to say, so I hold forth as best I can, trying to find a way out.    Needless to say, none of it makes any sense.    At regular intervals, Ghislaine passes on what I have written to Thierry.    He pronounces judgment: is it good or bad? She returns with the reply.    It is always bad!

On the third day, exhausted, I hear Tilly reminding Charles-Henri that I must on no account be allowed to sleep.    He confides in him that during my Thursday lunches with my friends – the last of which took place more than six years ago – I underwent hypnosis.    'If,' he explains, 'during these moments of great tension and psychological distress, Christine is allowed to go to sleep, she will wake up insane!' In spite of his medical training, Charles-Henri, once again, swallows this outrageous proposition, and becomes obsessively afraid of seeing me fall into a deep sleep.    In Tilly's absence, he tries to prevent me from sleeping by pinching the lobes of my ears, as he has seen anaesthetists do.    Then Tilly reappears, checks that I have not slept, notes my lack of progress, and, assuming an air of great menace, vanishes again.

Tilly's great skill, during all of this, lies in his having discharged the resolution of the problem on to two brothers and a sister. It's up to them, in other words, to get me to speak. It seems to me that there is some difference between the treatment the brothers receive and that of Ghislaine. She is absent for longer – to go and sleep, no doubt, and to eat. She is more favoured, in short. Besides, as Tilly will say to me later: 'The only person I trust is Ghislaine'.

This ordeal, in the gloomy little sitting-room, plunged into half-light during the day, and near-darkness at night, lasts for several days. Both brothers are at times, overcome by tiredness, inclined to fall asleep. Me too. But I am not allowed to lean back in my chair, nor to rest my head on the table. Occasionally, I fall on to the floor. I am promptly put back on my chair. Thierry alleges that I do it on purpose. I am 'a trickster and a liar!' He comes very close and leans over me: 'I'm going to flay you…You'll see! I'm going to put a bullet into you, right next to your ear. You'll wish you were dead, for it makes you go mad!' … 'Charles-Henri will be able to see his children, but as for you, you will never see them again'… He turns to Ghislaine: 'From now on she's not allowed to use the toilet!'

'Then I'll stop eating and drinking!' I say.

'Oh no, you won't,' he retorts, before leaving the room.

Charles-Henri and Philippe try to reason with me, exhausted, as they are too, by lack of sleep and food.

'Just give him the account numbers! What's the point of going through all this! It's terrible!'

'Do you realize what you're putting us through?

I invent some account numbers. Thierry checks them. He returns bellowing with rage: 'As for you, I'm going to put you into a brothel for negroes!'

Philippe and Charles-Henri react very badly when they hear this latest threat. They are both of them at the end of their tether. But my torturer couldn't care less. As for me, I now inhabit a different world, where I string together, from time to time, a few digits, a few names... Tilly loses his temper and, on several occasions, bursts into the room, punches me violently in the back and bellows wholly incomprehensible threats and demands into my ears. When Charles-Henri tries to intervene, he reassures him: 'Don't worry, she'll come to no harm. It's absolutely vital to counterbalance the influence of the hypnosis to which she was subjected'.

When Tilly leaves my room, he re-enters the real world, one in which his accomplice Jacques Gonzalez telephones him from Paris. He is, so he says, losing his patience. 'What on earth do these bloody fools think they're doing? If I get hold of them, they'll talk all right!' Which gives Tilly the idea of parading once again the threat of the prison cells and the physical interrogation in the crypt of the Invalides; which produces no better a result, and for a very good reason.

I really no longer know where I am, nor what I am doing. I'm drowning. Tilly denies me any possibility of washing or of changing my clothes. Informed of this, Amaury comes, on his own initiative, to help his mother, and to do some cleaning. It's not a matter of chance that Tilly has chosen to inform Amaury of this change. He knows how sensitive he is. Fearing he will be very shocked by what he sees, I decide not to submit so easily in future, not to take things lying down

Then Tilly brings Diane to reason with me. Which she does, frightened by the state she finds me in, but not understanding what she believes to be mere obstinacy on my part. She begs me to eat and to drink a little. And this restores at least a little of my energy. I try, with the best will in the world, to remember the transmission. Without success.

At which Tilly adopts his favourite method: malicious slander. Informed by Ghislaine of my history and that of my family, he pronounces judgment: 'So you think you are a good person, do you? A good daughter? But you seem to have forgotten that you let your father die in a retirement home!'

I have no intention of defending myself against so unworthy an attack: As I've already said, my father asked to go into the retirement home. But what was the point of explaining all that?

'At any rate' he continues, 'it's obvious you are lacking in family feeling. When you took Diane to Poitiers, you passed very close to Montmorillon. But you did not even have the curiosity, let alone the piety or the loyalty, to visit the tomb of your ancestors'.

These accusations distress and almost destroy me. They cut me to the quick.

Next, as though to step up the pressure, he profits from the presence of Ghislaine and her two brothers to deliver the final blow, the ultimate accusation: 'You might as well confess, too, that you have had intimate relations with your brother-in-law, Jean. There's no point in your denying it, I have videos and photos to prove it. He himself boasts of it openly'.

Set and match to Tilly: Ghislaine's rancour is increased tenfold, and Charles-Henri is devastated. In the state I am in, I am capable of confessing anything at all, I just don't care. But suddenly, as though in a vision, I see, in the corner of the room, a staircase. From the top stair, my three children are watching me. At which point, I retract, furiously, and I deny it the whole thing, protesting loudly that it is ridiculous, and completely false. Ghislaine slaps me in the face, bellowing: 'Confess! Just confess! He's got a video!'

At which point, leaving us in total disarray, Tilly departs, but only to return again a couple of days later and to unleash his final argument: 'There's no way round it. My boss can't do anything more for you. You'll have to pay for the case yourselves. You'll have to sell Martel'.

Martel, of course, is the family's most precious possession, dear to the heart, not only of Charles-Henri, but to that of his brother and sister too. All their childhood memories are there, all their traditions. To sell Martel would be to destroy the Védrines family. The three of them rise up as one. They will never sell Martel.

At which, Tilly retracts: 'I have just telephoned my boss. As a mark of good will towards you, he is ready to safeguard Martel, and has found a solution'.

For the first time ever, then, he beats a retreat. He accepts that, no, we will not sell Martel, but will instead take out a mortgage. Perhaps it is at this moment that the first little crack appears in the hold this monster exercises over us.

My sequestration lasts for several more days. The others cannot bear it. They end up by going out for longer stretches of time, and it is François who is left to keep watch on me. He does it with great kindness. As for me, I have reached the limit of my strength. I have become less than human – a 'sub-human'.

That is the last thing I remember: being seated at my table. Soon afterwards I lose consciousness. When I wake again Amaury and Charles-Henri are carrying me up the little staircase to the bathroom. Supported by Charles-Henri, I take a shower, and I wash my hair. The warm water revives me a little. But my feet are badly swollen, and I can't walk. My husband helps me to change, then I go back down to the sitting-room where, stretched out on the sofa, I fall asleep. I remain there for several days, unable to move, barely conscious, an inert wreck.

One morning Guillaume, on his way back from Monflanquin, joins us. Tilly and Ghislaine order him into the room where we are sitting, and he is immediately put on trial: 'It's you who have the transmission!' Guillaume is taken completely by surprise, but then he remembers an enigmatic remark communicated to him, in a whisper, by Tilly: 'Your family are planning to do you some mischief'. He's terrified. Tilly, in other words, bent on further destruction, is now trying to persuade Guillaume to lose all confidence in his own family.

I continue to be held hostage, guarded by Philippe and François, while Tilly takes Charles-Henri and our children to a lawyer in London. A loan against security is arranged. Martel is saved...! The nightmare is over!!

On their return, Tilly assembles everyone in the next door room. The partition is thin. Not a word escapes me. To my amazement I hear Philippe rebel, for the first time ever, against Tilly. He starts to go up the staircase to his room, shouting: 'I know I'm going to die,' before coming down again and regaining his composure.

Tilly decides to get Brigitte to come from Talade, so as to help to reassure Philippe. But on the day she is due to arrive, he summons us all and says, very sternly to us: 'This solitary confinement never happened, don't speak of it to anyone'.

We are all so exhausted and have lost so much weight that, when she sees us, Brigitte will of course realize that something has happened. And as for me, I am unrecognizable. But we say nothing to her...

Tilly wants to sent Brigitte and Philippe to Scotland. They refuse point blank and return to Talade. Tilly is unable to prevent this.

Charles-Henri and I stay on for a few days. He makes me take a daily walk, and little by little I recover the use of my legs. Except that I have gangrene in my hips, and that I limp. What I need is to be X-rayed and to see a doctor. But, since 2001, we have never seen one, nor have we looked after ourselves properly; so that I remain in need of proper medical attention.

On February 17th, we leave this house, handing it over to Ghislaine and the children. We go to a less central and more working-class neighbourhood, in the Cowley Road, and to a little apartment, a real dump. I have unbelievable difficulty in climbing the sixty stairs of a steep staircase that are needed to reach it. I am still weak and in shock. But Charles-Henri is very kind to me. And my good health soon helps me get over it. As for Diane, Guillaume and Amaury, they have been ordered not to have any contact whatsoever with us.

# 14

Robert Pouget de Saint-Victor, known to his friends as Bobby, is a character with a ruddy complexion, quite in the style of Falstaff. Charming and debonair, he has come to settle in England, where he has married. He has founded the Oxford Cheese Company, a food shop specializing in organic produce, and which also supplies restaurants, in particular one that belongs to his son, the Vaults and Garden, in Radcliffe Square, in the centre of Oxford. He also has a delicatessen, a little specialist grocery shop specializing in organic foods, and he sells English cheeses in the market, including two he has himself developed. Gastronomy aside, he is also a talented painter, a decorator and a very cultivated man. In addition to which he has a heart of gold, an excellent education and a powerful personality.

In February 2008, he places an advertisement: he is looking for a chef who possesses not only *savoir faire*, but also organizational skills. Tilly discovers this item in the newspaper, and decides it is time put me to work. As for Charles-Henri, he is already employed at the Oxford Garden Company, a business that specializes in the creation and maintenance of gardens. Tilly sends me, accompanied by Guillaume, for an interview with the 'Baron', telling us that Bobby has in the past been helped 'by our services, and that he needs someone like me'. And that it is Jacques Gonzalez who is recommending me: 'Christine!' Tilly says 'It is my boss who is giving you this helping hand'. He does not come with us to the interview, but waits in the car. That day, I had an unbelievable stroke of luck.

My CV and my experience in no way corresponded to what the advertisement specified. Bobby saw before him a cripple, not much to look at, and unable to offer a single reference. Obviously, he couldn't take me on. And yet, after he asked me if I knew how to cook and I said that I was capable of 'home cooking', he enquired as to the cause of my limp. I offered some vague explanation involving a bad fall. Was it his kind heart? Intuition? Curiosity? Whatever it was, the fact remains that he was willing to consider me as a candidate. While I, believing him to be associated with Tilly and Gonzalez, understood – or thought I did – the readiness with which he offered me the job.

He explained to me how the kitchen worked. Every day local caterers and restaurants put in their orders (in English, in the case of several dishes in particular, for which I had no recipe). What he needed was some vigilant person who would ensure the safety of the food chain. The latest health inspection report had been negative, so that we must above all avoid being closed down. I had two helpers, Brazilians, who were charming, but whose sense of time was, to say the least of it, imperfect. We started at seven in the morning – fortunately the kitchen was close to where I lived – with the preparation of the main courses and the fresh vegetables: falafel, chicken, vegetarian dishes whose ingredients came from an organic farm. Everything had to be ready by eleven o'clock and dispatched immediately in large metal boxes. In the afternoon I tidied up, and put in further orders for fresh produce, dried vegetables, rice, pastas etc. The early days were very hard work. Embarking on a professional life, after six years of isolation and the trials I had undergone, was not easy. On that first day, I did not even know what the date was, still less the year. I had to rummage in the drawers in the hopes of finding an up-to-date calendar or bill. I hadn't spoken any English for years and I was in a complete panic. I found even the routine work difficult. But Charles-Henri accompanied me to work every day and came to collect me afterwards. Tilly had – in the interests of safety and vigilance – ordered him to do so. I did not mind at all. It sometimes happened, even, that my husband stayed on for a while at the start of the day and helped me.

But I managed to adapt to this new state of affairs more quickly than I had thought possible. I was so pleased to have found this job, Bobby seemed so kind, and I was determined not to disappoint him. He had noticed, of course, that my methods were not those of a professional, even in preparing a salad. But he was determined to keep me on. He had understood that the social milieu from which I came was more like his own than that of a professional cook, and he wondered what reverses could have reduced me to such a situation. Observing me out of the corner of his eye, he sensed a mystery. I divulged nothing about myself. Nevertheless, in spite of my secretiveness, he appreciated my work, to the point of getting me to train as a kitchen manager so as to improve my competence and range. Then he employed Tim, an English cook who proved to be a good assistant and an efficient second-in-command. The random checks operated by the public health department were soon perfectly satisfactory, and we were allotted the highest grade.

When the Brazilians forgot to wake up in the morning, Bobby and his wife came to give me a hand. I managed to form an excellent relationship with them. One day when I was admiring a canvas that hung in his office, Bobby told me that he himself was the painter, that he had done it during the time he lived in Paris; and then he offered to give it to me. Today, it hangs in my sitting-room, and is a constant source of pleasure to me.

I was beginning to find again some pleasure in life. For the first time in ten years, someone was treating me with respect and had confidence in me. I had got back my identity card. I was earning £1,000 a month, of which Tilly took 90%. What of it? More important than the money was the fact that I was getting back some energy, and – almost – some hope. It even happened that I put in some extra hours in Bobby's grocery shop, where in the beginning I had some trouble in getting the change right, I who never myself had any money...

But not everything was perfect. My children were not continuing with their studies: all three of them were working, Diane as a waitress in a restaurant, Nandos, that specialized in chicken dishes, Amaury as a warehouseman in Zara, Guillaume still as 'slave' to Tilly, who not only did not pay him but had ordered him to find a second job. He had been taken on as a barman in the evenings, with hours that kept him at work until late in the night. Their cousins found themselves in the same situation: François was serving in a fast-food restaurant and Guillemette in a pizzeria in Bristol.  I raised the matter with Charles-Henri, saying that it seemed to me wholly unfair that our children, who had been promised a first-class education, should be reduced to this.  His view was that this state of affairs would not go on for long.  I felt a surge of anguish and anger arise within me.  But I still did not have enough strength to express it.

During all these months, Tilly appeared very rarely, and only then to collect his money.  There was no further pressure on me to recover the 'transmission', no more brutality or harassment.  But each morning I feared that he would again be seized by his obsession, and I remained on my guard.

One evening, climbing wearily back up our staircase, I found Thierry and Ghislaine waiting for us.  Ghislaine, who believed us to be in Lot-et-Garonne, had once again reverted to the notion that Philippe had tried to murder her by suffocating her with a pillow.  If she was to be believed, she had lodged a complaint against him.  Her brother had left Talade and no one knew where he was. No more, indeed, than they did Brigitte.

We now know what really took place... Yes, Philippe had certainly left Talade. After the proceedings in camera, the *huis clos* at Oxford, he could stand no more.  An altercation with Ghislaine had been the last straw.  And so he had made contact by telephone with his children, who had arranged for him to be taken into hospital at

Villeneuve-sur-Lot in order to get him away from Tilly's influence.  So, Mamie, Ghislaine and Brigitte were the only ones who were still at Talade.  When he was able to leave hospital, Philippe organized with his own and Brigitte's children an expedition to 'recover' Brigitte.

Luck was on their side.  It was a beautiful day.  All the doors and windows were open in order to let some sunshine into the house.  Ghislaine was sunbathing in the garden, stretched out on a bench.  The group had been able to sneak past her in single file, without making a sound.  The sight of her children had given Brigitte new heart and enabled her to act decisively.  They, for their part, had been able, at last, to hold her in their arms, to embrace her, and to persuade her to go with them.

I think that if Jean Marchand, too, had come that day, the same electric shock would have activated Ghislaine too, and the whole edifice elaborated by Tilly would have collapsed almost two years earlier than it eventually did.

And so they escaped, Brigitte and the children, leaving Ghislaine and Mamie alone.

Philippe, however, remained under Tilly's influence.  Even though he had no further contact with him, he lodged no complaint against him, for fear of reprisals.  Until my return...

Philippe, then, in his turn, was vilified.  Ghislaine returned to England with Mamie.  Tilly had asked Ghislaine to bring her to Oxford, no doubt to get her away from her oldest son, but also so that he could profit from her retirement pension.  So at the age of 96, Mamie had undertaken this long journey in order to be with Ghislaine. I was forbidden to go and see her, whereas Charles-Henri, for medical reasons, was allowed to on three occasions. Brave though she was, Mamie could not be left on her own day and night. So Diane was required to spend every night at her grandmother's. My daughter was already working very long hours, as she had been asked to take on new responsibilities in her restaurant. This additional commitment weighed heavily on her shoulders. But she could not, of course, refuse. Needless to say, nobody told me that Diane had been appointed night nurse to her grandmother. Mamie called on her three or four times every night to the point where Diane, greatly distressed, could no longer sleep.

Ghislaine and Tilly brought papers for us to sign: Philippe had apparently lent money to Tilly and, in the interests of family harmony, we must – on behalf of Tilly – undertake to reimburse him. Slumped on my sofa, exhausted by my day's work, I listened to all of this with a certain detachment. I observed that not only was this all a bit much to take, but also that it made no sense. Nevertheless, I signed. Charles-Henri, exhausted by his day of gardening, signed too, without making any objection. As far as I was concerned, these papers were of no value.

Since leaving England, Philippe had been the object of every imaginable slander on the part of Tilly. Next it was Guillaume's turn. He was, it appeared, responsible for the loss of his father's driving licence. He was supposed to have tried to hire killers to remove us. I paid no attention to all this nonsense. Behind it all there was a single motive: my oldest son had just found work that matched his abilities. He had applied for, and been appointed to, a position in a firm that offered advice on archaeological sites in Oxford. For the first time in years Tilly no longer had him under his thumb.

Tilly's hold over Charles-Henri and me, however, remained powerful: he managed to get us and the rest of the family to sign a letter to Guillaume's employer, accusing him of stealing from us, and another similar one to the Protestant church in Oxford. Even though the former expressed his astonishment to Guillaume, he took it no further and accepted his explanations, while the second took no action. But soon, under Tilly's control, our family launched six spurious legal actions against Guillaume. I know now that Guillaume feared opening his letter box every morning for fear of what new horrors he might find.

I had been working for Bobby for almost a year when I discovered that Tilly had put it into Charles-Henri's head that he was not Guillaume's biological father. Worse still, he repeated the same slander to the whole family, to the point where his cousins were quite ready to treat our son as a bastard. Guillaume himself quite simply rejected this lie. But, deeply wounded, he decided to break with the whole of the Védrines family, including his parents. As for Charles-Henri himself, he met this new slander by saying that, be that as it may, Guillaume would always be his oldest son; and that that was to be the end of the matter. Amaury, ignoring Tilly's orders, came to see me one day and disclosed the whole affair to me: Guillaume was, so it was alleged, not the son of his father but of his grandfather.  Not only was I supposed to have deceived my husband but, in addition, I had been guilty of incest... I was stunned.

I asked Charles-Henri, first of all, how he could believe such a horror.  He replied simply that, for him, Guillaume was his son, whatever his origins.  The slander had hurt me, but Charles-Henri's reaction was devastating.  While retaining all his affection for me, he nevertheless chose to believe Tilly rather than believing me.  I had already been ruined, betrayed, maltreated, humiliated.  I had accepted it all.  But an accusation of adultery, combined with incest... Too much, it was all too much.  At that moment, Tilly's hold over me cracked everywhere but did not explode.  Rather, like a drowning man who manages, thanks to a kick deep down under the water, to rise to the surface again, I reacted.  I summoned all that remained of my vital powers, of my energy; something deep within me awoke, as if my heart now beat to a different rhythm.  In the face of Tilly's disgraceful lie, my whole being rebelled, and the grief I felt on discovering my husband's reaction to it only strengthened my determination.  My maternal instinct, too, impelled me to act.  I could see only too well that Tilly was doing everything in his power to destroy Guillaume, who had always been a loyal and attentive son and brother.  I was going to fight.

The next day, arriving at the restaurant at 40 Stanley Road, I asked one of the kitchen staff who had internet access to find me the telephone numbers of my sister, my cousin and Marie-Hélène.  When he had tracked them down, I kept them carefully hidden in a drawer, waiting for a quiet moment when I could telephone them.

By chance, and at about this same time, Tilly made a mistake. He went to see Bobby and suggested they set up together a number of projects in fund management, as well as a consultancy in ultrasound. He said his wife was a midwife and, in Charles-Henri, he had at his disposal an excellent obstetrician. It would be an ideal partnership. I do not know exactly how the conversation went, but that same afternoon Bobby turned up in the kitchen, quite agitated: 'Do you know him well, this Thierry Tilly?' he asked me.

Since I knew nothing about their meeting, and still thought it possible there was some connection between them, I thought it best to be cautious, and gave an evasive reply.

'The man's a complete crook, neither more nor less!' he exclaimed. 'And besides, he's ridiculous, he's beyond belief, a real charlatan!'

Once again, I was evasive. I suspected a trap set by Tilly or Gonzalez, even though it appeared on the face of it highly unlikely that Bobby would have had anything at all to do with Tilly. Except that the previous nine years had taught me that even the most unlikely things were possible. Almost in spite of myself, however, I glimpsed a real possibility, thanks to Bobby, of emerging from this nightmare. But I said not a word of this to Charles-Henri who was still under Tilly's influence.

The next afternoon, while I was quietly on my own preparing the next day's orders, Bobby appeared suddenly before me: 'All right, sit down and tell me the whole thing. What's it all about, this story?'

I hesitated again for a few moments. But, after all, what did I have to lose? What more was there to be afraid of after these past nine years? And I told him everything. He could scarcely believe me. He shook his head, incredulous, astounded, horrified, but above all, uncomprehending. He was, moreover, the first person whose reaction to my story suggested that there were difficult times ahead. In order to convince him that I was not making anything up, I suggested that he go on to the Internet: 'Look up 'Reclus de Monflanquin', and you'll see...'. At which point, since Charles-Henri was about to return, I said no more but went home with the jubilant feeling that some real hope was at last on the horizon

Next morning, when Charles-Henri left me at the door to the kitchen, Bobby was waiting for me.

'Christine! I haven't slept all night', he said, 'we must do something – immediately!'

We abandoned the vegetables for the telephone, and I made my first call: to my sister. I got the answerphone. I left a short message, telling her where to find me. My brother-in-law replied almost immediately. This first contact with the outside world was decisive. Tilly had been so successful in persuading me that everyone had abandoned me that if I had sensed any coldness on the other end of the line I would have retreated into myself completely. But on the contrary, Jean-Michel was affectionate and very moved. I remember still the relief and the sense of calm I felt at this moment.

I explained the situation to him briefly. How, though, could nine such years be recounted in so short a time? Next, Françoise took over the receiver. We were both of us overwhelmed with emotion. All the love we felt for one another had never faltered during all this time. I asked her to telephone Bertrand and Anne, our cousins. And when I hung up, I was in tears. Of happiness. The first happiness I had known during these past nine years.

I next spoke to Anne, Bertrand's wife. And I heard in her voice too, unaltered, the same affection as before. She told me that Bertrand had been very ill, which was why she was doing the talking, but that they were going to get together with Françoise and arrange for my return. Then it was Marie-Hélène's turn. We were both of us so overcome with emotion that we could hardly speak. She told me that in 2004 she had contacted a barrister in Bordeaux, Maître Picotin, who was willing to help me. She gave me his telephone number. And so in no time at all a whole tissue of affectionate relationships had woven itself around me. Bobby, at this moment, was the focal point of all of this and from that moment on I felt supported and much stronger.

Bobby insisted that I use his office telephone again to call Marie-Hélène's barrister. It was March 20th, 2009. I wanted to lodge a complaint against Tilly, but I did not know where to do so. In Oxford or Bordeaux? 'Bordeaux,' was Maître Picotin's reply. 'Come back at once, and I will arrange a meeting for you with an examining magistrate'. Just as nine years earlier my life had descended into an infernal world of lies and unreality,

so that day it took off again in the other direction. I had
returned to a world where truth prevails.

I wanted to remain a few days longer in order to try
to persuade Charles-Henri to leave with me. Bobby and
I had a discussion on the matter. In his opinion it was a
hopeless endeavour: Charles-Henri would not be able to
disengage himself so easily from the hold Tilly exercised
over him. Indeed, if he was told of my plan he might even
torpedo it. And so, unwilling to run even the slightest
risk, I confided nothing of my plan to my husband. But
I did telephone Philippe. "Come back immediately", he
said, "I'll do everything I can for you." Having secured
the support of Charles-Henri's older brother in this way,
all that remained for me was to leave.

Aided and abetted by Marie-Hélène and Anne, Bobby
arranged my journey. On the morning of March 24th, and
with a heavy heart, I parted from Charles-Henri at the
door of the 'kitchen'. I left him behind with my children,
determined to wrest them from Tilly's claws, whatever the
difficulties. So as not to arouse suspicion, I had taken
nothing with me except all the relevant documents that
were in my possession, especially those I had written
during my various periods of imprisonment. Bobby and
his chauffeur were waiting for me. He paid me what he
owed me, urged me to write an account of everything I
had been through, saw me into his car, and instructed the
chauffeur not to lose sight of me until I was reunited with
my family. It was to be some time before those I had left
behind became aware of what I had done...

# Charles-Henri's story

It often happens in families that the older members hand down their spiritual witness, from one generation to the next, through lines selected from the Bible. For this purpose, my father had chosen chapter six, verse three from the Book of Judges: 'Go forth with the strength that you have'. These few words have greatly sustained me during these past dark years. They have helped me to live my daily life, but also to accept what is happening with a certain fatalism. Today they are helping me to rebuild myself.

In spite of the personality that I project, I am naïve, shy, and simple-minded. These are my weaknesses. Although I am prudent and pragmatic, once I place my confidence in somebody, I do not question it. If this person is dangerous, I am in trouble. To have faith in someone else is to give power to that person. What happened between Tilly and me was completely new to me. I had never before had to deal with lying and bad faith at such a level, nor had I ever encountered swindling. It was the worst episode of my life.

It is painful to have to relate both what I myself suffered, and what I put my family through. I am the one who introduced Tilly into my family, thanks to the trust I placed in my sister, Ghislaine. The length, the complexity, and the interwovenness of the situations that followed do not allow of any straightforward analysis or explanation of what we went through during this personal and family catastrophe. It is not my wish to seek to excuse myself, but to understand – and to help others understand – what happened, so that they will not fall into some similar trap.

One's perception of how a family functions depends very much on one's position within it. I am the youngest, spoiled no doubt, but very conscious of my place. My aim was not to be merely another link in a long chain, as my parents and grandparents had been. This is something that Tilly understood immediately; and he programmed everything so that I should become the weak link.

Am I, then, responsible for nothing? Certainly I am responsible, but I find it difficult to pinpoint the moment when my perceptiveness, and perhaps my courage, failed me. Even before he met me, Tilly had had every opportunity to observe how our family functioned, during three long years of acquaintance with my sister Ghislaine and her family. A letter that Jean Marchand wrote to Philippe, bears witness to this. As early as January 2001 he wrote: 'Ghislaine has gone out of her way these past few months to try to extricate you, along with Mamie and Charles-Henri, from a very risky situation, by immediately mobilizing the network and the effective but very friendly support system that, through her great energy and resourcefulness, she has been able to create at the Femme Sec'. Christine has already explained it, but I should like to emphasize still further the crucial role played by the support and the backing lent by Maître Vincent David, the friend who introduced Tilly to my sister and her family, in my being taken captive. He was recommended as a suitable person to handle the Lacaze case, the audit of the medical practice and the litigation that followed this, Philippe's divorce, and much more besides – a series of important events extending over several years. Without him, Christine and I would never, I am sure, have listened to anything Tilly said to us.

After the death of my father my main preoccupation was to keep Martel afloat, with Christine's invaluable help, and to hand on to our children everything that this place had meant to me.

Everything augured well. I reached an agreement with my first cousin, Antoinette, who was happy to sell the land she had inherited from her father. In this way it seemed feasible that the estate could be made economically more viable, and could be returned to what it had been at the time my grandfather owned it. Having led me to believe that he was going to help me finalise this transaction, Tilly did everything in his power to sabotage it. Through him, one part of this estate was sold to a third party. Our dream was shattered forever. This is, for me, a wound that will never heal, the more so since the break-up of Martel did not end there.

Meanwhile and in much the same way Tilly turned his attention to my professional life, and began insidiously to undermine it.

At this particular moment, I had been practising for several years, and my work was going well enough. But it was sensible not to rest upon one's laurels, but to use any opportunity that presented itself to consider my whole situation and to take stock. Tilly suggested that I undertake an audit of my practice, and I saw this as an opportunity not to be missed. It was, moreover, Maître

Vincent David who would be doing the audit on behalf of Presswell Ltd. In my view this was an important matter and one that would also be beneficial.

For purely historical reasons I was the person in charge of the management of the consultancy. I therefore proposed this project to my colleague, who trusted me and simply agreed that the work be done by Maître David. But then Tilly presented us with some absurd document, while assuring me that the rest would follow later. The bill when it arrived was pretty steep, which aroused the suspicions of my colleague who, quite reasonably, withdrew and refused to pay. The lack of communication between us, along with my attitude, already under Tilly's influence, resulted in a dialogue of the deaf between us, and an avalanche of legal processes of all kinds, by my business partner. In this way a pernicious atmosphere, skilfully sustained by Tilly, enveloped the practice. He said a number of very damaging things about my colleague, some of which ought to have raised my suspicions, but which, on each occasion, contained small grains of truth that masked the lies he was telling me. There again, everything was thought out in advance by Tilly, thus reinforcing my gullibility.

At this same time, using the internet, I had to make a variety of payments under various headings: day-to-day money for the children, insurance, business investment. My bank had supported me for several years, only to abandon me now, ruthlessly. A pitiless lawsuit ensued which it was impossible for me to oppose, forcing to abandon the struggle. It has left me, even today, with a bitter taste in my mouth. But anyway, it was another thing to manage, and very difficult to put up with, since it only strengthened the daily pressure on me, which was becoming more and more oppressive.

In this way, as the months went by, Tilly managed to exhaust me. He had no difficulty in making me take down my brass plaque and in making me disappear, like a plague victim, leaving chaos behind me. Abandoning my clinic staff and my patients so abruptly haunted my nights for a long time, although I had the feeling at the time that I had no other option.

Today, I have the pleasure of encountering again my former patients, and it comforts me to see the welcome they give me.

I have always met difficulties head on. I have fought for what I believe in. But, faced with a manipulative crook like Tilly, I did not know how to fight.

In 2003 I left Bordeaux for Martel. Various good friends managed to keep in touch with me, but as soon as they wanted to know more, I kept quiet.

As Christine has mentioned, Jean Marchand was vilified by his wife and children. Rejected, and certainly very unhappy, his attitude was nevertheless disturbing to us on several occasions. He left various messages for us on the answerphone at Martel, whose contents made Tilly's paranoid talk believable: 'You, the family Vé...vermin that you are'... 'We're going to see to you'... 'You're on your own, you're isolated and you're already done for'... 'The bailiffs will soon be there, you're finished'. These threats had a damaging effect on Ghislaine and her children and, by extension, on us too; while the mention of 'we' only reinforced the theory, so insidiously implanted in us for months now, of a plot.    Later on, the press campaign about the 'Recluses of Monflanquin' only strengthened the theory, propounded by Tilly, that we were surrounded.

I can scarcely find words to describe how I felt when the bailiff came to empty Martel of all its contents, without making any attempt to establish to whom the various objects and pieces of furniture belonged.  He put me in mind of a bulldozer, full of contempt for the memories of several generations of people, smashing them up without any trace of emotion.  It seemed to me to be a form of legal theft about which I could do nothing.  He was, of course, simply carrying out the task he had been given, but that need not have stripped him of every vestige of human kindness.  For me it was an act of great violence.  It was more difficult still to watch these events on the eight o' clock news on television, which strengthened again our feeling that there was some kind of conspiracy against us.

Christine has described our life in Talade.  We were together there, which made our day-to-day life more tolerable but also, perhaps, deterred us from taking any action.

The most painful memory we have of this time is that everything possible was done to try to distance us from my mother, to whom we had always been very close.  If this did not succeed with me, it was not quite the same for Christine...

Pacing up and down the courtyard in Talade, I often thought of my father walking round and round his prisoner-of-war camp in Pomerania. My situation was, of course, much easier than his, and this helped me to accept it.

My happiest memory of this time is of the hours I spent with Amaury in the workshop. I saw again, as it were, my own father teaching me how to use his tools. I saw, too, the birth of a new talent. The family traditions, the chains that link us, the ties that bind us, are not, perhaps, entirely severed...

Next came our enforced exile in Oxford. Three days which lasted three years... A period of time which, by removing us from Monflanquin – the only way there was of severing us from our roots – was necessary if we were to be stripped of everything.

At the beginning it was all rather pleasant, but very soon Christine's house arrest began to cloud unutterably our everyday life. Tilly kept up a permanent pressure, not just on us, but on his own family too. Jessica was required, I think without quite understanding the situation, to accommodate us and look after us from day to day. She was kind and welcoming to us, but Tilly gave her a terrible time, reducing her allowance for food every day. In order to keep me occupied, Tilly, in conjunction with the owner – having manipulated him too – got me to do some repairs to our wretched little home. The owner was later to take me to court, accusing me of having ruined his house And yet, all the work was done at his request and often with his help.

So during the day I abandoned Christine to her miserable lot, and found her again only in the evening, having been obliged to take supper with the Tilly family, while she ate alone in her room.

Why and how could I have accepted all of this? Without seeking to excuse myself, it must be said that for six years Tilly controlled our every action and our every movement, while all the while permitting us to hope for better things tomorrow, even though we had not a single centime in our pockets. It is true that I am by nature an optimist, and when I am busy I never envisage failure, another weakness that Tilly knew just how to exploit.

The days go by, without us being able to get any help from Guillaume, who lives opposite. Tilly requires Guillaume to stay very close to him: he must never, indeed, be more than ten feet away... We don't really know where Amaury and Diane are. In Oxford, Tilly has very skillfully ensured that we are kept apart from our children and from the rest of the family. Sometimes we don't see Tilly for weeks on end. He works, so he says, at night, or is away 'on an assignment'. We may take no decision without his approval. In this way he orchestrates our lives.

Now come the most horrible and the most hallucinatory moments of all, those that Tilly inflicted on us at 35 Church Hill Road in Oxford, where the experience was different for every one of us.

Under lock and key for two weeks, unable to leave the house, we experienced a nightmare whose horror and whose outcome was different for each of us. Tilly thought it all through: the house was characterless, without ornament or decoration, and from the kitchen you could see the Celtic Cross of the neighbouring cemetery. The whole scene was carefully calculated, and being deprived of sleep and food quickly reduced me to the state of a zombie.

Although I may appear to be a bit of a coward, it was something else during these fourteen days and fourteen nights that determined my behaviour. Tilly had at the very beginning anaesthetized me by persuading me that it was impossible that I knew nothing about the 'transmission'. He told me, moreover, that Christine had undergone sessions of hypnosis in Bordeaux, and that it was essential if she was not to lose her mind that she be prevented from falling asleep. If she went to sleep, she might become a 'vegetable'. Tilly entrusted me with this particular task, as he had done with others, to implicate me and to make me his accomplice. I knew nothing about hypnosis, I took fright on Christine's behalf, and I would do anything in my power to prevent her from sleeping, convinced that I was doing this for her own good. After several days, I ended up falling asleep myself. Some time later, I don't know when, I woke up, terrified by the danger to which I had exposed my wife.

Even if, at the start of such an episode, you are perfectly well aware that you are inhabiting some sort of insane nightmare world, you nevertheless very quickly lose all sense of time: reality is suspended, everything in your shut-in universe becomes hazy and formless. I am aware of Tilly, constantly on the watch, holding his breath, and spying on me, twenty-four hours out of twenty-four, from the next-door room. From time to time he reappears, to

check up on us, to pass on to us Jacques Gonzalez' latest
threat, and to tell Christine it is high time she stopped
making fools of us all, or to threaten her with the direst
of consequences if she persists in this.

Days go by, during which Christine and I are required
to re-live our past lives in the presence of my brother and
sister, in order to re-activate her missing memory. Christine
must remain seated, facing the wall. Her strength begins
to fail her, which no one quite realizes. Next, she is no
longer allowed to go to the lavatory and cannot control
herself. And so a hateful and humiliating scene takes
place, during which the adults present, beginning with me,
do not move. Nobody knows where this is all leading, but
the threat of the sale of Martel reappears, and a telephone
conversation takes place with Jacques Gonzalez, who
seems to be following the whole operation very closely.
There follows another strange scene, one that horrifies
everyone: a hysterical Tilly, while bellowing more or less
incomprehensible words into Christine's ear, deals a series
of heavy blows to her back with his fist.

Our children, very fortunately, did not witness these
scenes.

Things then became a little less tense, and Amaury
helped me take his mother upstairs to have a shower.
She was exhausted. We too were distraught. But then,
stupefied, I noticed that her lower limbs were covered
with bruises. She was unable to walk for several days.
My account of what had happened did not, later on,
convince the medical expert that there was any causal
link between what Christine underwent and the present

state of her hips, both of which need replacing. We ought to have arranged for an X-ray immediately after our imprisonment ended, but it was impossible for us to do this, partly from lack of money, but also because Tilly assured us that the doctors in Oxford were not reliable.

Tilly took me to London, with the children, to raise a mortgage on Martel, which was, according to both Jacques Gonzalez and him, the only way to save the house.

Christine remained a hostage in Oxford. Tilly said to me that if I did what he told me, my wife and my son Guillaume would face no further problems. The various doubts that my brother had awoken in me vanished immediately, so exhausted was I by these past two weeks of torment. It was January 2008 and I remained a total mental prisoner right up to the moment when the hair-shirt was removed from my back.

We were not aware of it at that moment, but this macabre masquerade had only one purpose: to marginalize us, so as to set in motion a devious and sordid scheme to sell Martel without my knowledge. This sale could not have been concluded without the knowledge and complicity of lawyers and businessmen, who were less than scrupulous, and also perfectly aware of our enfeebled situation, thanks to reports in the media. I hope that the law will allow us some recompense for this disaster – one that affects not only me, but the whole of my family.

Christine went to work with Bobby, whose decisive role in helping her save our family can never be overstated. As for me, I began work, but very reluctantly, with Wayne at the Oxford Garden Company. At first he was as sceptical as I was about how long this arrangement would last. But in spite of the barrier created by our linguistic and cultural differences, we achieved a genuine partnership, enhanced by mutual respect. I remember, too, with pleasure my days in the convent on the Woodstock Road where Sister Marie treated me to a good hot cup of tea, accompanied by little English cakes and pastries, which smelled and tasted delicious. I worked, too, with Dr. Hutchings the vet, whose wife considered us almost as friends. She also listened to me a lot and gave me moral support after Christine left.

Jessica had obtained permission from Tilly to rent an allotment. It proved to be, for her as well as for us, a haven of peace, because Tilly never came there. At the beginning it was a mess, but we ended with a well-tended garden, complete with a summer-house and cold frames – all of it made out of pallets and reclaimed material. Jessica brought out garden furniture and a parasol, and organized barbecues for the children. With typical British humour our neighbours nicknamed our plot 'Paris plage'. We had peaceful times there, forgetting for a time our everyday cares and worries. It was in this very place that I had a telephone call from Christine telling me that she had left.

Her voice was calm but determined. The call lasted thirty seconds, just long enough for her to say: 'I need some time to myself, I won't be coming home this evening. I love you'.

I was astonished, I couldn't grasp at all what was happening, and my first reaction was to send a text to Tilly to warn him of this. I wondered where Christine had gone. I was afraid she might have put herself in some sort of danger. I was quite certain she could not have left England, because Tilly's and Gonzalez's 'people' would have been forewarned of this by the Customs Officers at the frontier. This was my extraordinary mindset at the time.

Tilly took three days to answer my text message, and when I saw him he couldn't tell me where Christine was. And even this did not shake my confidence in him. In the end it is I who told him that she had gone back to France – which I discovered thanks to an indiscretion on the part of one of the people working in the kitchen.

As the days went by I began to view her departure as a desertion and also to become aware of how lonely I was. Amaury, very kindly, came every night and slept in my flat to keep me company. Christine was very soon vilified, and accused of being responsible for a search carried out by the English police in Tilly's flat on the eve of her departure. I cried a great deal. I was astonished and shocked by the critical things that Diane and Amaury said about their mother. I pointed this out to them; but this did not prevent me from accompanying Diane when she lodged a complaint against her mother. I was completely supine, and utterly incapable of any action.

And yet a petition for divorce got filed as well as a ridiculous but very serious action being initiated by us against Guillaume, who was already under legal attack, accused taking the family's money and goods, even when it was clear that this was impossible. Everyone who jumped ship was demonised.

Confronting one's own son in a court of law was a strange, deeply distressing and truly appalling experience. The more so since, in my heart of hearts, I knew that the alleged grievances were false, and that, even if they were not false, this was not the place to resolve them. It was a long time since I was at all familiar with the details of the case and so I had tried to catch up with them the evening before, or on the day itself, even, of the hearing, because during working hours I was busy gardening. Sometimes I went to the hearing without knowing what I was supposed to be doing there. Tilly directed operations, harassing Ghislaine and the children, day after day, with demands that they put together the necessary documents, while Guillaume, with great courage and competence, carried on a solitary battle. Fortunately, the Oxford magistrates knew how to deal with things in a correct and considered way, so that they were able to look at the entire case in all its various aspects; while Guillaume's fighting spirit resulted in a happy outcome of this whole trial. Nevertheless, the whole affair was very destructive, especially for Guillaume, but also for the rest of us. Harsh things were said, things that were not true. Even if they were uttered under duress, time will be needed for them to be forgotten.

After Christine's departure I returned to my work as a gardener and I went regularly to the allotment with Jessica and her children. In spite of Tilly's absence, at no point did either of us raise the question of Christine's departure, nor the legal proceedings against Guillaume. It is only today that I am able to assess the full gravity of the manipulation to which we were, both of us, subjected.

My mental liberation was achieved very slowly but was nevertheless wholly successful, thanks to Christine's persistence, but also to Marie-Hélène's obstinacy, and to the professionalism of Daniel Picotin and his 'exit counselling' team.

Christine and I are very fortunate to find ourselves reunited once more, and as happy as if we had only parted the previous day. I fully realize that it was her act of courage that saved us all. Christine is the only member of the family to have grasped fully the role that Tilly and Gonzalez played in this whole affair. Her decision to escape, and the action she brought, were decisive in the arrest of Tilly and Gonzalez. Without her, the full extent of what we have been through would never have been acknowledged by the law. That was the moment when I rediscovered with joy my wife and my three children, and that we were reunited once again. I was horrified to discover all she had been through those past months. And it would take many more months for us to recover our peace of mind.

I am discovering, too, the full extent of the human and financial damage inflicted on us during this diabolical encounter. I was incapable for eighteen months of resuming any professional activity at all.

# Guillaume's story

In August 2000, I am twenty-two years old.   Now that
I have  completed my course in business management at
Ecole Supérieure de Commerce at Marseilles, my graduate
studies are at an end.    I go to Martel in order to write
up my dissertation  in peace and calm.  I remember very
clearly the circumstances of my first encounter with Tilly.
As I always do when I find myself in Lot-et-Garonne,
I stop to take a coffee in Bordeneuve so as to see my
cousins, Guillemette and François.   I am the same age
as Guillemette, and François is only eighteen months
younger than I am.    I have always had a very special
relationship with them.   I have always been very close to
Guillemette, but also to François, to whom I have tried to
be an attentive and protective cousin, especially when, as
a teenager, he encountered real difficulties and suffered
genuine unhappiness.

When I arrive in Bordeneuve, Jean opens the door to
me with a big smile.   François and Thierry Tilly are just
behind him.   Thierry Tilly is introduced to me by François
as a colleague of Ghislaine, my aunt.   It is clear that my
aunt and Tilly are very close.   It is also thanks to Tilly's
help that François has passed his baccalaureate.   He has
also, it seems, helped out at the Femme Sec over various
legal matters.   Ghislaine and François are full of praise
for him, especially when they tell me how Thierry Tilly
protected 'Musique en Guyenne' when it was threatened
with a bill for unpaid taxes amounting to 2,000,000
francs.   Ghislaine is extremely grateful to him for his

help, especially since both her inheritance and Jean's would have been vulnerable to any such demand. Jean is no less fulsome in his praises. In short, I have no sooner arrived than the tone for the whole visit is set.

A few days after this first meeting, I am invited to dine at Ghislaine and Jean's house with François, my uncle Philippe, his children Frédéric and Lucille, and their fiancés. Tilly and his wife, Jessica, are also present. I greet Tilly. He talks volubly. Whatever topic he touches on, he gives the impression of having mastered the subject. Seated at either end of the table, Tilly and Ghislaine preside over the dinner. He has taken the place of the master of the house. Presented by Jean and Ghislaine as 'a person of the highest standing', he tells Lucille's fiancé that his property business is almost certainly illegal; with my cousin Frédéric, who is an engineer at Microsoft in Seattle, he discusses methods of encryption and impresses him with his knowledge. When he speaks of Gemplus, the world leader in the business of 'smart cards,' with whom I did a year's apprenticeship, he uses terminology that reveals a knowledge of information technology completely inaccessible to the general public. It is amazing. He seems, in every sphere, to possess exceptional expertise. He does not behave at all like a secret agent. At the time, besides, Tilly never presented himself to me as a 'spy'. I would have found that grotesque. He suggests merely that he works somewhere in the world of intelligence.

In reply to the question: 'But what do you actually do in life?' he replies quite crisply and with total self-assurance: 'My work is not something that is mentioned in the press'. He says nothing more specific than that he works with diplomats from the UN and NATO.

Jean and Ghislaine have always maintained a network of highly-placed people, both in France and abroad. Jean has been a financial journalist for well-known organs of the press: *La Croix*, and *Le MOCI*, where he was chief editor. Ghislaine was always telling us that Jean was the youngest chief editor in France. In view of his position, not only did he travel the world but he rubbed shoulders with political and financial personalities of the highest rank. The 'Musique en Guyenne' festival that he had been organizing for thirty years attracted musicians and conductors of international reputation. The fact that Jean and Ghislaine confirmed Thierry Tilly's pedigree earned him my complete trust. Both of them present him to me as an exceptional expert. He had obviously proved himself as far as Ghislaine was concerned. Jean too has benefitted from his advice, as well as that of Maître David. I have no reason to be suspicious of him.

Before going any further, I must say something about paranoia, which, as his chosen technique, is fundamental to the whole story of Tilly. The paranoid person, according to psychiatrists, functions normally in life but on the basis of a completely false set of propositions which become established fact. In our case, this paranoia was established in four stages: a first phase, seduction and the winning of trust; a second phase, the establishment of the system of paranoia; a third phase, the imprisonment within this system; a fourth phase, asset-stripping and destruction.

Tilly, a remarkable person, and 'guaranteed' first by my aunt and her husband, and then by my grandmother and my uncle Philippe, and finally by my parents, immediately won my confidence. In 2001, just before my departure for the United States and my voluntary civil service with Rhodia, I meet him again in Paris where I am staying for several days with Ghislaine and Jean. Immediately he issues a warning: 'Be careful of Jean Marchand. He's a warped individual'. This reminds me of various things Ghislaine and her children have been saying. According to them, Jean has been behaving in a very strange fashion for several years now. They have even tried to get him to seek treatment. 'He's a shady character! He despises you and thinks you're a little shit. He'll do anything to sabotage your work with Rhodia. He'll use all his connections'. And it's true that Jean has asked me some very specific questions about my mission to the United States. At that time, the managing director of Rhodia is the brother of a friend of Jean and Ghislaine. Paranoia sets in. I imagine the worst. What I don't know is that for two years now Tilly has been busy trying to destroy Jean Marchand in Ghislaine's eyes and to make him the Enemy Number One of the family, someone in particular whom we will be able to identify as being behind a plot that threatens us all. In many people's view, Jean is a person difficult to define, a seducer. His behaviour, on top of what his wife, his children and Tilly have said about him, has only reinforced my distrust of him.

When I arrive at Rhodia Inc, Phil M., my boss is not there. The job of project manager that I had been promised is nothing more than a training grade of the 'make the coffee, do the photocopying' type, and the promised office apartment is merely a co-tenancy with two other trainees.  Reacting as a good newbie paranoiac should, I tell myself: 'There we are then, it was only to be expected.  The community service volunteer has had the benefit, for ten years now, of an office apartment.  And by pure chance, the new system coincides with my arrival'. I can quite see that my reaction may resemble that of a spoiled child, but it is indeed a paranoid reaction that is being encouraged here.  Several weeks pass.  I speak to Tilly on the telephone: 'Be patient', he says, 'it will all be all right.  My boss and I will sort it out'.  Next, Phil returns from his trip.  He organizes a meeting with all the leaders of the e-business project team.  Some of them are on loan from the Paris office.  During the course of this meeting, he announces: 'I have decided that, for the first time ever, a community service volunteer will have an interesting project', and he appoints me as coordinator of a large-scale project.  I immediately think that Tilly is behind this.  This is all the more credible since I still remember the astonished reaction of the other members of the team.  This reinforces my conviction that the decision my boss has taken is indeed the result of some 'intervention'.  In actual fact, everyone at the top of Rhodia wanted to rein in my boss, who, as vice-president of Rhodia USA, had annoyed people.  With the benefit of hindsight, I interpret this decision of his quite differently: very conscious of the hornet's nest in which he has to operate, he wants to keep control of the project.  He has therefore had the good sense to take on for the task a little 'Frenchy' who is not one of the inner circle and whom he can trust.   This allows him to mastermind the project and to keep it under control.   Nothing at all to do with Tilly, nor with his boss.

During the course of 2001, Tilly persuades me to move to Manhattan.   He has an apartment in the centre of Manhattan.   The United Nations Hotel is at the end of the street.   Tilly is there only from time to time.   He explains to me that he holds business meetings where he meets diplomats.   The location of this apartment supports these claims.   He forbids me to go into his office, which helps to maintain the mystery.   His I.T. equipment is impressive.   I sometimes wonder about it all, but I trust him.   And taking advantage of this he persuades me to open up to him.   A good and kind listener, he gets to know me well:  my enthusiasms, my hopes, my plans, but also my frustrations.   He manages, little by little, to win my confidence.

His status as an exceptional man influences me, definitively, some months later when he introduces me to a certain Charles F., who has an extraordinary background.   Rescued from a concentration camp during the war by a French couple, he made a fortune in the United States.   As the owner of some twenty high-rise buildings in Manhattan, he is one of the most influential property developers in New York.   One day, I have the opportunity to meet him in his office on the Upper East Side.   Very kind, courteous, and a Francophile, he reminds me of Sydney Pollack.   It's obvious to me that this is a man who is not very approachable.    It's quite incredible: the walls of his luxurious office are lined with innumerable photos.    There he is, in particular, with the president, Jimmy Carter.    Thierry Tilly had introduced him to me as an influential member of the World Congress of Jews, and a generous patron of a number of humanitarian foundations.    It's for this reason that Tilly has approached him, to solicit his help with various projects launched by the Blue Light Foundation (the BLF). Charles F. seems responsive and well-informed.    Their discussions will go on for more than a year.    Charles F. will even meet Jacques Gonzalez in London.

Charles F. has exercised, without knowing it, a terrible influence on my story.    The respectability he lent Tilly, the amount of time he spent with him, to the extent of he and his wife inviting us to one of the classiest restaurants in Manhattan, not only reassured me definitively as to Tilly's standing, but accorded a real status to the BLF of whose existence I had only just learned. Which is of course how Tilly operates. Charles F. is an exceptional person. Therefore, those who do business with him must belong to the most exclusive circles.    The fact that Charles F. trusts Tilly, and cooperates with him in the BLF, has swept away my last doubts.

Moreover, Tilly shows me the internet site of the BLF, where I find recorded a contract worth several hundred million dollars between the Foundation and a Chinese medical centre.    The BLF is represented by the President of the Association for Franco-Chinese Understanding. Pursuing my researches further, I discover confirmation of this project on the site of the Consul General of Quebec. That the BLF is licensed in Montreal drives the nail home fully for me.

I am at this time very worried about my brother Amaury. Tilly gives me the decided impression that he is helping him, which reinforces further the immense trust I have placed in him.

Tilly is a crook. But he is a sophisticated crook, one who exploits very skillfully the emotional weaknesses of his victims. He is a predator. Within a few minutes of meeting you he identifies your profile and goes on the attack. And if he manages to achieve control over you, he pushes this to the limit. You may well be extremely intelligent, very well educated and yet have emotional flaws: a lack of self-confidence, a need for recognition, the feeling of having had your place in the family taken from you, or the desire to give back to life what it has brought you by helping others in need, as is the case with Charles F. As far as I am concerned, Tilly is the Hannibal Lecter of manipulation, possessed of everything that is Machiavellian, terrifying and perverse in that character as played by Anthony Hopkins. Tilly is a crook who, on top of everything else, displays a terrifying psychological profile, that of a narcissistic pervert. Manipulation taken to extremes is his favourite weapon. He seduces, then controls and stifles you in order to obtain what he wants (which is to say, everything you own). Finally, he destroys you.

When I return home in 2002, I find the whole family distraught. The diabolizing of Jean, pursued to its limits by Tilly, has been taken over by Ghislaine and her children. They claim that he wants to abandon them.   Next, Ghislaine throws Jean out of their house, in the presence of Philippe and of my father, which leads Jean to leave threats against the whole family on the answerphone at Martel: 'You Vé…vermin that you are… We'll see to you, never you fear'.  This leads us to believe that we are the victims of a plot.  A plot instigated by Jean.  These threats echo, terrifyingly, what Tilly has been telling us for months.  Unfortunately even if, today, I understand the terrible state Jean was in, these very violent threats reinforce my wish to help Ghislaine, my cousins, and my own family, all of whom I believe to be in danger.

The ban on declaring the taxes to which she is liable, which Tilly has imposed on my grand-mother – the motives for which were quite unclear to me at the time – has provoked a cascade of proceedings against us.  We find ourselves with twenty actions against us lodged with a lawyer in Montauban.  These proceedings only feed our paranoia.  Why have the tax authorities seized the contents of the house at Martel belonging to my father, his brother and his sister in order to settle a debt of my grandmother's? Why, since the tax debt was paid in time, has all this furniture been sold by the Treasury bailiff? I have still, today, received no reply to these questions. We have, moreover, launched an administrative appeal. When the senior police officer in Monflanquin tells me, several times, that not everything in our case is entirely clear, and that he will keep a copy of his own enquiry into the matter, so as not to be accused of irregularities later

on, I begin to wonder.   The police show no leniency in
anything that concerns Jean.   They seem, however, very
protective of us.   We are now at the start of 2003, and
all of this  lends credence to the idea that there are people
who have a grudge against us.   This is what moves me
to remain close to my family.   For me, the threat is very
much there and very real, and reinforced everyday a
little more by various concrete pieces of evidence.   This
threat is perhaps being orchestrated by Jean.   And since
Jean is in touch with our relatives, we end by suspecting
everyone.   I cut myself off even from my friends.   They
had been in contact with Jean, had seen him.   Today, they
still wonder why Jean advised them at the time not to get
in touch with me.

Finding themselves in this litigious atmosphere, my
parents, my grandmother, and my Uncle Philippe are
completely out of their depth.   They are 'country people'.
They are not used to devious scheming.   Ghislaine, who
is, as she says, always ready to have a go, directs the
warring parties with energy, even if she also complains
a great deal.   Tilly manages to make me think it is quite
normal that I should wish to help my family, that 'this is
nothing to be ashamed of'. Confronted with the evident
distress of my family, I accept this mission, while hoping
to be able to devote myself to my own projects in a little
while.   In the meantime I have to manage fourteen of
these legal actions, which is nothing if not a full-time
job.   I am obliged to put my professional life on hold, in
order to help my family.   And so I conceal a weakness,
which  is to prove to be catastrophic in this affair: a need

for recognition on the part of my family. I have always craved their appreciation. We belong to a family in which we do not compliment one another much. When everything is going well, this does not matter. But, when someone makes a mistake, the criticisms and judgments that follow can be quite severe. In a family where clannish sentiment is quite powerful, I needed, at the time, some recognition. But instead of this, we were made to compete with one another, and I suffered from this.

Ghislaine never stopped saying that I was 'a little bastard', that, without her interventions with Tilly, I would be with 'the other lot'. This merely reinforced my wish to find my place within this family.

Brought up to have a sense of duty, I therefore abandon everything else without hesitation in order to offer my services to my family. But, mindful of how it will look on my CV, the passage of time is creating a gap that disturbs me. And so I sign up for a correspondence course in law with the University of London, so as to derive some benefit from this period.

So here I am, at the age of twenty-five and twenty-six, lugging unreliable documents about the place, going with Ghislaine and our tax lawyer to see the Paymaster-General of Lot-et-Garonne. The preparation of many contentious cases is entrusted to me, a task that, given my age, is overwhelming. The rest of the family know that they can trust me, that I will not balk at the task. And besides, my collaboration with our lawyers is intellectually enhancing. I am learning things that my studies in law validate. I finish by persuading myself that I will, in the end, profit professionally from deploying these skills. Optimistic by temperament, I even persuade myself of this.

I remember, on one occasion, working for almost thirty hours at a stretch helping Ghislaine, Philippe and Brigitte to put together some documents. At this time Ghislaine had announced that she would no longer do anything for anyone else except for herself, her children, and Mamie. And that it was quite out of the question that she should do anything to help Philippe and Brigitte. Having a genuine affection for my uncle and his partner, and finding Ghislaine's attitude very regrettable, of course I helped them. And I slaved and slogged over it. Their very genuine gratitude towards me only reinforced my feeling that I had done the right thing. My grandmother clearly felt the same, when she said to me: 'I am so pleased that you are there, my dear. You will be able to help Ghislaine too, because I am so very worried about her. She is not well. She talks to me, you know, for hours every evening. When you are there, the atmosphere is so much calmer'.

Tilly having left for London, then Oxford, I go backwards and forwards between England and Lot-et-Garonne, which involves some fourteen hours on the road each time, so as to discuss with him whatever documents are currently relevant. But as time goes by I begin to find these comings and goings physically exhausting. And the pressure of the work ends by undermining me psychologically. All the more so since Ghislaine, always busy but never productive, has no scruples about unloading it all on to me. But I know that the help I give Ghislaine helps to keep her calm and to ease the atmosphere in the family. My aunt was beginning to complain a little less, which made matters more restful for everyone and especially for my 93-year-old grandmother.

This lasted from the end of 2002 until October 2008. Six years. I was twenty-five when this insane task was allotted to me: that of helping my parents and other family members with their judicial proceedings. All these litigations confirmed me in my belief that we were under attack, and I felt under an obligation to do whatever I could to ease the situation. This task stripped me of what should have been the sweet years of my twenties. My professional ambitions, like my ambition to start a family, were destroyed. But the evident distress of my family and my own sense of duty prevailed. And Tilly exploited this with remarkable skill, making me feel guilty whenever I displayed any desire to be done with it all. Besides, I could not in any case abandon my parents, my 16-year-old sister and my brother, just when troubles were looming on all sides. It was quite simply impossible. In taking over our family collectively, Tilly made each one of us individually a prisoner by playing on the weaknesses and the strengths he knew each of us to have. What an artist! Bravo!

When I am not on the road, nor in Talade, I live with Tilly, I take his children to school, I prepare for my lectures in English law, and I manage the legal casework. But very soon this causes financial problems: the means we employ to protect ourselves from Jean and his network of contacts and from all those who threaten us is costly.

And there is always rent to be paid. At which point, Tilly threatens me: 'Guillaume, if you don't find a way to earn money, and my family finds itself on the street, that will all go very, very badly!' Not long afterwards, in 2007 in Oxford, finding ourselves on the High Street and outside the Berlitz school, he suggests I apply to be a teacher. I am accepted. I give lessons in French. My day now begins at 7 o'clock. What with taking the children to school, my courses at the Berlitz, then my job as a barman in a cocktail bar which occupies me from 7 p.m. until 4 a.m. and supplements my income, and on top of all this my work with the family papers, I sleep between three and four hours a night. And Tilly takes almost all my money. But I have passed my law exams, to the great relief of my parents. His strategy depends on one thing above everything else: maintaining discord among the de Védrines. He's been telling me for months now that my family is about to make some very hostile move against me. And yet, my involvement with them is enormous, while their gratitude is minimal. Everything that I am doing for them is taken for granted, especially by Ghislaine and my grandmother. I feel very bad about this. And I can't take any more. All this clannishness oppresses me. But my reluctance to abandon my own flesh and blood is stronger than all of this. In spite of which, I do distance myself a little from my nearest relatives. For me, that is not what family is. A certain withdrawal on my part takes place.

January 2008 marks the beginning of that sinister period when Tilly demands that we meet as a family in order to put everything on the table, or, as he puts it 'to make the peace of the brave'. He tells us to stay behind closed doors, without sleeping or eating. My mother must reveal to us a family secret. At which point, I rebel and retort crisply that it is out of the question that I take any part at all in this farce: why would my mother hide such a secret from us? He replies drily: 'We will talk about this again at the end of next year'.

It as at this point that he sends me to Martel with François to rejoin Mamie and Ghislaine who live there all year round. We are to find some money, raise a mortgage on Martel, an order that is accompanied by a threat: 'If you don't come up with some money, there will be deaths!' It is during this period that François accompanies me wherever I go, supposedly for reasons of security. I will later learn that at this point Tilly has been saying for months to Ghislaine and her children that I am a traitor. In other words, François is watching me.

A little while later, we all meet in Oxford. It is during this time that Maman is tortured for days on end. I didn't see anything of this, but only noticed, when I returned, that she was in a dreadful state. I worry about her. When I see her again, she is so exhausted that I have the impression that her jaw is broken. Ghislaine, as mistress of ceremonies, says to me: 'We have thought it all through, and it's not your mother who is in possession of the transmission, it is you'. At which point I am seized by a dreadful anxiety. Seated in the middle of the sofa, surrounded by members of my family, I tell myself, completely terrified, that they are planning to play some warped trick on me. I am exhausted, physically and psychologically, by all these years of hard work. There will be no end to it, I will never be allowed the space I need to follow my own plans and live my own life. My anguish is the greater in that I had recently met a young woman I liked. All my hopes of freedom take flight within a few seconds. I understand nothing about this story of a transmission and, above all, I am terribly frightened. A few minutes after this sinister event, Tilly takes me to one side: 'You can now see for yourself what I told you was so, that only two people can protect you: my boss and I. If you want us to help you, to protect you from Jean's and from your family's threats, you must follow, to the letter, the orders you are given'. Whereupon he recovers all his power over me. Weighed down by a burden of anxiety and terror, devoid of the strength to resist, my critical faculties no longer function. My defence mechanisms are dulled. I have become a puppet.

One of my pupils at the Berlitz school runs an advisory service for tourism and the commercial development of archaeological sites. Oxford University is a partner in this company, which employs three hundred people. It is an excellent concern, a European leader in this field. We get on well and, several months later, he offers me a job there as a business consultant. I am beside myself with joy: a job, at last, that is in line with my own aspirations. A chance to make up for the gap in my CV that I have been worrying about. I who have been out of circulation for six years now. At last, I have bounced back professionally. And Tilly's reaction?

'Do you remember when I suggested the Berlitz to you? Well, there we are then! My boss and I had already organized everything'. This remark is all the more effective in that Tilly has already reasserted his hold ever me to a frightening extent. He repeats endlessly that the work I have done recently for my own family has enabled me to improve my professional capabilities.

The financial director of the company in Oxford needs help in setting up and developing a subsidiary company in France. The work I have been doing for some years now allows me to play a really useful role for him, not only in the legalities of setting up a subsidiary company, but also in the management of work contracts, of invitations to tender, and in meeting the requirements of the Ministry of Culture.

After three months I am offered a permanent contract. I love my job. The company is expanding and ends by employing some hundred people. How gratifying. Surrounded by distinguished researchers, working alongside and valued by a boss who trusts me, I am experiencing what many French people find in the Anglo-Saxon world. A real professional development, where your progress depends upon the quality of your work, your personal merit, and where the only limits are those you impose upon yourself. My relationship with my boss is excellent. Working alongside a Frenchman, and moreover one from the South, this typically phlegmatic Englishman, who, thanks to his small pointed beard, has a somewhat dry air, becomes more of a Latin every day. As for me, his English pragmatism appeals to me more and more. In short, this excellent professional environment is just what I need.

It is in fact my breath of fresh air, my oxygen, my living space, for I have to continue every evening managing the 'family papers'. And Tilly appropriates 90% of my salary. Several times he asks me to negotiate advance payments with my boss, who always grants them. I explain to him that I need money so as to be able to help my grandmother, which is true. For example, I have bought her the electric armchair she so badly needs, since she has to remain seated all day and everyday. And every morning, I have to be at Tilly's disposal and look after his children, of whom I am very fond. Also at this time I have a girlfriend. Tilly's influence on this relationship is little short of monstrous. Since I am obliged to manage the family papers, I am only allowed to see her at the weekend. And so I cannot wait for the weekend to arrive, all the more so since, when I am with her, I rediscover a life that is normal and soothing. But very often, at the last minute, Tilly tells me I must go to Paris to deliver documents to his boss. I leave then, inventing some useless excuse and I deliver the papers to 'the great man', to adopt the hallowed terminology which we have been talked into. At other times, Tilly informs me at the start of the week that it is very likely that I will have to go to Paris at the weekend. I am fed up, frustrated, sad. But then, at the last moment, 'kind' Tilly tells me he has done everything he can to spare me this journey so that I can see my girlfriend. And so I am full of gratitude towards him. He uses me and exploits my desires and my disappointments in order the better to control me. I have not forgotten what he said to me several months beforehand. I must do as I am told if I am to have any hope of being calm some day, free from the wicked machinations of my family. My critical faculties, my defence mechanisms are increasingly impaired. Physically and psychologically exhausted, I can no longer hold out. And so I give in. A classic case of mind control, typical of 'the Tillyan method', which, during the trial the public prosecutor renamed 'the reptilian method'. Which is entirely apt, for this method adapts itself to every situation, uses every possible means to maintain its control over its victim and possess him, as a snake does its prey.

And then, in October 2008, Tilly throws me out of his house, giving me four days to 'restore to my family everything I had, so to speak, stolen from them'. Not long before this I had found lodgings elsewhere, a room which I rented with other lodgers in a very pretty redbrick Victorian house. The next day, I receive the formal demand from the whole family, summoning me to return to them the profit on every sale I had made. Ghislaine forwards to me a copy of the letter she has sent to the police in Oxford, according to which I am a crook and it would be appropriate to arrest me. Another letter is sent to my boss in which it is alleged that I have stolen 2,000,000 euros from my family. It also claims that the advance payments on my salary that I had requested were nothing more than a pretext, designed to cover up the true situation. All of this shows to what extent Tilly had planned everything in order that I would be revealed as a thief. Had he not warned me that we would talk again 'in a year's time exactly'?

It was my aunt who, at Tilly's instigation, orchestrated the whole thing, with unbelievable callousness. The years 2008 and 2009 were atrocious. Having spent so much time trying to defend my family, I found myself in court, facing it alone, except for Maman. I spend my evenings combing through the thousand pages of conclusions which I have had to have translated into English: my whole salary is eaten up by the costs of this process. And I wear myself out putting together legal papers in English. When I go away for the weekend with friends and a hearing is to take place the following week, I take my papers with me. I devote all my days off to sitting in on hearings. In total, six actions are launched against me. And to crown it all, my cousin François comes round almost every day and harasses me, to the point of saying I am a bastard and banging the courtroom door in my face. According to him, I am not my father's son. I have never believed this, but his violent aggression dealt me an added blow.

When Simon, my boss, received this 'very disturbing letter' with its false accusation, sent by Ghislaine, he immediately summoned me to his office and asked me to explain myself. Terrified at the idea that he might dismiss me, I explained that 'my family were telling lies' and I asked him to give me 'the benefit of the doubt'. Which he did, and this gesture of confidence gave me very great comfort. But every morning, I go to the office with a sinking stomach. My immediate reflex as I go in to wish my boss good morning is to size up his attitude. Has he received any further defamatory letters?

Every evening, too, I return home sick with apprehension. My landlady leaves any post I have received on my desk. I can hardly bring myself to open the letters I receive. Another summons? A threatening letter? Notification of another visit from the bailiffs, prompted by complaints made by Ghislaine, so that I will be obliged to pay her council tax and her electricity bills? It's a nightmare. For months now, every time I see a police car, I imagine it's been sent by my family in response to some false allegation or other. I am convinced that, thanks to a great deal of effort on their part, they will end by getting what they want. Did not Ghislaine warn me, when she said very aggressively to me, in court, 'You haven't forgotten, have you, that I know my legal papers inside out?'

I was quite alone; but I had the support of three people: my boss, my girlfriend Lynn, and my landlady. She was very maternal towards me. A professor at Oxford University, this highly-cultivated and sociable woman provided me with a domestic environment that was both enriching and restful.

Having to confront the hostility of my own family was a terrible ordeal. I was very conscious too that the situation in which I found myself might influence, unfavourably, the judge's opinion of me. I was afraid of finding myself alone, once again, and in the dock. So Lynn very kindly came with me. Her presence was a very great support and comfort to me. But without my professional and social background, I would not have stood my ground. Tilly's intention was that I should lose my job and end up on the streets. Maman had seen this quite clearly. It was mainly this that had given her the strength to go away. And it is here, too, that life for me reasserted its claims. Besides, the people around me also believed in me and supported me very generously. I kept my job. I kept my room. And I stood up for myself.

But why, at that same moment, were my eyes not opened as to Tilly's character, since it is at this same time that Tilly throws me out like a dog, snarling at me: 'Clear off, why don't you, that's fine by me'. For some days, I can't make up my mind. After all, wasn't I used to this? And then I receive Ghislaine's statement detailing what it is I am accused of. It's perfectly clear to me that it's full of false claims that it would be easy to disprove. In particular, Ghislaine claims the proceeds of the sale of the houses at Bordeneuve and Fontenay, neither of which has ever been sold. This leads me to believe, once again, that Tilly is helping me.

Tilly never left anything to chance. The only person to whom he has ever been obliged to yield is Ghislaine, who is a difficult person. He knew that he could get her to 'do whatever it takes,' as he was overheard saying to Gonzalez. I would say to myself: 'He's letting her do whatever she likes so as to give her the impression that she's engaged in some new battle'. I thought that he was channelling her energies and letting her make mistakes, because he knew that after all these years I could look after myself. In point of fact, I was refusing to accept the idea that Tilly had been deceiving me for years.   It was easier for me to believe that he was doing what he had promised:  protecting me against the underhand tricks of my family, and especially of Ghislaine's.   This illustrates the extent to which mind control can produce perverse effects.   The moment comes when you find yourself alone when you don't want to face reality.   At that point you clutch at whatever is reassuring, somewhere or other, at certainties one chooses not to question:  'I trust Tilly because he is obviously a good person'.   This control, even at a distance, continues to function.

In spite of this completely crazy situation, I resume my social life.   I work.   I go out with colleagues and profit in full from the many fantastic things Oxford has to offer.   But I go on constantly feeling under pressure. I am like a hunted animal.

## Amaury's story

I have been, I think, too easy a target.   Since the age of fifteen I have suffered from a genuine existential malaise, without being able to put it into words.   I remember writing poems at the time, a real cry of despair which no one heard.   Later, on holiday, when I went out with my friends, I took refuge in silence.   I was numbed. At home, we didn't have time to talk to each other. My father was never there, no one ever stopped for a moment to ask themselves questions.   All alone, without any contact with my parents, I therefore asked all the questions and gave myself all the answers...

When I was twenty and a student in a commercial college in Bordeaux, following a course in which I had at the time no interest whatsoever, I suffered the same malaise as when I was fifteen, and I smoked cannabis. People talked of an artificial paradise, and artificial was certainly the right word for it.

My older brother, my minder, has gone to do a course in Toulouse. My parents are worried and don't know what to do with me. I am a worry to the whole family. Enter Tilly. On the kindly advice of my aunt and godmother Ghislaine, he passes himself off as a therapist for the whole family. He listens to me, and replies in language I understand. There is kindness, a sort of disinterested benevolence, and an absence of judgment in the way he listens to me. He becomes my confidant and helps me get by. This earns him great credit with my parents, my brother and me.

In fact, he didn't save anyone. He was later described 'a delinquent therapist', especially where relationships are concerned. He used my cannabis habit to secure his control over me. He saw immediately that I was fragile, with nothing going well either in my head or my life. He adopted a posture that inspired confidence and respect in me. After which, he could tell me anything he liked, and I would believe it. And he didn't hold back: 'The people who are selling you cannabis are adding much more dangerous substances to it in order to destroy you...', 'You were hypnotized in 1998, by your cousin, without your knowing anything about it'. I had told him, without seeing any harm in it, the story of how, returning from the

United States, I had run into a cousin and we had shared a joint together. Implicating my cousin whom I liked very much and claiming that he had added heroin to the joint he offered me, plunged me into chaos and brought on a change of direction: belief in the 'plot'. 'I am not, then, responsible for my problems, my own malaise'. Tilly's people had been informed of this, and he predicted that ten years without any medical therapy would get me out of it, as long as I follow his methodology.

There are three episodes in particular that allowed him to exercise a mental hold over me. At the very moment this whole story begins, I was, as I remember, twenty years old and my personality was as yet unformed. Lacking any points of reference, I welcomed Tilly as a kind of saviour and gave him my total trust and respect. I have always been attracted and fascinated by top people.

In the year 2000 he sent me to Oxford, to go to a school there, OISE, in order to learn English and to get me off 'drugs'. I came to life again. It was a good moment for me. At the time, I wasn't really aware of any notion of a conspiracy, but simply enjoyed a happy and carefree life. Tilly advised me to cut myself off from my friends, which I did. But one day in my English class I was surprised to see someone I knew from Bordeaux, for whom I had no great liking. Tilly then told me that this person had come to keep an eye on me, that he was part of a network that wanted to destroy us. He told me that this network was very powerful, for, in spite of the trouble his people have taken to 'hide' me, the enemy has found me. Without my really grasping it, this episode was my first warning that I should be on guard against the outside world. I remember his leitmotif, which was: 'There is no such thing as chance'.

Second episode: We had got into the habit of meeting up in cafés. One day, Tilly and I go into a café with my cousin and I find myself face to face with a girl from my lycée to whom I had declared my love and who had rejected me. Petrified, I sit down and I ask Tilly if he realizes what this means to me. He replies very calmly that he understands very well and that it is time to pack up and go. Two streets later he launches into a veritable debriefing session: 'This was not a chance meeting, Amaury. I knew she would be there but because I sense that you are not really aware of things, I wanted you to see them for yourself. This girl is part of the network, she has been sent to seduce you and to destroy you. So there you are. You now understand my profession better. I have spent two months organizing this whole thing'. I am appalled by the methods of the enemy camp, who are, it seems, lawless and faithless. But then, daily life takes over again.

Third episode: I am an inveterate romantic, and, one day, while I am still attending these same English classes, I meet a French girl on the internet. I of course tell Tilly about it, who informs me that it is not she who is corresponding with me, but 'my family in the enemy network', who are trying to lead me astray and destroy me. I listen but go on exactly as before. Still feeling attracted to her, I get the girl's telephone number and we talk for hours on end. She becomes my confidante,

I tell her everything. So much so that I decide to go to France to see her. So, again, I tell Tilly about this, to get his approval. He tells me it's a trap, that they are going to kidnap me and give me some kind of injection. So I break off all contact with her. I was in the habit of going to see Tilly in London, so that he could give me some money, and to discuss with him my future. I loved these visits. But on this particular day, he 'receives' me in a café and, to my utter amazement, he proffers some torn up photographs which he lets fall on to the table, while lashing out at me. I am completely taken aback. He tells me that they are photographs of his own family. The mother of the girl I met on the internet is apparently a senior police officer and she, too, is part of the network. This envelope and these torn photographs should be read as a threat against Tilly and my family. And all of this is my fault. I don't understand what I have done wrong, but he has achieved what he set out to do, because the only thing that I take away from all this is that I can no longer do as I want, which is to live a carefree life; my actions have consequences for the whole group, including some top people. I am caught in a trap.

I think that after these three episodes my grasp of reality and my ability to think clearly were put on hold, for I was supposed to have acquired all the evidence and proof of the existence of this so-called plot.

In 2004 or 2005 I find myself in London sharing a flat with my cousin François. Tilly issues us with very strict security instructions, which I more or less observe. I later discover, during the investigation, that François

had been ordered to watch me. My English course, life
in London, a well-placed flat, it is all very pleasant. Then
suddenly Ghislaine and her daughter Guillemette move
into our flat, only thirty square metres, and immediately
take charge of everything. All of this on Tilly's orders,
though they do it all with great enthusiasm. They ruin
my life, to the extent that I contemplate suicide.

I implore Tilly to get me out of there, and as a result
he sends me to the office of the Blue Light Foundation and
I am imprisoned there for fourteen months. During this
period, I wrote a great deal. I have preserved everything
I wrote. Tilly came to see me and took away what I had
written 'so as to read and discuss it with me'. He returned
the writings to me without ever discussing them, except
to say that I had not done enough and that I must give it
all much more thought. At first he presented this to me
as a form of therapy. Later, he said it was a punishment:
I must understand what it meant to be all alone. I was
in fact dying of hunger and loneliness, even though I was
not sorry to be deprived of the company of my cousins.
I slept on the floor in a sleeping bag. I was obliged to
wash in cold water in the toilets of the apartment block.
My days were shaped by my one and only meal which I
divided into portions to try to overcome my hunger and
my anguish.

During this time Tilly tried to drive me mad, so as
to destroy me once and for all, and I reached the point of
doubting everything I believed, so he almost succeeded.
I later understand that what I went through amounted
to a real act of torture. This technique resembles the

methods the CIA uses against terrorists in Guantánamo Bay. It is what is called sensory deprivation. Its effect on me was very powerful. For example, one day when Tilly was telling me about his people he let slip that 'they are a year ahead of civil society'. At which point I asked him if they had a special relationship with God. He replied, gravely: 'You, Amaury, have already grasped many things. I will tell you everything in ten years' time!' I was trapped forever. Tilly had become not just my tutor, he had taken on the role of a father and of God himself.

Later on, in Oxford, I work: boring little jobs, packing shelves, gardening. Like everyone else, I hand my pay over to Tilly, who gives me back some 'pocket money'. All spending on treats, on bars of chocolate for example, is forbidden. When I do buy one I feel that I am doing something wrong. One day, when I remark to my cousin that Tilly does not see everything, that he does not know that I allow myself a treat from time to time, he retorts that I am quite mistaken: Tilly knows all about it, but is saying nothing for the time being (which illustrates perfectly his power of persuasion together with the ability to exercise a mental hold on people). This reply of course makes me very anxious. My Marchand cousins and their mother have always been well in with the regime established by Tilly. They have benefitted from milder treatment, and he has allowed them certain powers. As I see it, my aunt and my cousins have been Tilly's go-between as far as my little sister and I are concerned. My aunt's behaviour was little short of thuggish.

The most extraordinary thing about this whole story is

that we had our doubts, all the time, about what Tilly said and did. But such was our conditioning that, whatever the truth of the matter, we tried to validate every one of his assertions. For example, in Oxford as in London there were surveillance cameras everywhere. His 'people' used them, apparently, for our safety and to watch and protect us from any danger. Subconsciously, we knew that we were trapped in a fantasy world and at the same time we were not quite certain, and this idea haunted us. It created fear and anguish. It undermined us, powerfully reinforcing the psychological hold Tilly had over us. To be perfectly honest, if it were not for our mother's fighting spirit and her love for us I would still be there.

## Diane's story

When this story begins, I am fifteen years old and am still at school. I am a perfectly normal and ordinary girl. In spite of a slight lack of self-confidence, quite usual at my age, I am a happy teenager, full of plans, who joins in everything in my search for what it is I want to do later. Before I'm grown up, I have very little contact with Tilly except, for example, when I go on a tennis course in England with his daughter Natacha, who is four years younger than me. Up until this time I know Thierry Tilly through what other people say of him. They are almost all under his spell.

Even if I don't communicate directly with him, this does not mean that he is not 'taking an interest' in me. Like a spider, he is weaving the web that will imprison us for years.

I have always been very close to my parents and my brothers. The family means a great deal to me and, as the youngest and smallest, I have always admired Guillaume and Amaury. I modelled myself on them.

When Maman goes to Martel and leaves me in Bordeaux with Papa, I am at first torn between various different feelings. For the first time in my life, I am going to have my father all to myself. What good luck! But at the same time, I won't have Maman and won't be able to tell her everything that has happened to me that day in school. In the end, things turn out for the best and I establish a special relationship with my father: there is nothing more important for a daughter than that she should get on well with her father. And of course, I think that this is thanks to Tilly and that all of this is being done in everyone's best interest and for everyone's good.

Later, everything goes wrong. I don't like Tilly's plan to send me to a boarding school for girls during my last year at all: I have never been away from home before. Tilly is very insistent. I end by letting myself be persuaded. His daughter went there and loved it. The worst thing is that in the end I was even persuaded that this whole idea had come from me. Every weekend I join the whole family at Martel, and then leave them again on Sunday evening in tears. When Maman asks me if my bag is packed, I resent this, and feel that she is sending me away. The web is beginning to close about me. My resistance takes the form of tears, a gift for Thierry Tilly which he will make use of again several times, saying that I am only a little girl, that it is best not to cry, that any sorrows which I have are due to my mother; I get over it. The worst of it is that these remarks are supported by people whom I really trust: my aunt and my cousins.

I should point out that if there are certain things one has believed, even if they are fantastical, they are believed because they have been passed on by trustworthy people. To give one simple example: when Jean is being vilified it's not Thierry Tilly whom I believe but what my aunt and my cousins say, who have been living with him, as they tell me of his behaviour, various things he is supposed to have done in the past. All of this was consistent with what Thierry Tilly put forward, so that no one challenged what he said.

One day during the school holidays my aunt says, in my hearing, that Thierry Tilly is very anxious about me. I am, a 'borderline' person, and he doesn't know what he will be able to make of me. I take fright. I don't want to be marginalized. I want to show them that this is not so. I do everything I can to be perfect, unless it goes too much against the grain.

At the age of eighteen and having left secondary school, I go to London to a college which prepares students for university entrance. It is a place where Natacha, Tilly's daughter, is also studying. Who, in such circumstances, would suspect anything at all? What parents would not be happy to see their daughter admitted to a college of this kind, with an excellent reputation and preparing its students for university entrance? As for me,

I feel very privileged.  No one could imagine that Tilly's only objective is to separate me once again, and a little more, from my parents and my brothers.  Very soon, François and Amaury and then Guillemette join me and we all live together.  The rent on this flat has not been paid.  Obviously, I don't know this, and my parents send money to Tilly, believing he will take care of everything.

Tilly, in fact, who is supposed to be sharing out between us the money our parents send, is keeping most of it for himself and gives us as little as possible on the pretext that the rent and the cost of various security measures absorbs the greater part of it.  It is at this time, too, that Amaury is sent to the office in which he is held prisoner, and François and I take him his meal every day.  I can see that my brother is very unwell, and this worries me dreadfully, to the point where, when I knock on his door and he takes some time to open it, I am terribly afraid that he may have tried to commit suicide.  I sometimes even find myself looking at the pavement under his window.  However, the atmosphere in the flat itself isn't bad.  We are used to being poor.  We forge strong links and a real bond unites us, Guillemette, François and me.  On Sundays we go to supermarkets where products that have passed their sell-by date are sold very cheaply.  At the end of the day the price is sharply reduced.  We laugh about this, and I tell myself that, later on, we will have good memories of this time.  I go to my course every day, and basically my life appears perfectly normal.  At the end of the year I win a place at Edinburgh University.  I am very proud, and impatient to begin.

Then, in July we are obliged to return to France: we have been evicted from our flat for non-payment of rent. We arrive in Talade imagining that, after a month's vacation, we will leave again in September. In the past, we never knew when we would be leaving, nor for how long, but, on this occasion, we were quite certain that we would be staying only for a month, in order to be present at the start of the new academic year in the UK. This month, however, gets extended and prolonged until it becomes three years. At first, when I ask questions about my departure for Edinburgh, I'm told there are difficulties in the enrolment in my course and that there is a possibility of late entry to it. After a while I stop asking Thierry Tilly through Ghislaine (which is how such things are done). I have realized that I will never go to Edinburgh, that they have been telling me stories.

I am, in life, a positive person: I try to get the best out of everything. At Talade, I establish good relations with my grandmother. I look after her, relieving my aunt who has been doing it up until now, during the day at least. I have always been very close to Mamie. I accept this task very willingly, and enjoy the company of my grandmother. We strengthen our already close relationship. She teaches me how to run a household, and a bond of mutual trust, which already existed between us, is reaffirmed.

There is, however, one hitch: I spend the greater part of my time with my aunt and my cousins and soon avoid all contact with my parents. I try sometimes to act as a buffer between 'the Marchand clan' of which I am a member, and 'the others'. I am, in point of fact, under the influence of Ghislaine, who acts as Tilly's agent.   In a very insidious way, everything that is said is designed to separate me psychologically from my parents and my brothers: 'Your parents don't love you, your brothers would have preferred a different sister, you've been spoiled and at Guillemette's expense, who is eight years older than you!  Your mother is jealous of you.   You were very badly dressed as a child...'  In a subtle way, I suppose, they were sowing a seed and letting it germinate. And it worked very well.

Tilly acted in a different way with each of us.  In my case, I felt like a kidnapped child who keeps on hoping that one day her parents will come and find her.  But the days go by, and nobody comes.  During this time the kidnapper keeps on telling the child: 'They won't come. They don't love you'.  It's the principle of the drip, drip, drip of water, of which a little more accumulates each day.  In the end the vessel overflows, and the child believes what she is being told.  This is what happened to me.

Even if at the start you resist and rebel, after a few months or even years you bend the knee and you accept what you are being told.  But above all you develop a thick skin: 'If they don't want me, so much the worse for them.  They will be the losers in the end'.  And you begin to envisage a life without parents and without brothers at your side.

Moreover, another idea took root in me: that if you are not with the Védrines – with, that is above all, Ghislaine and her children – you are against them.  My aunt had said to Amaury and me: 'I fight for myself and my children; whoever loves me follows me'. Not to do so is to be a traitor. At the age of twenty-one you do not want to seem to be a traitor to anyone at all. Besides which, the Védrines were in practice my only family. I no longer have maternal grandparents, and Maman's sister lives in Paris. At that particular moment, moreover, all relations with her were severed. Looked at from this viewpoint, one could say that Maman and I have each made every effort to be accepted by the family, while at the same time everything possible has been done to alienate us from each other.

In Oxford I have truly lost any autonomy. Tilly insists that I find two jobs. I work ninety hours a week and sleep for three hours a night, on a very thin mattress. The story is always that the money is needed to pay the rent and to ensure our security, but also to make the savings necessary to fund my coming year in Edinburgh. Tilly, however, pockets the lot. He keeps me under control by telling me that his boss and he are very proud of me, but also by claiming that what I am doing is helping my parents. And so from day to day I go on. At the time I am living on my own with Natacha. When one of my employers proposes to promote me so that I would become a manager and thus no longer have to work set hours, I accept, even if I am very soon exhausted. It is decided that I should go and live with Ghislaine, my cousin, Amaury and my grandmother. I must under no circumstances see my parents. And the only time that I broke this rule, I had the immense joy of seeing my parents but also an unforgettable dressing-down from Thierry Tilly.

From the moment I arrive in this house, everyone adopts a negative and sometimes unkind attitude towards me. I am constantly criticized: I have put a little money to one side, and am therefore a traitor, a crook who thinks only of herself. Tilly gossips about me behind my back, repeating spiteful remarks, doing me down in the others' eyes, whereas, when he is alone with me, he is all encouragement. Seeing me very upset, but above all in total incomprehension as to what is going on, Amaury tries to smooth things over.

My cousin joins in. She compares our two situations, emphasizing the fact that she has always gone out a great deal, has had lots of friends, whereas I have had none of this. I don't know what she is talking about: when she was the age I am now I was only thirteen. And in Oxford, there is no question of going out, or of making friends, still less of love affairs. I begin to think that, even if I am not abnormal, I am certainly good for nothing. Little by little, I lose all my self-esteem.

Added to which my cousins are treated very differently from me. To give just one example: François's working day ends at 5.30pm. If he gets home at 6 or 6.30 pm, no one says anything. Mine ends at 4.30pm. But I have to return home immediately. So anxious am I to get home, for fear of being accused of something or other, that I have almost had a bicycle accident an unimaginable number of times. Moreover, Thierry Tilly made a point of arranging meetings with my aunt at a time when Mamie was on her own, which I found unacceptable. The only solution was for me to get home as fast as I could. This caused a great deal of friction.

When Mamie arrived in Oxford I didn't look after her straight away but began to do so little by little, starting by getting up during the night to help her. My room was on the first floor, whereas hers, and that of my aunt which adjoined the party wall, were on the ground floor. And so I had to run downstairs several times every night. I had been told that this was part of my punishment for having 'betrayed them'. Like Amaury, whom Tilly had condemned to live on his own in Regent Street in order to put the screws on him, I too now deserved special treatment.

Then, little by little, I took over the whole of my grandmother's daily routine, which I had to organize so that it fitted in with my job. I prepared her meals in advance so that all my aunt had to do was to heat them up, and I did all her washing.

Looking after my grandmother had its positive side, but was also very hard work. I would go to bed, afraid I would not hear her calling me, but often hardly had I fallen asleep but my grandmother woke me, which happened several times every night. I remember one night, when she needed me, I was feeling so exhausted that I felt certain I had not the strength to get out of bed. Except that, when you know that the person you are in charge of cannot get up without your help, you are ready to move mountains. You find a strength you did not know you possessed, and you get up.

Besides which, if it happened that Mamie slept a few minutes longer than usual in the morning, I was afraid of having to announce to the whole household that Mamie had 'gone to sleep for ever'. I don't at all regret having looked after her, even if I sometimes said to myself that, since her daughter was around, it was not really my responsibility. One thing, however, is certain: my grandmother was happy that I was there. And later, when we were released from the nightmare, and had returned to France, I remember how her face lit up one day when I came to visit her. She used to call me her 'little nurse'. And no one can ever take that away from me.

In spite of all this, I nevertheless had my doubts, and an impulse to rebel. The day when Ghislaine pronounced that it was I who possessed the famous 'transmission', I protested: originally it was supposed to be Maman, then later a male of the family. And besides, I was the youngest member. François put forward an opposing argument: it must be a woman. I replied that, in that case, it was certainly his own mother, and would they stop pestering me. And when they asserted that Guillaume was a bastard I objected: the photos of Papa and Guillaume as small children prove this accusation to be wholly false. They are so alike that you cannot tell one from the other. This was obviously an idea of Tilly's that they had taken over.

Finding yourself in such a nest of vipers, you end by confessing anything at all so that they will leave you in peace. This is how I came to lodge a complaint against Maman. One day I happen to mention that, when I bought my first bra, she came with me. Ghislaine leapt up: 'That's appalling; it's disgraceful…' And I end up by making this enormous accusation, which I know to be untrue:

that she interfered with me. 'That will get them to leave me alone about this whole business of the transmission', I think to myself, 'they will even be nice to me'. Today, I think that Thierry Tilly knew how to use members of my family as if they were pawns on a chessboard. He succeeded in getting me to lodge a charge against Maman, and to attack Guillaume in the courts. Tilly got me to sign papers at midday in the restaurant where I worked, when I was completely up to my eyes in work, and exhausted. That was his great speciality. Anxious to get rid of him, I signed without realizing what it was all about. Subjected to such methods, you end by doing anything you are told. As to the sale of Martel, I discovered, at the time of our liberation, that the property no longer belonged to us, whereas, as far as I was concerned, all we had signed up to was some sort of mortgage agreement. Our awakening was very painful and still is.

With my brother Guillaume (and, in fact, Tilly and Ghislaine) I was imprisoned briefly under suspicion of money laundering, after a lot of cash in our names, from the sale of Martel, turned up in a Money Shop. For someone like me, who suffers a little from claustrophobia, being frisked is not a pleasant experience, any more than it is to have fingerprints taken, or to be interrogated, or to hear the sound of prison keys being turned...

At the time, I said to myself: 'It's a test, you must show how strong you can be'. But then, on the wall of my prison cell someone had written in large letters: 'Tell the truth. That will reduce your sentence'. But what truth? I could not understand what was happening, except that

I was accused of money laundering, when all I had done was to withdraw a large amount of cash in order to give it to Tilly.   At this same time I told myself that I must not, whatever happened, betray him, he who having been arrested along with me had had the nerve to whisper in my ear: 'Don't worry, I got myself arrested with you on purpose'.

This is a trial it takes time to recover from.   I remember that I could not afterwards walk past the restaurant where the arrest took place or see a police car, of which there are many in Oxford, without feeling afraid. But, in time, with the help of strength of character and willpower, you rise above it.

Tilly's two magic phrases were: 'The worse it is, the sooner it passes' and 'There is no such thing as chance'. He always bounced back and was always able to land on his own two feet.   I never saw him display a moment's uncertainty.   Not long before I was arrested with him, Maman had passed by the restaurant where we were working.   He later whispered to me that she was hoping to see her daughter in handcuffs, that she was a sadist. Maman, however, was simply returning home from work by her usual route, her flat being only a few blocks away.   But even if you are listening with only half an ear sometimes, the worm is in the apple, and you begin to believe anything at all.

I remember, too, the moment when I found myself confronting my older brother in court.   Giving evidence against him was extremely difficult, horrible even.   But if I objected that I didn't agree with all of this, or that

I didn't want to get documents together, or to work on them, I was reprimanded, and indeed criticized as selfish. So that, to avoid all of this, I submitted, and did what I was told, feeling sick at heart. Especially during this time when I was obliged to behave in a particularly docile way, in order to prove that I was not a traitor.

After all these years I realized only too well that the situation was hopeless. Either I must run away riddled with debts, ignoring what has been dinned into me for years, that I am utterly useless, and that if I go away again no one will help me, in which case I will have abandoned and betrayed my family. Lose-lose, in other words. Or I stay with my father and my brother in a wretched situation, under the thumb of my aunt, and with the only person who is nice to me and whom I look after every night, my grandmother. Since I neither want to, nor can, leave her, I don't go.

**Part Four:** Escape

# 15

I had no sooner arrived at St. Pancras Station than a man approached me. The chauffeur, worried, intervened. False alarm: it was Stanislas, my cousin's son. Anne was there too, with Marie-Hélène. I flung myself into their arms. They clung to me, so overcome with emotion that Marie-Hélène, usually so expansive, was unable to speak. We went through security and boarded the Eurostar. And only then, for the first time, did I feel the enormous weight that lay on my shoulders lift: I was no longer afraid of Tilly. Not in the least. I was free. I would never, ever, have been able to do that on my own.

Sitting opposite me, Marie-Hélène and Anne observed me, appalled by the way I looked. The difficulty I found in walking, my emaciation, my hair, greying and hanging about my face, the terrible state I was in, my clothes even, everything about me indicated more than any words what I had been through, which they did not yet understand. I tried to tell them, but my words at times got muddled up, and at others failed me.

When at last we arrived in Paris, there was only one thought in my head: to find my sister, and ask for her forgiveness.   We embraced, held each other tight, and wept.   My cousin Bertrand and my brother-in-law Jean-Michel, who were waiting with her, were both of them visibly moved at the sight of me, both because we were reunited at last, and also because of what I had become. Several hours later I left a message on my husband's answerphone: 'There it is, then, Charles-Henri, it was all too much, much too much.  I had to get away.  I love you'.

I stayed on in Paris for several days:  I needed time to recover, to switch off.   Françoise looked after me, made me rest, gave me clothes, money and everything I might need.   Then I met Maître Daniel Picotin: he was waiting for me at Bordeaux.   When Marie-Hélène was first in touch with him, in 2004, he had explained to her that there was nothing she could do to help me, since she was not a member of my family, and since French law accepts only complaints lodged by the victims themselves. In my opinion, this restriction to the About-Picard law of June 2001, which itself, for the first time, recognizes as a criminal offence the abuse of weakness, is regrettable. This anomaly, indeed, is what lies behind the whole of Maître Daniel Picotin's present campaign: he is proposing to reinforce the law, so that it may be made more effective in the assistance it gives to victims of manipulation and brainwashing.

Marie-Hélène's choice of lawyer could not have been better.   President of the Info Sectes Aquitaine, an association opposed to brainwashing, he was wholly familiar with the mechanisms of manipulation and mental domination.  Before I arrived he had already approached the examining magistrate, M. Lorentz, with a view to arranging a meeting with the least possible delay.

When I arrived in Bordeaux, I went at once to Maître Picotin's chambers.  Brown hair, green eyes, about fifty years old, athletic in appearance, and with a penetrating intelligence, he at once inspired confidence in me.  He had been involved in politics, had had a career as a radical deputy from 1993-97, and had been a member of the group 'Sectes' in the Assemblée Nationale.  Then he had returned to the bar in order to specialize in cases involving the abuse of weakness, as well as mental manipulation.  I spent several hours in his office, telling him, down to the very last detail, everything that had happened to me.  He understood it all without my having to spell it out: this case was exceptional for its length and the number of people involved, but it had much in common with the practices of certain sects: manipulation, as well as psychological domination attained by identical techniques.  But the prime objective was different, being neither religious nor ideological, but economic and financial.  Tilly's sole aim was to strip us of everything and then to dominate us, so as to continue to live entirely at our expense.  The lawyer presented his conclusion in the following terms: 'There is no sect without mental manipulation, but there can be mental manipulation without any sect being involved'.

We were not a sect, but a perfectly normal family to whom something abnormal had happened.

On the 29th March 2009, at ten past three in the afternoon, and with a pounding heart, I entered with my lawyer into the office of Judge Lorentz. I was motivated from then on by a powerful desire for justice. I wanted to bring the truth to light and to save my family. The first question the judge put to me went to the heart of the problem:

'You have expressed the wish to be heard. Can you explain to me the circumstances under which you have been led during the course of the last few years to part with the whole of your inheritance?'

I began by making it clear that although I was sure of the facts of the case I was less so of the timing; and then I told him everything. This took quite some time. And, very frail still and without having had the time to prepare myself properly, I broke down several times. The need to speak of my children and what they had been through distressed me unutterably (and, besides, I did not know, even then, the full extent of it). I was overcome with a sense of guilt. Compared with what they had endured, the fact of our having lost all our property seemed to me negligible. I would have given everything to have spared them. This session lasted until seven o'clock in the evening. By the end of it, the charge had been decided: abuse of weakness, sequestration aggravated by acts of cruelty, abuse of trust, fraud.

The judge asked me to avoid the media and to find lodgings outside Bordeaux. I had, in any case, no place to stay. Marie-Hélène, who lived in the country, insisted on taking me home with her and surrounding me with every comfort. She wanted me to enjoy again everything I had been deprived of: a pretty room, delicacies and tit-bits, cosmetics in the bathroom, and, above all, affection and attention. Together with her husband Dominique, she did everything in her power to make me feel loved and supported. She bought me a watch and a diary, so that I might rediscover my temporal points of reference. Little by little, I began to come to life again. But with every step I took I continued to feel pain. It soon became obvious that I must arrange to be operated on very soon. But I had nothing left to live on. I had to register for social security and sickness benefits.

Daniel Picotin took me in hand: emerging from a situation such as I had just experienced required psychological support. He found a psychoanalyst who helped me to put into words what I was feeling, and to distance myself from the past. As the days slipped by I became more and more impatient: the only thing that mattered when it came down to it was to save my children and my husband, who were still suffering. My lawyer explained to me that rescuing my family could not be considered without a long and meticulous preparation. Without this, we would be sure to fail. Guided by him, I met a criminologist in Paris who was a specialist in the handling and exfiltration of victims. I decided first of all to maintain contact with my children and my husband. I wrote to them regularly. I tried several times to speak on the telephone to Diane, who immediately hung up. Another obstacle arose: we must not think of doing anything at all, until Judge Lorentz had put Tilly in a place where he would be prevented from harming us.

Because of discrepancies between our legal systems, the English judiciary proved, at first, reluctant to collaborate with him.   But on the other side of the English Channel, Tilly already had several convictions, among others for money laundering, as well as for matters concerning the Blue Light Foundation.   There had been a raid on his premises by Scotland Yard; they had even confiscated his identity papers to prevent him from leaving the country.   But matters were dragging...

Besides which, impatient though I was to see my family again, I needed to take care of myself and recover my strength.   In September, I had a hip operation.   I had no choice but to accept this delay: I could not go to Oxford unless I was totally fit. I had also to find again a way of life that was 'normal'.   It was three years now since I had last driven a car.   The very idea of taking the wheel terrified me to the point of inducing vertigo. I had to relearn everything.   My sister, her husband, my cousins, and my friends were extraordinary.   They even formed an association, designed to come to my aid financially and materially.   Persuaded, however, that it was up to me to make the first move, I gradually renewed contact with all those people with whom we had broken off communications during these past nine years.   I approached some of them uncertainly, but was always warmly received.   In this way I found again my brother-in-law Bernard and my nephews.   My reunion with Jean Marchand was tinged with emotion.   He bombarded me with questions about Ghislaine and his children.   I reassured him as best I could. My own immediate family had been supporting him throughout this whole time, materially as well as emotionally, and I was very pleased about this.

Finally, having learned by tapping his phones that Tilly was planning to go to Switzerland, Judge Lorentz found a solution to the delays caused by the English judicial procedures: he asked for Tilly's identity papers to be returned to him. He hoped that since he was now able to do so Tilly would flee. And he was right: in October, Tilly, abandoning his wife and children, flew from London to Zurich where as he left the plane he was met by police and dispatched to Bordeaux. He was arrested and committed to prison in Gradignan.

Thierry Tilly contested his arrest vigorously, uttering vague threats and insulting the judge to the point where a further offence, that of contempt of court, was added to the initial charge. Moreover, confident of his own judicial expertise, he refused any legal representation. Hearing all this in Oxford, however, Mamie, Ghislaine, Charles-Henri and the children were convinced that for some unknown reason he had organized his own arrest. His influence had not waned.

As for me, reluctant to be dependent on anyone else, thanks to a friend I found work in an organization specializing in reintegration into the community, and began preparing the rescue of my family.

# 16

Daniel Picotin's practice specializes in helping victims of brainwashing, either supplying legal representation or exfiltration itself.   I discover that these operations are planned well in advance and demand a team of specially trained people.  This procedure is called exit counselling. Even before embarking on such a course of action, my lawyer retraces with me the whole history of the affair. Since I am to be a complainant, he is anxious that I understand properly the whole procedure.

Between 1970 and 1980, there was only one practicable method of rescuing victims of brainwashing from the circle in which they found themselves trapped, whether this was a sect or some other form of power play. Up until then, they were abducted, and specialists or their own families 'deprogrammed' them, subjected them, in other words, to a type of brainwashing designed to bring them back to reality.  There was nothing voluntary about this brutal 'deprogramming':  the survivors were obliged to undergo the treatment, usually by being confined.   The description they were offered of their time with the sect was wholly negative, a caricature, indeed.  This procedure met with a number of failures: sometimes, the people involved returned to the sect after being released; while those whose eyes were opened often suffered numerous after-effects.  So towards the end of the 1980s, 'deprogramming' was strongly criticised, and many specialists turned to a different process.

Thus it was that 'exit counselling' came into being

in the United States, formulated by an ex-member of the Moonie sect, Steven Hassan, who had developed his own method after studying psychology in the USA. He himself had been snatched from a sect by his family, who confined him in order to 'save' him. This episode had utterly traumatized him, even if, afterwards, he had readapted well to normal life and had never been tempted to return to the Moonies. So he subsequently devoted his energies to the development of a less violent method of exfiltrating followers of sects.

In contrast to 'deprogramming', *exit counselling* is based on a gentle approach and on the consent of the victim to the help he is being offered. But this method requires time, teams of specialists, and the active participation of the victims' families. Nevertheless, it has already rescued more than a thousand people, who have been able to readjust, more easily than after a 'deprogramming'.

To set such a process in motion, and before organizing the journey to Oxford, it was essential that the whole team should know our story, as well as the psychology of every one of us, and Tilly's profile. With Philippe and Brigitte, I undertook to record these years of sequestration, describing the attitudes and the behaviour of each of us, in the minutest detail, along with the changing nature of relations that prevailed between the different members of the family. I also drew up a chronological account of the facts, conducting my own inquiry as it were. Then on 4th April 2009, a month after my departure from Oxford, while we are celebrating Marie-Hélène's birthday, Jean reveals something to me that makes my blood run cold: 'You know, don't you, that Ghislaine never liked you. As early as '99, she was saying to me: 'As for that creature, I'm going to make her eat dirt...' At the time, I refused to believe him, but unfortunately the testimony of two of Ghislaines' friends has since borne out what Jean told me.

This process was long and extremely demanding, but soon the team knew almost as much about the whole affair as I did myself, and we could at last begin to set the whole enterprise in motion. But as Daniel Picotin had warned me: it was possible that my children or my husband would refuse to return. In which case, no one must threaten or coerce them. For a moment my heart almost failed me: could it possible be that my family had reached the point when they would refuse to return home? Then I decided that, no, they would of course come back, and of their own free will.

I understand better now the tight constraints on time that underlay the whole process the team was engaged on. During this period of preparation I wrote very regularly to my children and my husband. I wanted them to know that the affection and the respect I felt for them would never falter. In spite of the fears of those around me, I was convinced that I would succeed in this.

But it took nine months – of hope and, often, of uncertainty and discouragement. Nine months without turning round in the street when someone calls out 'Maman'.

But, I am fortunate. It is a time when I am surrounded by friends and family. I go from house to house, but

having as my base Les Annereaux, with Marie-Hélène
and Dominique.   My sister and her husband are much
in evidence.   My cousins too.   Little by little I rebuild
myself.   I am not afraid of Tilly;  but, all the same, taking
a train on my own, using my debit card, administering
my affairs, all of this requires a great deal of effort on
my part.

At this same time, I am tormented by one question:
when should I arrange to have my hip operated on?  I do
not want to be immobilized at the very moment when
our trip to Oxford needs to be made.   I even telephone
the judge to find out what stage the legal proceedings
have reached.

And, suddenly, the date for my surgery is fixed.  It is
to be carried out on September 2$^{nd}$, 2009 at 10 o'clock.

It almost breaks my heart, having to go through with
it without being able to warn my family.   It causes me real
anguish: suppose I don't wake up from the anaesthetic?
Am I never to have the opportunity of saying to my
children that everything that has been said about me is
untrue, that I love all three of them?

But, strengthened by my desire to go through with
it, by the medical team, and by my friends (with especial
thanks to Marie-Aude and Véronique), I recover quickly.

The 'exfiltration' operation had a name, "Bow-
Window 1," and a date, November 2$^{nd}$ 2009.

We called the exfiltration operation, 'Operation Bow
Window', because of Ghislaine's habit of looking out of
her window on alert for the next threat.   There were a
lot of us involved: Philippe and Brigitte, Marie-Hélène

and her husband Dominique, Ghislaine's husband Jean, a criminologist, a psychologist, Daniel Picotin, and me. Shortly before our departure, a journalist from the *Sud-Ouest* had written an article about our story. I had been able to read it before it appeared. Daniel Picotin gave him permission to accompany us. Except for this vital group of people, no one knew anything. I had not even told my sister about it.

On November 10th, we all meet on the Eurostar. Happy to be at last in action, and very conscious of having arrived at an unforgettable moment, I go from one to the other of them in the carriage. Philippe and Brigitte, who have been separated from their children for nine years now, understand only too well my feverish anxiety. Marie-Hélène reminds Jean, jokingly, of their daily telephone exchanges at the time when, without Ghislaine and his children, he was feeling desperately lonely. Daniel Picotin and his whole team are optimistic.

On our arrival in London, we persuade Jean not to accept an invitation to appear on the eight o-clock news on television. Our plan can only succeed in conditions of the utmost secrecy. We arrive at last in Oxford. Once we are there, the specific plan must be carried out step by step without any rush. We go to bed, but I am beside myself with impatience. I force myself to remain calm, but sleep will not come. I am afraid of failure, afraid in case my husband and children reject me. At the same time, nothing on earth would persuade me now to retreat. I say to myself: 'If they refuse to talk to you tomorrow, they will talk to you the day after tomorrow, or in a few days time...' When I at last fall asleep, I feel a visceral certainty that I am going to get my family back.

The first of them that I find again is Guillaume, an unforgettable moment for me, and what joy to hold him again, at last, in my arms. He talks to me at length, telling me everything he has been through. He says how traumatic it was for him to find himself the target of numerous legal proceedings initiated by his own family, but all of them in fact orchestrated by Tilly. Having no money to employ a barrister, he defended himself alone in the witness box, as well as he could. I can tell he is both relieved and exhausted.

When we part, late that evening, we know that we have found one another again, and that we are going to fight together, side by side.

But then we faced a setback. An English newspaper article compromised the plans for exit counselling by revealing the operation and attempting to photograph or interview family members, which disrupted their ability to recover from what they have been through. This also meant that Ghislaine could get at those members who were still under Tilly's influence and ruin any positive contact they might have had with us.

The rescue team halted the mission but promised to return eventually to rescue those members of the family who were still in Oxford. Nevertheless, the game was far from being won: at the very moment that we arrived at St. Pancras to board the train for home, Jean, who had been delayed, arrived. He tried, on his own initiative, to see Ghislaine, but this had turned into a domestic dispute,

with shouting and threats.   As he left, he even finished
by shouting: 'You will end up in prison', with the result
that his demonisation in the eyes of those family members
still under the influence of Tilly was reinforced.   In going
it alone in this way and unfortunately distancing himself
from the rest of the team, Jean risked that any future
operation would be compromised.

After his psychological liberation, Guillaume had
said he would see us again in Bordeaux.   He was taking
a week's holiday, and arrived by car, bringing with him
a trunkful of documents.   We went straight to the judge
and his whole deposition corroborated everything I said.
Then he went back to Oxford:  he wanted to keep his job,
because he was enthusiastic about it and valued by the
people he worked for.   I reflected that, at this moment,
free once more, he needs time to reflect and to recover.
He also needs a regular life, balanced between work,
love and leisure.   We remain in contact by telephone and
e-mail.   The happiness I feel, reading his messages headed
'Dearest Mother', is beyond words.

But we, too, will need to return to Oxford soon.
Organizing 'Bow-Window 2' is complicated:  everyone
has to set aside some time, and getting the dates when
each of us is free to coincide is tricky.   Meanwhile, I am
still working at a society for helping with  reintegration,
AMOS.   My cousin Bertrand has lent me a studio, where
we meet regularly to plan the second operation.

The nights are long.   In my head I replay the
film of our stay in Oxford.   I think again of all those
people, private and public, who helped in the practical

organization of this mission.   But I am shattered by a complaint lodged by Diane, who accuses me of interfering with her, and of touching her inappropriately.  Of course, I see Tilly's signature on all of this and I know perfectly well that,when she has emerged from this nightmare she will withdraw the charge.  A perfect example of 'induced false memories'.

In the middle of December the same team, except for Jean Marchand, returns to Oxford.  We use a car with a driver rather than taking public transport, to conceal our journey.  We choose another hotel, more central than the earlier one.

We are to launch this second mission with a meeting in the French embassy in London, arranged by Maître Picotin.

We attend, all of us, with Guillaume.  The consul, Edouard Braine, has heard of the affair and proves extremely helpful.  We are all won over immediately by his warm personality and his vitality.  This charming and intelligent man indicates that he was posted for a while in Algeria.   So that a conversation about Oran takes place – inevitably – between him  and Marie-Hélène... The atmosphere is perfect.   Next, we meet a French liaison judge attached to the embassy, who is responsible for all judicial matters in both countries that involve French nationals.   Finally, there is also a representative of the English police present – we need someone from Scotland Yard to ensure the smooth running of operations. Reassured about the judicial framework of our expedition and its policing, we leave for Oxford.  Operation 'Bow-Window 2' can begin.

The team make contact again with members of the family who need to know of this new venture. First of all, the specialist is able to approach each of them individually, with the aim of getting him or her to see things as they really are. As a result, they begin to rediscover little by little their familiar points of reference and reality itself, becoming fully aware of Tilly's swindling, his lies, and the false memories induced and distilled by him. During a second stage, the mission allows, at last, a family meeting between Philippe, Brigitte and me.

Charles-Henri, who had not understood the reasons for my departure, accepts these reunions without hesitation. Eager to see me again, he regains his former self. Amaury is very disturbed emotionally by these revelations, but he, too, is very eager to be reunited with us all. Diane has regained most of her perceptiveness, but still wonders about various things.

Having obtained their agreement, the criminologist joins us in the early evening at the pub, where she finds us waiting for her and for her help in facilitating these various family reunions. Brigitte and I are very anxious at the prospect of seeing Ghislaine again, but are supported throughout by our friends and by the whole team.

When Philippe, Brigitte, M. Picotin and I arrive, the atmosphere becomes very charged: it is nine months since I last saw Diane and Amaury. My daughter is still very reserved. She needs to understand. And besides, there is the complaint she has lodged against me, under duress, it is true, but which still stands.

It is an intense and complicated occasion, with

moments of general hubbub and chat, and then of silence, while groups form and reform. There are tears, and laughter too. And, over and above all of this, an impression of floating, of drifting: where is the reality? Who are we? What has happened to us? To say that we have awoken from a long and atrocious nightmare is too reductive, banal indeed. In these cramped surroundings, constrained and lonely, I recall, in sudden flashes of memory, life in the big house in Caudéran, which I always thought so secure, Martel and our easy and happy summers there, Pyla, which the children adored... I don't miss the material ease and plenty we enjoyed then, but I will always mourn those nine years of existence so cruelly taken from us. Charles-Henri, very moved, takes me in his arms, and the children gather round me.

In finding her oldest son again, Mamie also understands the full significance of the occasion. An immense weight seems to have been lifted from her shoulders. And she is to spend her first undisturbed night of sleep in years.

That evening, in Oxford, we rediscover our life as a family: a father, a mother, and their children, all of them broken, exhausted, burdened with questions they will not be able to answer for a long time if ever, but reunited.

The moment has come for the family photograph, one that will bear witness to our joy at being reunited, and to our gratitude for the sensitivity and tact with which the professionals have extracted my nearest and dearest from this impasse.

*The reunion of the de Védrines in Oxford.*
*Left to right: Charles-Henri, Christine, Philippe, Diane, Guillemette*
*(seated), Amaury (behind), Maître Daniel Picotin, Ghislaine,*
*François, Brigitte. (Guillaume was not present)*

After a very long and emotional evening we part company, so as to get some rest.

We meet again the next morning to take up again the conversations begun the previous evening. Mamie, Charles-Henri and the children ask Monsieur Picotin to promise he will take on their defence, and deliver their testimony as witnesses to the magistrate of the court in Bordeaux. Marie-Hélène and Dominique rejoin us and get a hero's welcome from Ghislaine in spite of their years of demonisation.

Later that evening I am anxious to leave this house, so that I can enjoy to the full the company of my own family. We decide to go out to dinner, the children, their father and I, with Marie-Hélène and Dominique. Seeing my family assembled, Ghislaine is suddenly aware of her own isolation. She wants to come with us, trying some emotional blackmail. Diane at once offers to stay at home with her. We refuse: Diane is having dinner with us. In the end Philippe and Brigitte agree to spend the evening with her, along with Mamie, François, his girl friend, and Guillemette.

We discover a little Italian restaurant, and settle down in front of a table of pizzas and pasta. I feast on the sight of my three children. Amaury can still hardly believe what he is discovering about Tilly. It is a gross betrayal of friendship, a wicked deception, a fraud. He had placed, unreservedly, his trust in Thierry Tilly. He says, his head in his hands, over and over again: 'It's simply incredible. I can't believe it!' Diane cannot contain her anger. Perhaps she blames herself; she certainly blames us, the whole world, as well as the conman himself, and everyone who could have helped us, and did not. Guillaume is happy to be with his family again, but cannot quite forget the family pressure he has been under these past few years. Charles-Henri says least. I think it is he who will suffer most, and longest, for having yielded to Tilly's influence and led his family into this trap. Worse than the guilt he feels, an insurmountable sorrow, a sense of being broken forever, is gradually taking him over. I feel it in him. But I reject with every fibre of my being the idea that my husband can be destroyed. I am convinced that, however slowly, time heals and repairs. Later on, we will talk, and little by little...

Left on his own with Ghislaine, Philippe is happy: he has discovered his mother again, who, for her part, lets nothing impair her joy at seeing him once again at her side. We part, that evening, exhausted, and postponing until the next day all the decisions that must be made.

Next morning, we organize a meeting of the whole family, so as to decide what to do next. Diane and Amaury both want to resign from their current employment. From now on what they earn will be theirs to dispose of, and life will be a little easier for them. Ghislaine hopes to stay on in England with her mother, so that they may be there for the birth of the baby Guillemette is expecting with the nice young Italian she married in 2009. She would very much like it if Charles-Henri could stay on with her. But there is no question of our being separated again, and in any case Charles-Henri must lodge a complaint as soon as possible. We return to France together. Later, on our return to Bordeaux, the whole family will lodge their legal complaints.

On arriving in Bordeaux, we move into a large apartment lent us by Marie-Hélène and Dominique, where we can receive our children when they return. I go back to work. Charles-Henri continues, little by little, to understand the full extent of the catastrophe that has overtaken us, without being able to put it behind him entirely. Immediately on regaining her freedom, Diane withdrew the charge she had made against me. I told her I did not in the least resent what she had done, nor hold it against her. On the contrary, I feel still closer to her. I understand the force of the pressure she was under from having lived through it myself. I understand, we all understand, that this manipulation had as its first objective to set us against one another and so destroy us.

Our relationship, as mother and daughter, grows stronger every day.

At Christmas, we all return to Oxford to spend the holidays with Mamie. I cannot help remembering our last Christmas in Monflanquin, in 2002. We were – on the face of it at least – a numerous and close-knit family. Our disagreements seemed to me at the time serious enough, but it never occurred to me that they could not be resolved, with a little more mutual good will. I now know that Tilly exploited all our differences in order to set us at loggerheads with one another, and to profit from this. I am no longer now as I was then. Ghislaine, by contrast, is the same as ever. What she thinks and what she says are exactly as they always were, to the extent that, during one mealtime, I explode in anger: 'That's quite enough, Ghislaine. You've been ruining my life for years. I won't put up with it any longer!'

'I quite understand your reaction, of course' she replied, 'the *in camera* proceedings of January 2008' (the 'transmission' episode) 'were difficult for you… But they didn't bother me!'

'Of course they didn't, but as for me, they very nearly killed me!'

And, miraculously, she is silenced. She has understood that the balance of power she has relied on ever since my entry into the family no longer exists.

Similarly, when I discover that all the houses rented out since 2006, even her own, were leased in the name of my children, I explode.   I insist that she take on her own responsibilities.  Her reply is totally evasive.  But I don't let her get away with it.

But other matters are much more important than disagreements of this kind.   My husband and I are very anxious to re-engage our children in discussion of various serious matters.   Talking to Diane, I discover that the brainwashing she underwent was as insidious as it was ruinous.  It began during her first stay in London: she was persuaded that she was more spoiled and more favoured than her cousin Guillemette.   At the same time an attempt was made to destroy the very good relationship she enjoyed with her own family: because she was a girl, she was told, her parents loved her less than if she had been a boy, while her brothers would have preferred another sister, different from her.   And she asserts all of this quite openly, as if it were a statement of fact.   How does one respond to such a thing?   It's tempting to deny it, to shrug one's shoulders:  since how on earth could we love her less than anyone else, our only daughter? But a simple denial is not enough: these false memories, these deeply implanted and false convictions, must somehow be dispelled. Talking will not dislodge them.   Above all, Diane needs her family's love and reassurance.  We have all been wounded.  Our brains have been stuffed with lies: lies that are instilled in us like a poison.   It will take months for us to recover, and be repaired.

Moreover, Diane is exhausted: she works all day and looks after her grandmother at night. For reasons that are not at all clear, Ghislaine is opposed to the idea of Mamie returning to France. But Mamie needs looking after: she is by now completely blind, and becoming weaker every day. At the beginning of 2010, we arrange for her to come home. It is not easy to move a person of her age, whose health is the more fragile in that she has not seen a doctor for the past ten years. We end up by going to collect her by car, Diane, Charles-Henri and I, with a professional driver who specializes in such matters. All of which is very expensive, leaving us short of money. Hospitalized in the Polyclinique Bordeaux Nord-Aquitaine, where Charles-Henri has worked for a long time, her health improves rapidly, and she is finally operated on for her cataract. Along with her sight, she soon recovers her serenity. Philippe takes her with him to Talade where she feels much better. We go there every weekend and during my holidays in order to relieve Philippe. During this time, we see little of Ghislaine who is pulling herself together again and re-establishing contact with Jean. In November 2010, at the age of 98 years, Mamie dies in her sleep. She is happy to have seen again her grandchildren, her great-grandchildren, her son-in-law Bertrand – the widower of her daughter Anne – and various friends she had shunned for years. Ghislaine, too, was able to take her leave of her, as a result of a telephone call from Charles-Henri.

Her funeral at Monflanquin also provided an opportunity for her closest family, deprived of her presence for ten years, to gather once again around her, an occasion described in a poem written by a great-granddaughter.

In June, Amaury returns from England, followed in September by Diane. It has taken us a year to come back to life. During these long intervening months, we have endured an extraordinary sense of weariness. A perfectly normal phenomenon, so it seems. We were, in fact, convalescent, and made uncertain progress: good one day, not so good the next. Guillaume, finding again his role as the older brother, has been very helpful to Amaury, who, won a scholarship and resumed his studies. He has since rented a studio flat, and has succeeded in taking control again of his life. Diane has embarked upon a course in chemistry.

For Charles-Henri and me, the whole process was harder. In the first place, we were older and therefore more vulnerable. Charles-Henri had never quite understood that he was completely ruined. He realized the full extent of the disaster only when he returned to Bordeaux. This plunged him into great disarray. As did a question that haunts him still: how could he ever have believed the lies of his own sister and of Tilly? I try to explain this to him, using the formula adopted by Professor Zagury, which I have often repeated to myself, to the effect that 'our intelligence was made to lie fallow'. But this is not enough for him. He is deeply wounded, and very unhappy.

Thanks to a friend, I, for my part, worked with an organization that reintegrates problem children in society. I adored what I did there.

Fortunately, the brainwashing we suffered has not destroyed everything, but simply tested our resilience. We have never stopped loving and respecting one another...

And, last of all, we are fortunate indeed in the help and the hospitality – the weekends, lunches, reunions, excursions, holidays – lavished on us by family and friends alike.

Such support has been beyond price.

# 17

The trial took place three years after my return to France. I was confronted with a difficult choice: should it be before the assize court or a magistrate's court? One of the allegations I had made – 'illegal confinement with acts of cruelty'– required the assize court, the rest could be judged in a magistrate's court. In the assize court, the proceedings would be long, the penalties imposed very serious, amounting to tens of years in prison, and the sentence would depend on the decision of a jury. Such a procedure would, moreover, have required us to re-live, in detail, and in front of the jury, these nine years of martyrdom. I was absolutely determined to spare my children this painful experience. In the magistrate's court, the grounds for a court of assizes would be reassessed, and it would be up to the magistrates to judge and to deliver the verdict. The penalties would be less severe, not exceeding ten years of imprisonment.

It was vital that we look things squarely in the face: in any version likely to appear in the press, or even to emerge from the evidence offered by witnesses, our story was on the face of it difficult to credit or even understand: an aristocratic family, very well off in the eyes of today's average citizen, lets itself be duped by an insignificant and unattractive person, swallows whole all the nonsense he utters, and ends up being totally subjugated by him.   Our helpless naiveté might even provoke a smile.   As for us, even we, when we looked back over the whole affair, were incredulous.   And yet, it had happened; and we were ordinary people, with an excellent level of education.   Impossible: things like that only happen to other people.   Even the evidence offered by the professionals, however convincing it was, might not succeed in explaining what had happened, nor influencing a jury in our favour.   But at the very least, we wanted men like Thierry Tilly and Jacques Gonzalez to be prevented from doing any further harm.   After thinking it all over carefully, and after listening to our lawyers and discussing the whole affair with the family, I opted for the magistrate's court.

On September 24th 2012 the first hearing begins. The courtroom turns out to be too small to accommodate the public:  there has been a great deal of interest in the media, and we are well known in Bordeaux.   Right from the start I notice, among the close friends who have come to support us, relatives I have not seen for a long time. We ourselves are numerous, tightly packed along the bench reserved for litigants.   The president of the court, an experienced magistrate, has to assert her authority – not that she lacks it – from the very first day.

Throughout all the years I have known him Thierry
Tilly has displayed the talents of a quick-change artist.
I have seen him as a young teacher in ill-matching sports
kit, as a self-confident businessman in a three-piece suit,
as a kind and gentle father in navy-blue pullover and
white shirt, and as a torturer you might almost take for
a Nazi. I wonder what face he will put on here. Will
it be his own, the true one? He appears in the dock in
black trousers, a black Lacoste T-shirt, his tow-coloured
hair combed to one side, his eyes indistinct behind his
small glasses. You might take him for some sort of low-
grade clerk. He listens to the charge against him, then
the president begins her cross-examination.

We did not know everything about Tilly, far from
it, but now we discover his true origins. Every aspect
of his life is embellished with some commentary, some
anecdote of his own devising. Even the factual account
of it which the experts give is transformed into an airport
thriller once it is his turn to speak. He was born in Bois-
Colombes on March 29th 1964. His mother 'had been
liberated by General de Gaulle'. He was brought up by
his two grandmothers, one of whom 'held a salon, where
she received Mitterand and Georges Marchais'. Next, he
claims that his mother was so young that she could not
help him with his school homework: barely more than
a child, she was nevertheless a woman who 'inspired
trust', she was 'the wife of only one man, although my
father himself was fickle. My mother, if she had not
had me, would have been a champion ice-skater, my
father was a naval frogman, who afterwards worked in

the special services of the Ministry of Defence, Category A Secret-Defence, like his two brothers.   It would be improper for me to say anything more about this'. Tilly had been beaten, at the age of two, by his father, which had provoked nervous convulsions and left him with a squint, which had been operated upon.   Now he wears glasses, which 'prevents him from playing tennis, and he doesn't risk driving'.

But he claims, too, that he likes 'first-class tennis, as well as skiing, which he has enjoyed since the age of two years' and that he 'parachuted from a military plane when he was twelve years old'.   He concedes that he was never at the military academy of Saint-Cyr-l'École, but he was in primary school at Saint-Cyr, and spent two years in a military training school.   He failed the competition to enter the Navy.   The account he offers of his schooling, from which an obsession with education emerges, is completely confused: he has followed various different courses, studied a little law, then was enrolled in a 'centre for higher diplomatic studies with a special dispensation, permitting him to enter it under age, in a school reserved for diplomats and soldiers engaged in intelligence, which has allowed [him] to have a notebook of addresses'. He has also 'undertaken post-graduate study' gaining 'a doctorate in marketing so as to become a specialist in measures to control counterfeiting'.   He has 'attended his final oral examination in Geneva for the Cartier Foundation'. He also has 'an MA in property management and administration from the school of building and public works... a DEA in international economy and in intelligence concerning codes of investment in relation to corruption…'. There is, however, no record anywhere of any of these qualifications. This is because he was at the time either 'too young' or 'too good' to have received them into his own hands. One of them was supposed to have been awarded by Bernard Kouchner, another by Alain Minc.

He adds an infinitely long list of other qualifications he has acquired, with very vague titles. He confronts the questions the president of the court puts to him with remarkable sang-froid, trying to submerge her in a torrent of information, of dates, and of places – and sometimes succeeding – all punctuated by claims that 'I can prove it'. He displays, indeed, a stupefying memory for places and dates, mingling historical references with his own story, to the point where the president asks him to be silent and even his own lawyer ends by interjecting: 'Do be quiet, can't you see that you are irritating the president?' But none of this discomfits Tilly, who describes in minute detail the humanitarian activities of the Blue Light Foundation, whose headquarters have been established in Canada. He makes constant reference to 'Monsieur Gonzalez', thus implying that this man is the principal coordinator of his activities, and of the whole affair that concerns the Védrines. Gonzalez had apparently put him in charge of Blue Light, and in particular of the task of getting this foundation recognized by the United Nations.

The courtroom listens to this great tide of words, sceptically, then openly mockingly, and sometimes laughter breaks out. This laughter worries me. Watching him going on and on endlessly and with his usual arrogance I sometimes glimpse again the Tilly I first knew. Sometimes, too, I tell myself that he is acting a part. But it isn't as simple as that. Hearing him under interrogation in a court of law, it strikes me that, while he may sometimes stumble, his delivery is rapid, his ideas well-constructed, he digresses, splits hairs, evades the point at issue, but only to return to it later, obliquely. He hints at great affairs of state, persecution, secrets and their disclosure, but always within the context that 'I cannot say more, my mission would be compromised'. At times I am really uneasy: he offers no proof of what he is hinting at – no more than he has ever done – but, unless his interlocutor is determined to confound him – may finish by sowing doubts. By the end of the day, the president looks exhausted.

Next day, we witness a confrontation between Thierry and his father, Alain Tilly. The latter's testimony completely contradicts that of his son. No, he has never been a naval frogman, nor a member of the secret service, he was a driver for the Ministry of Defence, and is now retired. As for his wife, now deceased, he has no memory of ever having seen her compete in figure skating. She was a nurse, nothing more. He does not deny that his son is intelligent and endowed with a remarkable memory, but adds that he is difficult. He has no recollection of him ever having acquired any diplomas, but only of him having failed entry into the naval college in Brest. He liked history, yes, that's true. But Tilly *père* becomes angry when he learns of the accusations of violence levelled against him: 'It's all deception and distortion', he bellows from the witness box. 'He had convulsions when he was two and a half and was treated for this, he had problems with his sight and was operated on... that's all'. And he concludes his testimony with the bitter remark that 'If I had been harder on him, things wouldn't have come to this!'

Philippe's children, Lucille and Étienne, are the next into the witness box. Étienne relates how, in the summer of 2001, when he went to see his father in Talade, he found him changed. He seemed very anxious, talked of enemies, and threats of psychiatric internment. He barricaded the house, and refused to give his son the number of his new mobile phone. At the same time, Brigitte had confided to Étienne's wife that they were all in danger. This provoked such anxiety in the children, Étienne and Lucille, that, with Caroline, Brigitte's daughter, they had arranged to meet in order to discuss it. At the time, the two girls had heard some talk of Thierry Tilly, who seemed to count for a great deal in the family and who had promised their father returns of 10% on various investments. All of which elicited from Étienne one word, and one name, only: Madoff! They looked up Tilly's entry on the Internet: he is, it appears, the manager of ten companies, all of them in compulsory liquidation. Étienne immediately informed his father of this, who replied, crisply: 'Tilly is a remarkable man, you don't know what you're talking about!' He then telephoned Charles-Henri, who is not only his uncle but also his godfather, but who responded to his anxiety by retorting: 'Tilly is helping us and we trust him.

Don't meddle in things that don't concern you; just go away and leave us in peace'. Étienne made one last attempt and went to Martel. Ghislaine and his cousins barred his way and prevented all his attempts to see his grandmother whom he adores. He ended by obtaining an interview of five minutes with her, during which Mamie sent him packing: 'Stop pestering us. Why don't you just clear off, you little monster!' Étienne tells us how he got into his car, started the engine then stopped for quarter of an hour, too upset to drive away. He did not see his father again for eight years. Philippe, meanwhile, the first to have escaped the family imprisonment in Oxford, was nevertheless still under the influence of Tilly, and in a state of intense terror and psychological confusion, he was persuaded that to have stood up to this man amounted to a veritable suicide. Which explains why he lodged his complaint only after I had done so. Lucille, equally terrified by the atmosphere in Talade in the early 2000s, did not at all understand what was happening. Her father spoke of a plot that was being mounted against the Védrines and said that Tilly was helping them to decipher various pieces of evidence of this that were to be found about the place. According to Philippe, Tilly even had a list of the people involved. Lucille did not know how to deal with this paranoia. According to her, Tilly had become 'the master-mind of the family'.

As for Brigitte's daughter, she too remembers seeing her mother abandon everything in order to go and shut herself away in Lot-et-Garonne. She said she was in danger; she seemed persuaded, in particular, that 'one of her family was trying to have her interned in order to seize her property'. The young woman adds that her mother had made her promise not to mention this to anyone. She had agreed to this at the time, but bitterly regrets it now. Afterwards, it was too late. But the hardest thing of all for her was the thought that during that time her mother had refused categorically to see her or speak to her. In short, she lost her mother for eight years.

These moving statements remind me once again of the gravity of the collateral damage inflicted on the members of the family who remained outside Tilly's influence. Relatives on whom we had turned our backs and who had done everything they could to try and rescue us…

On September 27th, Maître Vincent David enters the witness box. This 68 year-old lawyer, who first introduced Tilly to Ghislaine, expresses nothing but regrets. He met Tilly during the 1980s, and they remained quite close throughout the following fifteen years. He, too, has been the victim of various manoeuvrings on the part of the accused: 'At first I found him congenial. He asked me to sort out various accounts, which, it turned out, could only be done through their liquidation. Without this, the company concerned would have had to close. I discovered quite late on that he won people's trust, got them to sign contracts, and then took matters no further. He wanted to dispose of a considerable number of companies whose articles of association remained vague'. For some time Maître David provided his advice to Tilly free of charge because he imagined him to be a young man trying to take his first steps in the world of business.  He did not know where Tilly derived his income from, nor what exactly his work was.  He nevertheless found him plausible, to the point of investing in a scheme he had embarked on to build several apartments in Albiez in the Alps.  Tilly had promised him a return on this investment that would handsomely reimburse the fee he was owed.  He had also arranged a meeting between Tilly and the heir to a *maison de champagne*.  Tilly defrauded the heir, who, however, had never lodged a complaint.  It was probably at this time, not having yet realized how dangerous he was, that Maître David, who had children at the school, took Tilly to the Femme Sec and introduced him to Ghislaine.

He never recovered the money he had invested in the Alps.  Worse still, he had stood security for the rent of an apartment for Tilly, who had never paid the rent, but simply disappeared, obliging Maître David to settle eighteen months of unpaid debt.  So this lawyer appearing here as a witness is also a victim: 'He was living in my house.  Fortunately, my wife threw him out. He went to Nice to draw up an inventory of property belonging to her family.  She realized before I did that his objective was to get his claws into rich people and to live off their capital.  He is brilliant, there's no question about that, but he employs his intellectual faculties in a scandalous manner.  He manages to manoeuvre people into a position of veritable intellectual subjection...'

Tilly will have none of this, but, raising his eyes to heaven when he hears the damning evidence of the various witnesses, protests, and describes once again his various important missions. Only when the presiding judge resorts to a sharp 'Do be quiet!' does he fall silent.

Unfortunately, neither Maître David nor his wife thought to warn us of Tilly's criminal activities, which they themselves had endured. During the trial, some of the lawyers implied that Maître David could have done a lot more to come to our aid...

During the next two days, Charles-Henri, Diane, Amaury, Guillaume, and I are required, as witnesses, to speak at length of what happened during all those years. For me, having to listen to the suffering, the fear, and the anguish my children went through is a sort of trial too. I cannot rid myself of a crushing sense of guilt, even though the accused not only denies all responsibility, but allows himself the liberty of himself passing scornful judgment on the children. He continues with his lies. According to him, it was the Védrines who first sought him out, hoping he would help them with some tax evasion!

The second week of the trial opens with the testimony of Tilly's co-defendant: Jacques Gonzalez, who, until this moment, has been the subject of grave accusations on the part of Tilly. He is the instigator, the *deus ex machina,* of the whole affair. Thierry speaks of him as 'his boss' or as 'the president'. None of us has ever seen him before. Except for Ghislaine. She had dinner with him in London when Tilly moved there. In his presence, however, Thierry Tilly, usually so voluble, is silent, even adopting the demeanour of a small boy. At the time in question, he says, Gonzalez, who was domineering and using him for his own purposes, poured forth slanderous remarks about the Védrines family, insinuating, for example, that Anne, the older of the two sisters, who had died of a brain tumour in 1997, had been murdered.

Before the trial opened, an American journalist had managed get in touch with Jacques Gonzalez.  In a long article, he describes him as an elegant little man with grey hair who speaks fluent English.  Gonzalez did not, however, allow him inside his house but on the doorstep had calmly denied knowing Thierry Tilly. Nor did the names 'Blue Light…. Védrines….. Oxford' mean anything at all to him.  The very fact, however, that Gonzalez showed no curiosity, that he neither asked him the reason for these questions nor precisely who he was, surprised the journalist, who came away with the impression that he had approached the wrong person. After all, Jacques Gonzalez is a common enough name in France.

But he is, most certainly, the person in question.  We watch as an invalid appears, seated in a wheelchair, both his feet amputated, and with a weak and monotonous voice.  An ageing and sick man, who in no way appears to correspond to this terrifying 'boss', on first-name terms with the high and mighty of this world, and who exercises power and influence in every domain.  And yet, if you look at him closely, his profile – that of a bird of prey – and his pinched lips belie the apparent frailty of this reticent man, cold and distant at first sight, but who expresses himself coarsely enough.

Gonzalez discloses that he was a car salesman until 1990.  After which no one, the tax authorities in

particular, knows anything about him.   He reappears
several years later, transformed into the founder and
president of a foundation with a humanitarian agenda,
the Blue Light Foundation, based in Canada.   Tilly had
already told us a great deal about this organization,
claiming that he was, on its behalf, 'responsible for
relations with the United Nations'.   Gonzalez concedes
that the grandiose projects envisaged by his foundation
have never been realized: these include a hospital in
China, bulk purchases of alfalfa intended to alleviate
famine, opencast coalmining… 'Time has not been on our
side', he says, regretfully, in the witness box.   He claims,
too, that, being in possession of several hundred bonds
belonging to shareholders of the American railways in
the nineteenth century, he was proposing to use them
as guarantees to finance his foundation through bank
borrowings.   In spite of the fantastic contacts he claims
to have, he was badly informed, and the only person still
to believe that these bonds had the least value.   It was
at that moment, he says, that he met Tilly, who made a
good impression on him: 'He knew a lot about judicial
matters, about banking, and information technology.   He
said he could help me.   He spoke of the Védrines family
as potential patrons'.   At which point he slips into the
role of the victim, offended that anyone could imagine he
had despoiled an entire family: 'I believed the Védrines
to be generous', he protests, 'in the manner, that is, of
various other old French families.   I was mistaken.   If I
had known what Thierry was doing, I would never have
gone along with it.   A foundation cannot be launched on

so uncertain a basis!' His own, indeed, never got off the ground. After they had arrested him, the police carried out a search of his home in Paris. They seized Rolexes, three Patek Philippe watches, a collection of haute couture dresses, lithographs, a BMW 645, a cellar of vintage wines, 34,000 euros in cash, and, in a suitcase, a further 86,000 euros… With the money we had sent in padded envelopes via our children, our nephews, and Natacha, none of whom ever saw any of it, he had lived for almost ten years in great style. The total amount pocketed by Thierry Tilly was close to five and a half million euros.

And then, fairly and squarely, Gonzales goes for Tilly, who is trying to catch his eye and to whom he pays not the least attention. His relationship with him was entirely humanitarian in its intention. He sums up his relationship with Tilly in a single sentence: 'When I trust someone, I trust him!' implying, in this way, that he knew nothing of what was going on. Tilly, in the dock, assents with a vigorous nodding of his head. But Gonzalez is reminded in court of something he himself said in the course of a telephone conversation during the period of my imprisonment: 'I've had it up to here with these people. They must cough up the cash – if not, things will turn nasty! Execution…' Gonzalez protests that this is no way proves his complicity: Tilly had promised him money provided by the Védrines for his foundation! He will concede only that 'when he gets worked up, he can be a bit brusque'. Since all of the money he received had been sent by Tilly, he is not responsible for the manner in which it was acquired, and concludes: 'He can think

what he likes, I know what I did, and what I did not do!'
But the president of the court reminds him of a telephone
conversation he had with his girl-friend at the time his calls
were being monitored, in which, referring to Tilly he said:
"Either he's ill, or he is totally mad'. Gonzalez concurs.

Tilly gets to his feet again, and an expression of
panic passes across his face. Gonzalez's next remark
drives the point still further home: 'He didn't just ruin
the deal,' Gonzalez asserts, 'but the whole thing'. Tilly
gets up again and, his voice becoming ever more shrill,
tries to intervene: Gonzalez has betrayed him. It is he,
Gonzalez himself, who is the chief coordinator of the
masonic plot that has pursued him since 1999. And he
has just understood this. The president orders him to
be silent, and he obeys, choking with anger. Gonzalez
returns to his wheelchair. He has convinced no one of
his good faith.

Next it is the turn of the experts. Judge Lorentz
had consigned us to the care of Professor Daniel Zagury,
a highly-respected psychiatrist, an expert in court
proceedings, and well known to the magistrates. Tilly,
for his part, has been examined by two psychologists
and two psychiatrists. The concluding remarks of the
latter two – Drs Serge Bornstein and Roland Coutanceau
– describe a personality capable of doing precisely what
he inflicted on us.

They speak of 'the consummate skill of this person,
who specializes in fraud – a particular form of theft which
consists in obtaining from other people the transfer of
property by exploiting their credulity by various means.

This supposes on the part of the perpetrator a degree of intelligence and of competence, but allied to a distortion of moral sense ('bad faith') and a certain perversity ('intention of creating moral damage').

'In Tilly's case,' the psychiatrists say, 'there emerges, too, a distortion of this type arising from vanity and from a fondness for money, and above all from mythomaniacal tendencies complicated by a criminal intention, involving the fabrication of a story and the realization of a chimerical scheme designed to subjugate or tempt. In these cases, the person's imagination allows itself free rein by manipulating a hermetically isolated and vulnerable family group. One often sees, in the perpetrator of such a crime, as well as a specialization in a particular type of fraud, a tendency to repeat it, since a second such offence very commonly occurs.

Is he deceiving himself? This is unlikely, but he must have revelled in his success for a while, satisfying his vanity and taking pleasure in being able to deceive other people. The mythomaniacal hoaxer, when he finds willing ears, can even become the centre of a collective suggestion of great influence. He has thus been able to satisfy his greed for gain, and even after his fall he tries – against all likelihood of success – to cling to the remnants of this personality, all-powerful for a day.

Once the curtain has fallen, he is in reality a well-orientated, well-informed person, in tune with his surroundings, free from delirium-inducing, interpretative or hallucinatory material, without depressive or extrinsic antecedents, and so able to take responsibility for his actions'.

Professor Daniel Zagury gave evidence by video link. He began with a reflection that was full of good sense. One which has doubtless occurred to the majority of people who have heard about this affair: 'I said to myself: "Ten years! This must be a somewhat inadequate family, they must be very odd people!" But not at all! They're perfectly normal'. And he went on to explain, in simple terms, the mechanism that had allowed a single individual to gain power over a family, 'with failings, like everyone else, but who are normal people, with a great diversity of profiles'. He observed, first of all, that he had rarely, if ever, encountered so great a talent for manipulation. Then he repeated what he wrote in his report of the psychiatric examination I underwent with him, included as an appendix (p. 309), defining what he called 'abusive transference' as a perversion of the kind of transference that takes place in psychoanalysis and some other one-on-one relationships, where the desires and feelings felt for a parent in childhood are revived and directed towards a different object.

Professor Zagury then went on to say:

'A certain number of techniques used in brainwashing are also employed in abusive transference.

- The made-to-measure rather than the ready-to-wear. It is striking to observe the degree to which all of the victims are pursued through their weaknesses, their vulnerability, their singularities. This demands a knowledge of the history of the family, of the latent conflicts within it, of the disagreements, jealousies, rivalries, as well as of the family values that characterize it, and of the place within it that each member occupies.

- The institution of a functional paranoia is an essential part of the technique of manipulation. The word 'functional' is used here to indicate that it is not at all the case that the personality of the victim must necessarily be composed of the typical characteristics of a paranoiac personality (psychorigidity, mistrust, poor judgment, projectivity, hypertrophy of the self, which is to say, self-aggrandizement). Everyone becomes to some degree paranoid during an episode of this sort. Nothing is a matter of chance any more. This is what Tilly, moreover, used to repeat as a leitmotif. This loss of the category of the fortuitous is the very essence of paranoia. The manipulator uses it to reinforce his omniscience: "I always told you it would be so". Events then reinforce his credibility and his image of omnipotence, a process that is further assisted by a degree of self-reinforcement. In conjunction with the tutelary powers and the forces of destiny, he knows about events before anyone else does. It was in this way that he was able to persuade the family that he had foreknowledge of the events of 11th September 2001.

- Group paranoia.  This involves instilling into everyone the idea that it is vital that they stand together against the external world, adopting a kind of siege mentality. The notion that they are threatened by some sort of plot or conspiracy against them also allows each person to be assigned to a particular role that he must not abandon if he is not to put himself into danger. Besides which, to break rank is to demonstrate that one is a traitor.

- On the other hand, this group paranoia is also designed to combat the enemy within. The identity of this latter changes according to various needs and unknown factors. It is in this way that, at certain moments, Thierry Tilly has allowed himself to use some truly Stalinist techniques against one or other of the group.

- Having the answer to everything. All the protagonists describe this well: Thierry Tilly is a man who was never at a loss, never taken unawares. He had the answer to everything. All the others, then, could only reproach themselves for having doubted this, and become reinforced in their conviction that Thierry Tilly was always right.

- Suppression of every direct contact: a system whereby a member of the family can no longer communicate directly with any other, even if their relationship is close. Each of them communicates with the others only through the intermediary of Tilly. Even if he is not present in person as the interlocutor, what he thinks or could have thought if he had been there is implicitly or explicitly present in the relationship.

- The world according to Thierry Tilly. Everyone having lost his or her critical judgment and autonomy of thought, it is through the beliefs held by Thierry Tilly that the world is henceforward viewed.

- Reinforcing or severing relations between members of the group. From his commanding position Thierry Tilly issues his orders: this or that person is to move, go to such and such a place, shut him- or herself away, work, do two jobs at once, divorce, lose his or her temper, go away or come back. The purpose of all this is simply to destroy long-established relationships in order the better to subjugate.

- Destroying each person's sense of self-worth. "Your wife is unfaithful…" "Your husband is cuckolding you…" "Your son is not your son…" "Your mother abused you…" Everything becomes possible. When one has lost one's independence of thought, one's own free will, when one has a poor opinion of oneself and of one's ability to judge the world, everything, when it is the all-powerful person who articulates it, is credible.

- The astrologer's technique. The procedure is well known. Everyone will interpret what they hear or read in the light of their own preoccupations, their own hopes, illusions, or resentments… and since emotional considerations will always override those of the intelligence and reason, the event will serve to reinforce the conviction that Thierry Tilly, decidedly, was right yet again.

- The technique of waxing hot then cold. All the protagonists describe periods of disgrace and then of rehabilitation, of destructivity and then of restoration. Like their mothers who, when they were very young, alternated between gratifying and thwarting them, Thierry Tilly was adept at displaying magnanimity, and at granting favours, after a period of punitive severity. This was a yet another way of ensuring and encouraging subservience, since, if he were to exhibit unremitting hostility, this would end by provoking an irreparable rift.

- The continual use of the group. Whether Thierry Tilly controls this himself, or whether everyone turns spontaneously towards the group to seek its approval, the group is there as a substitute for the individual, to validate some piece of information, to threaten expulsion, or to reinforce obedience of an order.

These various forms of manipulation support one another, reinforce one another, facilitate one another... all of them serve the abuse of transference'.

In court, everyone can now understand and reconcile every episode of our story with the techniques described. All that remains for the lawyers to do is to present their closing arguments. The sentence was passed some weeks later: Thierry Tilly was sentenced to eight years in prison. The public prosecutor had called for ten, which is the maximum allowed under the law. Jacques Gonzalez was sentenced to a fixed term of four years.

At the end of the last session, Tilly stood up and said: 'You have passed sentence on the French citizen but not on the English citizen! This is not, believe me, the end of the matter'. And they both lodged an appeal, although Gonzalez withdrew his.

**Part Five:** Aftermath

# Guillaume

In October 2009, Maman comes to find me. She tells me that Tilly has claimed to the judge that he has done nothing, that it is I who am in fact behind the whole thing. I immediately grasp the situation and within seconds I have dismantled his whole Machiavellian scheme. This time, it's final, or rather, it is just beginning. He has stolen nearly ten years of my life. I very nearly died. But here I am, more alive than ever. And so relieved. For I am no longer alone. Justice is on my side. I lodge a complaint and at once begin to prepare for action.

Tilly has over-reached himself. This sinister manipulator reserved, just for me, a particularly brutal treatment. The judge said that Tilly treated me like 'a flunkey, subject to endless and merciless exploitation'. And his perverted manipulation of me has had effects that go far beyond the family, provoking reactions, judgments and rumours that have caused me to suffer dreadfully.     And which even today affect me still.     I have suffered a great deal from what the press felt able – mistakenly – to say about me at the beginning.     I was almost immediately dragged down by the family connection, for the context lent itself to this.     Then I got involved psychologically and emotionally, thinking that this would help my family, without realizing that my involvement was giving the impression that I was playing a role that  had never been mine.     In a family where respect for one's elders is paramount, I have only done what was asked of me: worked.

Fortunately, the judge grasped the situation very quickly, and we were able to have a number of excellent exchanges.  As my story unfolded, I noticed that the judge was becoming increasingly appalled by what he heard.  I was very pleased to see that he understood everything. Remembering the smallest detail, placing everything in context, using concrete examples to illustrate what I was saying, all of this constituted a very difficult exercise.  For something very important was at stake:  to describe facts accurately and in such a way that they could subsequently be expressed in legal language.  To be effective the case for the prosecution had to be augmented, because the subject of brainwashing is not well understood.  My aim was very straightforward:  to help to clarify every part of the case papers, however obscure.  At the request of the police and the judge, I took the time to go over Tilly's papers, which I discovered at that time, with a fine-tooth comb.  This allowed me to achieve an accurate assessment of the damage he had done. These hundreds of hours of work, these sleepless nights exhausted me. I had the impression that I was once again taking on a completely unreasonable family burden. And it was here that my various legal skills were of immense value to me. I often say that studying law has saved my life. It was in this way that I discovered that Tilly had repatriated our money through companies registered in England, Luxembourg, and Belize. What madness. I learnt too that the solicitor who had acted for us over the sale of Roquefère and Monflanquin had made out a cheque in the name of a company in Luxembourg that had as yet no legal existence.

When the authorities came to interview this man, he invoked professional secrecy, taking no account whatsoever of the interests of his defrauded clients. I was stunned. As for the lawyer who had arranged the 'sale' of Martel, he was investigated during the course of the inquiry. He was summoned by the authorities in Toulouse to face charges I laid against him, but he never came and was never pursued. I was astonished.

I was, however, soon completely reassured, for the case was going well. We had had the good fortune to find exceptional investigating officers, as well as expert and very meticulous lawyers. Simultaneously, I was having to regularize my affairs in England, following Tilly's disastrous lawsuit against me. Four years after action in the English courts, the situation is completely resolved, but immersing myself once again in the papers, devoting so much time and energy to them when I was looking for

work again has been extremely trying. The trial itself
was a very difficult time, especially given the exceptional
media coverage. The stakes too were very high: I had
to restore the good name of my family and prove that we
had been brainwashed, even though we have never been
involved in any kind of sect. After three years of struggle,
the verdict has helped us to make a fresh start.

My family has deep-rooted rural origins. They
have always, on both sides, lived in the countryside,
according to the rhythm of the seasons, handing on from
one generation to the next the simple and fundamental
values of work, honesty, sharing, and openness to others.
These simple and solid values have not taught us how to
protect ourselves against trickery, depravity, or deceit. We
have certainly been too naïve. Because of that, placed in a
context that creates paranoia, exacerbated by a situation
that is itself disconcerting, we ended up as prisoners.

Today, I sometimes have the feeling that I do not
have the right to be viewed in the same light as everyone
else: 'After all he has been through, there must be some
aftereffects'. Sensing that a judgment without the right of
appeal has been pronounced on you by certain people is
very wounding, especially when, at the same moment, one
is struggling to establish the truth and to rebuild one's life.
Like everyone else, I am scarred. But, at the same time,
this episode has shaped and strengthened me, as adversity
always does. I still have the energy of a twenty-year-old,
but I have also acquired a certain maturity as well as
strength enough to move mountains, and, quite simply,
the determination to be happy, free of any bitterness,

and with a genuine confidence in the future. Sometimes wounds reopen, but I have learned, as does everyone else, to live with that and to move on while trying to put to good use whatever life offers you.

I have got back all of my friends and some of my cousins. Our friendship was restored within five minutes and our relationship has emerged the stronger for having been put to the test. I was very touched by the welcome they gave me, after this long interlude, even if I also experienced some painful moments: finding my friends married and surrounded by their children often made me aware again of a sad truth. Tilly and Gonzalez robbed me for good and all of all those moments that, with a degree or one's first earnings in one's pocket, and without a care in the world, one shares with friends: all the marriages, all the births I was unable to be present at. I who, since my teenage years, wanted to be a father but was not able to achieve any of this, until recently when this happy ambition was finally fulfilled. Fortunately, I still have my family and my friends. My best friend has asked me to be his daughter's godfather, as though to remind me of our friendship and the happy years we spent together in Marseilles. Life is reasserting itself.

And I tell myself, besides, that this episode has been the occasion of my meeting some very fine people. I should like to thank, in particular, Edouard Braine, who was consul general in London at the time, and whose help meant so much to me...

And finally, I set up a year ago an advisory service in social and family protection. Very caught up in my work,

I also have the opportunity to work with my clients in their fascinating projects. My next priority: to construct my own family unit. I have so many plans...

Various people have encouraged me to write. I hope that this book will answer the questions they are perhaps still asking themselves. That is what I wish, with all my heart.

## Amaury

What saved us was love. It was our mother's love that got us out of this trap. Love was the only power against which Tilly could do nothing. He nevertheless used it against us: at first he divided the family, by cutting off any communication between our parents and us, as far as was possible. Then, using induced memories, he severed our emotional ties: our parents didn't love us, they were capable even of poisoning us. As for our parents, he gave them to believe that their children were to become part of an international élite: Guillaume would work at the UN, Diane would study in Edinburgh. Loving parents are ready to sacrifice anything to be able to offer this kind of undreamt-of opportunity to their children. But he reckoned without the resources and the energy that her love for us had given our mother. Nor did he take into account the love we all of us had for each other, that powerful and unifying bond that lay hidden deep within every one of us.

Having returned to the real world, I have had the good fortune to find myself just as I was before, when I was twenty years old. We remained, all of us, faithful to the values, both of our family and of our Christian faith, values of courage, purity of heart, humility, sacrifice and generosity to others. I could even mention the ideals of chivalry if this were not somewhat outdated. As to religion, I am still asking questions. I practise none. Dogma and the institutions of religion trouble me nowadays, because Tilly, who claimed to be a practising and devout Catholic, used them as part of his quest for power and domination. I reflect a great deal, however, on the universal links between all religions. I am attracted by philosophy and world religion. In short I have a profound sense of the sacred. During that whole time, I never lost it, it even helped me to rise above myself and to resist, and I developed an instinct for survival thanks to the power of faith.

Nevertheless, readjusting to the real world after I returned to Bordeaux has not been easy. I went to live with my parents in the flat that some friends had lent them. My perception of reality had been greatly affected; but the most curious part of it all is that, during these nine years, I was persuaded that I was firmly grounded in reality. We watched television, read the newspapers, went into town. When I realized that I had been living a lie for nine years, that the whole thing was simply an illusion, this discovery provoked immense anguish in me, along with a powerful need to find some reassurance, to rediscover some points of reference and a congenial environment, and to be able to live at last at my own pace, to restore to its proper perspective what I had been through.

Afterwards I had to start again from scratch, with nothing to offer except my degree. But, thanks to my psychiatrist, I started by securing a social and administrative position in order to help me reintegrate into society. I signed up for incapacity benefits and filed a CV with a charity, ACTE, in Bordeaux. I rebuilt my life slowly by living, psychologically, more or less from day to day.

Today I am doing a degree in business change management and working in a vineyard, a *grand cru classé*. I think that, professionally, I will pull through, but, psychologically and emotionally speaking, things are more complicated. It will require courage and willpower, but in the school of life the most difficult lesson for me to learn is patience. What I am proudest of is to have found again a network of friends of real quality and humanity, and a family that I love more than anything else in the world. In short, I am surrounded by affection and respect. I am beginning to be happy again, which in my eyes is a great privilege. I want to look towards the future and to live in the present. It is not possible to forget, but I must use what I have lived through to reconstruct my life. I have a duty to rise above my memories; my aim is to turn lead into gold. It is through failure that we build our lives. My experiences have taught me to be sensitive to the sufferings of others, and to increase tenfold my love of life and of other people.

## Postscript for English edition

I write this in November, 2014. It is almost five years since I broke free of that false reality, thanks to the courage and love of my mum. Starting afresh from that kind of experience is hard to do, but I really do now have the opportunity to discover and enjoy things that were barred to me for ten years.

I have met a nice, kind and genuine girl. She is helping me to learn how to accept love again. I am trying to give my trust again to a dear companion. She is the closest person I have.

I still have issues in perceiving people's real intentions, the masks and illusions of appearances. But now I have another view of things. I am very cautious when it comes to sharing my deepest weaknesses with people. Psychiatrists, family and friends are also helping me to relearn a belief in my own choices and protect them. I am also helped a lot by a few mantras that I received from my grand-parents:

- Being happy with what you have is a treasure.
- Living is an endless fight.
- Out of problems comes progress.

I am still trying to act on those mantras, as they are so profound to me. As long as I am alive I will try to live happily and face reality, even though I have such a fear of facing devastating suffering again.

# Diane

When she learned from the newspapers that Tilly was in prison, Ghislaine asserted that he was not guilty, but that he has his own reasons for accepting the situation. She told me that 'Thierry has told her that this would happen. No one should worry about it, but should carry on as before. His boss Jacques would look after everything'. She even took the same line with Natacha, Tilly's own daughter, who confirmed everything that was said in the press. As for me, I began, once again, to have doubts about everything.

One thing strikes me as I write these lines: when she was told that Thierry Tilly was in prison Mamie did not wake me up a single time that night. When Maman comes with my godfather and his wife to collect me I say to myself: 'That's it then; it's all over at last'. Then, when we are all together again, I curl up in a corner of the sofa and I say to myself: 'OK, it's finished. But I need a little more time and space in order to believe what they're telling me'. I no longer trust anyone. I need to regain confidence in myself and other people. It is a difficult moment.

Our great strength, one that Thierry Tilly underestimated, is the love that exists between us. The proof of this is that, when he asked Papa to seek a divorce, after Maman left, Papa was unwilling to have anything to do with the papers. It was Amaury and I who were landed with it. Going to collect papers for the divorce of your parents is something it is very hard to do.

At the time, what struck me was that Papa had not turned his back on his marriage. I, a deeply wounded daughter, abandoned by her mother, could not understand this. When I asked him why he was sticking by it, he replied quite simply: 'We entered into it, the two of us, on the same day; if your mother wants a divorce, the two of us will have to abandon it on the same day'. I realized that there is such a thing as real and true love, in spite of all that had been said, over and over again, for years.

I return, in due course, to France. I want, above all else, both to prove to myself that Tilly has not destroyed me, and to get my life back. Today I am doing a course in chemistry. It looks on the face of it as if everything is going well, but you do not emerge unscathed from such a story. For years we were, above all, not allowed to show any weakness or to complain; even today I find it difficult, when something is going wrong, to acknowledge it. Besides, although life has reclaimed me, I am still apprehensive about my future. When you have been brainwashed, when someone has planted false memories in you, it is difficult to break out of this mentality. When I emerged from it, I got in touch again with my cousins who had not been dragged into this history, and with my godmother in particular. I talked a great deal to her, asked her endless questions, sometimes in different ways, in order to check that she gave the same answers. She has helped me, enormously, to unravel these tangled memories. I am very grateful to her. Today our relationship is strong, and very genuine. At the age of twenty-seven, I have the feeling that I have been robbed of ten years of my life, years that are essential if one is to lay down a sure foundation for the years to come.

I sometimes feel utterly exposed. The experiences I should have had when I was younger are missing. For fear of being manipulated all over again, I need to test people. And above all I am afraid of being abandoned. During my ordeal I was separated from my parents against their wishes. And I felt abandoned. It's no good my telling myself that this was utterly and entirely against their wishes, I am still haunted by this memory.

As with many children, it is from my parents that I seek answers to the questions I ask myself. In my case, for more than ten years I relied entirely on what Thierry Tilly, my aunt and my cousins told me. No one confirmed or denied what was said to me, and this left the door wide open to the false memories which had been planted in me, some of which I am still trying to disentangle.

I am filled with the most bitter resentment against Thierry Tilly. He turned us into executioners and victims. He made me believe things that were untrue and that have affected me deeply. It will take me a long time to rebuild myself, but I will get there. I have discovered within myself a strength of character, and an instinct for survival, which I will never lose. He interfered with every aspect of my life. He ruined my parents financially, and also took a malicious pleasure in trying to destroy our family. Because of him, I have learned the facts of life, 'the hard way', but above all I have had to deal with wholly abnormal situations.

I remember one day, during the hearing, when I began to laugh without reason. It was a nervous reaction: either I laughed or I burst into tears, as sometimes happens at funerals. What were we doing there ?

Thierry Tilly knew perfectly well that, to take us over, he must separate us from our parents. The strength of this family, but also its weakness, is the gap between the generations that exists at its very heart. I am the youngest of the grandchildren, and my nearest cousin is six years older than I am.

We are a family in which certain members have an opinion on everything and everyone, and in which comparisons are readily made between people of the same age or the same sex. I was often compared with Guillemette who is eight years older than I am. I certainly always wanted to grow up too quickly, but when you find yourself surrounded by 'grown-ups', with no one of your own age, this happens quite naturally. Differences in age are completely forgotten. And, since a young girl of fifteen will never have had the same experiences as a young woman of twenty-three, this leads to a loss of self-confidence.

Our strength and our weakness has been that there were eleven of us caught up in this sinister system. We all of us had moments of doubt and of impatience. When one or other of us lost his or her nerve, there was always someone to help them back into the saddle. I remember on one occasion trying to cheer up Guillemette, who was fed up with the whole situation. If it was not I who was cheering her up, it was she who was cheering me up.

In this history we have all been, after all, very lucky. My parents, it is true, have lost everything. Yes, Tilly has robbed us of ten years of family life, but we have the good fortune to belong to a loving and forgiving family, as well as heaps of friends, and lots more years to live together and enjoy one another's company.  I know that my parents are worried about their own future and ours, even if I am convinced that the worst is behind us.

Fortunately, I have found again, not only my parents and my brothers, but, intact and unaltered, their affection too.  We now talk more freely among ourselves.  This is perhaps because the most important thing that our troubles have taught us is that there are no longer any taboo subjects between us.

We will do anything for each other, the five of us: we will move mountains.  Just as we were able to count on our parents to look after us until we became adults and responsible for ourselves, so we, their children, will be there to give them everything they deserve and need. What pains me in this whole story is to see that, for years, I forged ties which I thought were very strong with my cousins and my aunt whereas, since our liberation, they do not seem to want to maintain this contact, which makes me very sad.

## Charles-Henri

Today I am re-establishing contact with a wider world. Will I be able to re-establish myself? Why not, given that my financial situation leaves me no choice in the matter? Unlike Tilly, who will be able to live with complete impunity with the money he has stolen from us, I will be forced to work until my dying day.

I don't blame anyone for anything.  I don't know what my reaction would have been if I had viewed this history from the outside. Regret serves no purpose, but we do need to understand. Why weren't the numerous interventions by members of our extended family, some of them highly placed, able to avert this disaster? Would we, without my immediate family's insistence, have laid ourselves wide open to Tilly's cruelty? These are questions we must ask ourselves. But first we must think of today and of tomorrow.

I emerge from all this bearing the guilt of not having had the perspicacity to avoid falling into the trap. Nor have I lived up to the trust that my parents and parents-in-law placed in me by preserving and maintaining what they entrusted to me. Throughout these ten years I have believed I was fighting to protect my family, whereas in fact I was forcing them back against a wall. Today I remain somewhat damaged, but not destroyed. My energy and force are diminished, but I am recovering my resilience.

I am fortunate to be where I am, surrounded by my family, and in a position to write these few lines. Today, my strength prospers and grows, with five of us to strive together and together to have faith in tomorrow.

## Christine

Neither for me nor for my family was this story finished after the sentence was passed. But we were glad that on appeal the sentence was increased to the maximum, ten years.

But we still have unanswered questions. What, for example, has happened to the money Tilly stole from us?  We now know that he gave part of it to Gonzalez, who has profited from it immensely.  He put the rest into accounts in England and in Belgium.  But doubtless in other places too, in tax havens to which we know he has gone on several occasions.  Tracfin, the Ministry of Finances service for fighting money-laundering, has followed up various leads, and made some calculations: there remain unaccounted for about two million euros. Two million hidden somewhere which will be ready and awaiting the crook when he leaves prison.

The loss of Martel remains a grievous wound in Charles-Henri's heart.  Not that he was ever attached to the place for its material value, but he felt himself responsible for it.  Martel had not been given to him, it had been entrusted to him.  His duty in inheriting it amounted to maintaining it, making it prosper and then handing it on. As the first Védrines ever to lose land and property belonging to the family, he feels guilty.  He has decided that his duty to his children consists in recovering this asset and is doing everything he can to have annulled the two sales that have taken place since we left the property.  The sales were strewn with irregularities, but the task is arduous and uncertain.

I understand this and I support him in his new fight.  But in addition to this I am preoccupied with somewhat different things.  Ruined though we are, we still possess an inexhaustible and indestructible treasure, but which must nevertheless be maintained : the affection and loyalty of our friends, and of my family.  When, under Tilly's influence, we shut the door on them and then completely disappeared, they never abandoned us in spite of the pain we were causing them. They simply increased their efforts on our behalf, and never faltered in their loyalty towards us. And at the first call for help, they came at once, without the least reproach, the least hesitation, and surrounded us. They saved us, and still help us to live and to rebuild our lives.

Above all, we have recovered our three children, who are taking on, with great courage, what we have put them through. I am very proud of them.

The little fault-lines that existed between us, as they do in all close-knit tribes, were exploited and aggravated by Tilly for his own ends, and none of us was able to offer any resistance. Every one of us has been manipulated, but the treatments inflicted on us have been very diverse. And, with the ordeal now behind us, Charles-Henri and I are the only ones to have lost everything. His sister and his brother can return to their previous existence in their own homes, which were spared when disaster struck.

Today, we must all of us reflect upon what it was that drew each of us in turn into this maelstrom. We must analyse, as objectively as possible, what this implies about each of us, so that we may be able to forgive ourselves.

As to our family unit, ourselves and our three children, I think we never really lost them even at the worst moments when, under pressure as we were, there was a great danger of our becoming estranged from each other. It seems to me that there is a reason for this: that deep within the heart of each of us there remained, ingrained, the certainty that we loved one another.

And in spite of the wounds we have received, and the suffering we have endured, I believe that we will succeed, all five of us, in remaining a family.   Fragile, damaged, but united.

I have set myself a task:  to help my children and my husband come back to life again.   This is not an easy undertaking.  We have to ask ourselves questions we would doubtless have preferred not to face, and to confront our failings and our contradictions.  It imposes on us a curious kind of dialogue: one that is no longer between parents and children, but between adults.   My children have passed from childhood to maturity  under the most brutal and distressing circumstances imaginable. From now on we will always be a family that shares a strange and painful experience.

Every one of us has, at one moment or another, used the same words to express this: that we must 'turn this failure into a strength'.  It's not a question of us erasing the past but of making a new start.   Nothing in either family, nor in our own characters had prepared us for such an experience.  We should like to forget it, but we cannot.  We should prefer to be free of the weight of the memories, to be rid of them, but they return, unbidden, by night or by day, like wounds that, unexpectedly, re-open and bleed.   Nothing but the happiness of my children can cure me.  I have faith in tomorrow.

## Postscript for the English edition:

Today, in 2014, in my Bordeaux apartment I turn over in my mind the events that made up our family tragedy. It is difficult to express my true feelings, but the trial and its psychological aftereffects have allowed me to understand better what has happened.

Even so, the daily round is not always easy to deal with: there are still a few regrets, a shared guilt and a sense of injustice. As well as having ruined and humiliated me, Tilly, by the barbarity of his actions towards me, has left a mark on my soul, and the damage to my hips means that I have been compelled to stop working. I am trying to distance myself from those events and experience a kind of 'happy nostalgia.'

I am helped and comforted by the presence of our friends and certain members of the family who support me unstintingly when I am feeling low. The first step in rehabilitation has been our recognition by the justice system in our country as victims, in the course of the two trials which I hope will lead to new laws concerning brainwashing.

Like many mothers it is the future of my children which shapes my determination and my energies. I am proud and touched by the courage which my three children have displayed since their return to reality. Guillaume has continued his studies in Paris. He invested a great deal in the preparation of the court cases in France and England before setting up his own practice providing an advisory service for social and family protection. Life has returned to normal, both emotionally and professionally thanks to his unfailing energy.

Amaury has bravely and successfully resumed his university studies, and rejoined the job market with good qualifications. Every day, he fights successfully to heal the wounds resulting from Tilly's destructive activities during his confinement.

Diane, having completed her chemistry degree, is preparing to complete her studies in management training. Her natural energy is what the drives her to carry on.

All three have refound groups of friends who have help them to rebuild social, professional and emotional lives.

My husband has resumed his private practice in gynaecology. He values his good fortune in being able to recover the type of professional practice he loves, even though he sometimes regrets not being able to carry out the plans which he had prepared so painstakingly, particularly for Martel.

Tilly's diabolical schemes compel us today to face costly and exhausting legal proceedings. Each time, we are plunged back into the nightmare of the past.

Our story is without parallel and we are regularly called upon to retell it, both in France and abroad. My aim is to try to bring out the reality of the brainwashing we suffered so as to prevent others falling into a similar trap.

My happiness today comes from being surrounded by my family and rediscovering our reserves of family love.

Charles-Henri and I are going to celebrate our fortieth wedding anniversary next June. Now, I entrust the past to Mercy, the present to Grace, and the future to Providence.

# Acknowledgments

Our rescue was made easier by the exceptional help we received from all sides. Bobby – Robert Pouget de St-Victor – for example, who, it can safely be said, played a decisive part in the escape. Our counsel, Maître Benoît Ducos-Ader, Maître Daniel Picotin and Maître Nathalie Pignoux, have stayed with us and supported us throughout the whole of the investigation and the hearing, unstintingly, and with the utmost competence and humanity.

We should like to thank the family and the nephews who supported Amaury and Diane financially, so that they could resume their studies. Nor can we forget the ANF (the Association for the Mutual support of French Nobility), for the scholarships they gave our children, or some of the individual members who, of their own accord, helped and stayed with us. Our thanks, too, to the circle of family and friends who organized continuous prayer meetings to try to extricate us from our difficult situation.

All of this has meant a great deal to us, and has touched us profoundly.

A great deal is owed to the support of the French Medical Association for Charles-Henri's professional life.

The greatest thanks to our family and friends who welcomed us back and helped us reestablish ourselves in 'real life.' In particular, Dominique and Marie-Hélène Hessel who among other good deeds put us up for many long months.

Our thanks also go to:

The association, 'Friends of Christine de Védrines'.

Coralie, Diane's godmother, for long and affectionate conversations over cups of tea which allowed me to separate myself from so many 'false memories.'

Edouard Braine, Consul General of France in London, who was often present at our side.

Alain Juppé, mayor of Bordeaux, Alain Rousset, President of the Regional Council of Acquitaine, and Philippe Madrelle, President of the general Council of the Gironde. It is thanks to their financial support that we were able to organize the second 'exit counselling' and recover the whole family.

The exit counseling team, who acted with such great professionalism and humanity and with respect for everyone.

Tom Sackville, president of FECRIS (Fédération Européenne des Centres de Recherche et d'Information sur le Sectarisme)

CCMM (Centre Contre les Manipulations Mentales) and its regional branch, INFOSECTES Aquitaine

UNADFI (Union Nationale des Associations de Défense des Familles et de l'Individu Victime de Sectes)

MIVILUDES (Mission Interministérielle de Vigilance et de Lutte contre les Dérives Sectaires)

The community of the Sisters of Notre Dame, Oxford.

Dr. Daniel Zagury for everything he has done to help us, including his perceptive analysis prepared for the Court and included as an Appendix.

# Editor's Note

On November 13<sup>th</sup> 2012 Thierry Tilly and Jacques Gonzalez were sentenced by the Criminal Court in Bordeaux to eight and four years imprisonment respectively: Thierry Tilly for the illegal arrest, kidnap, imprisonment or arbitrary detention of a hostage within a seven day period in order to facilitate an offence or crime, for violence against a vulnerable person, for the criminal exploitation of the ignorance or the weakness of a person in a state of psychological or physical subjection, and under the further pressure of having suffered, through some means, some impairment of their judgment; Jacques Gonzalez for complicity in the criminal exploitation of the ignorance or the weakness of a person in a state of psychological or physical subjection, resulting from some form of pressure or some technique of a kind likely to impair their judgment; and for repeated receipt of stolen goods. Tilly appealed and this case came before the Court of Appeal in Bordeaux on 22<sup>nd</sup> April 2013. The Court of

Appeal issued its decision on 4th June 2013, when they confirmed the verdict and increased Tilly's sentence to ten years, the maximum allowed.

The civil parties to this lawsuit were: Philippe de Védrines, Brigitte Martin, Ghislaine Marchand, François Marchand, Guillemette Marchand-Delfino, Charles-Henri de Védrines, Christine de Védrines, Guillaume de Védrines, Amaury de Védrines and Diane de Védrines.

Thierry Tilly is now appealing to the highest court in France, and says that if necessary he will take it right up to the European Court of Human Rights.

# Appendix:
## Report of Dr. Daniel Zagury

At the request of the examining judge I have questioned the ten members of the Védrines family, including Christine de Védrines, at the time alleged victims of Thierry Tilly. My role as an expert witness to the court prevents me, of course, from revealing anything I have learned in confidence, from making any value judgements, or from commenting in any way on the legal process. It means that I can draw only upon what has been said publicly during the course of the trial.

Having, many of them, travelled a long way, sometimes from abroad, each member of the family expressed in his or her own way the wish to be understood, but also to understand, after ten years of a terrible experience, ten years in hell. Like everyone else, I am, before being a psychiatrist, an ordinary person who watches television, listens to the radio and reads the newspapers. I had then, naturally enough, my own prejudices, and I imagined an ancient and degenerate family, clinging to its grandiose myths of past glory, taken for a ride and duped by a crook. I imagined them, then, to be naïve, and not very intelligent. To my great surprise, what I found were two generations of men and women, more or less united, in spite of the conflicts and wounds that exist within every family. I encountered a diversity of types of personality among the parents' generation and also among the children, cousins to each other. It is, moreover, this common adherence to a family myth, and the bond this creates, that raises the question of 'family transference'. But before defining 'family transference' it may be useful look into what we mean by 'transference', that phenomenon described by Freud himself, the father of psychoanalysis, as so strange.

In my experience there is an essential element, which is common to the relationship between the guru and his followers, between the pseudo-therapist and his patients, and between the crook and his victims: this common element we call abusive transference, a distortion, that is, of the transference relationship, a kind of influence that one mind exercises over another mind. I cannot stress this too much: there is nothing magical nor supernatural about Christine de Védrines or any of the others becoming victims, there is no abracadabra, there is no bewitchment. The Védrines were not hypnotized for ten years. All these descriptions are too weak. It was not a question of people being under some mental subjection, under some influence, of them being objects of mental manipulation, but rather of them being victims of psychological enslavement and subjugation, of totalitarian subjection, of them being denied any autonomy whatsoever.

What do we understand by 'abusive transference'? Sigmund Freud noted the existence of transference, first as an obstacle to treatment, then as the principal instrument of that treatment. Francis Pasche, in 1975, defined transference thus: 'it is a re-living of desires, emotions and feelings experienced towards one's parents in earliest childhood and directed towards a new person.' We are speaking here of normal feelings, but which are exacerbated during psychoanalytical treatment. They exist in everyday life, for example in the relationship between doctor and patient or master and pupil. Transference recreates the earliest time of life, when everything the child needs for survival depends on parental love. Transference is therefore stamped with the seal of the unconscious, the infantile and the irrational.

The power that was exercised by Thierry Tilly over the whole of the family can be considered, therefore as a form of abusive transference. A person works his way into the family. Very quickly, he dominates it. He is at one and the same time elevated and co-opted. He is 'assumed to know', in Lacan's formulation, through an omnipotence which is attributed to him, and the illusion of which he does everything in his power to maintain. He gives proofs and evidence of it. It is essential to understand that this all-powerful being is also the intermediary of tutelary powers that are greater than he (God, destiny, fate…). He is the saviour, the guardian and protector. Very important people, moreover, even international institutions, know everything about you and are watching over you. It becomes essential, then, vital, to submit in order to exist.

Everyone finds himself in a position of infantile regression, of subjection. And so rationality, logic, intelligence, the critical faculty, or quite simply autonomy of thought, disappear.

Intelligence is always present but as though it is lying fallow. It is inhibited. This, in particular, explains why, when the control is lifted, the subject very quickly finds again his former points of reference and his critical faculties. He has always known that he was the victim of illusions and mirages, but this knowledge was not consciously available to him, because it was repressed.

At which point the dominant impression will be that of the end of a long parenthesis, during which the autonomous subject had disappeared. This was also the case with his values and his ideals. The intensity of infantile regression is such that a wife can impugn her husband, parents can institute proceedings against their children, a father believe that he is not the biological father of a child, a daughter accuse her mother of sexual abuse... However monstrous these fabrications, if the guru, the saviour, the guardian and protector has said that it is so, it is because it is true, and moreover every subsequent event will support the suggestion, and turn it into conviction. By occupying a central place, the person who abuses transference within a family deprives everyone of their role and their place, subverting family ties. Everything then becomes possible, since in the absence of conventions and constraints the abuser can indulge in play involving every conceivable fantastic possibility. Nothing any longer causes surprise.

Christine de Védrines, like all the other members of the family, has remarked upon Thierry Tilly's great skill in listening to his interlocutors, and in giving them the impression that he is promoting their welfare. He has, in a sense, acted like a completely deviant therapist. It may seem shocking to compare transference as it is used in psychoanalytical treatment with the power employed by the guru or the conman. But when referring to abusive transference we must bear in mind that, while its springs are the same as in those other cases, there is, obviously, a total divergence of outcomes. Psychoanalytical treatment aims to restore to the patient his or her freedom and autonomy of thought. Abusive transference has as its objective to enslave and to exploit.

Let us consider some of these differences:

- During psychoanalytical treatment, one regresses in order to progress; during abusive transference, one regresses in order the better to be exploited.

- During psychoanalytical treatment, what is sought is the autonomy and the freedom of the patient; during abusive transference, what is sought is his or her enslavement.

- During psychoanalytical treatment, the rule that consists of saying everything and doing nothing is a mark of respect for the inner life of the patient; during abusive transference, there is a constant manipulation of the patient's inner life in order to increase his or her dependency.

- During psychoanalytical treatment, the personality of the psychoanalyst is effaced in order to become the screen that receives all the projections of the patient; during abusive transference we find, inversely, the hyper-presence of the guru, the saviour, the providential man. It is no longer a question, merely, of an omnipotence that is projected on to him: he *is* omnipotent. He invades the entire living space of the patient.

- Psychoanalytical treatment, founded on the analysis of transference, is protected by a framework, by rules, and by a professional code of ethics; abusive transference is secretive and is unanalyzed. It is the pure and shameless exploitation of a subjection that is implicit in the relationship, without any protective framework, any exterior supervision, or professional code of ethics. Its aims are money, sex, or power, and sometimes all three at once.

But the tragedy of the Védrines family cannot be reduced to the sum of the various individual cases of abusive transference. We miss the essential point if we take no account of the importance of the family transference itself. The mistake that this united family made lay without doubt in its shared belief that they were of noble lineage. In 1982, Alberto Eiguer defined family transference as being co-extensive with regressive behaviour arising from the shared psyche of the family, involving only instinctive primitive desires and what they have inherited from a long-established family tradition. It involves those parts of the individual psyche that resonate with all members of the family. It is doubtless because he perceived this family weakness, and this collective area of the family's subconscious, that Thierry Tilly derived the essential basis of his power over them. Thereafter, he was able to deploy the full range of manipulative mechanisms, adjusted to, and 'tailor-made' for, each member of the family. Everything, for this family under siege in the middle of a hostile world, had to be mediated through him.

But readers can now understand for themselves the innermost workings of all these processes. There is no substitute for personal witness, the detail that allows us to grasp immediately, without straying into the byways of theory, the very essence of the phenomena in question. Christine de Védrines' account is illuminating because it teems with details, details that are worth a great deal more than any long treatise.

Anyone hearing this story might well believe that none of this could happen to him or to her; that it is all too monstrous. Perhaps. But, before we reach such a conclusion, we ought to read Christine de Védrines' own testimony.

*Daniel Zagury*

# Index

## L

Lacaze, property sold by de
Védrines family 10, 13, 15,
17, 31, 176
Le Monde, French newspaper 52
Lorentz, Judge 238

## M

Marchais, Georges 261
Marchand, François 14, 40, 41,
69, 73, 91, 98–99, 115, 117–
118, 145–146, 148, 159–160,
166, 190–191, 204, 209, 216,
222, 226, 228, 253, 308
Marchand, Ghislaine 9–11,
14–16, 18–19, 28, 31, 33,
37–38, 40–42, 57–61, 64–71,
73–83, 87–88, 90–94, 96–100,
103–106, 108–110, 112–115,
119–121, 145, 148–151, 153–
155, 157–159, 161, 166–168,
175–176, 179, 188, 190–193,
198–204, 208–213, 217,
223–225, 228–229, 240–241,
244–247, 250, 252–255, 257,
266–269, 292, 308
Marchand, Guillemette 1, 2, 11,
65, 67, 69, 74, 78, 88, 91, 98,
101, 108, 115, 117, 119, 166,
190, 217, 222, 224, 253–254,
256, 295, 308
Marchand, Jean 11, 57, 59, 67,
68, 88, 167, 176, 179, 193,
240, 249
Marie-Hélène, Christine's friend
– see Hessel, Marie-Hélène
Martel, de Védrines family
château, near Montflanquin
10, 12–14, 16–17, 28–29,
33–34, 40, 42, 51, 65–68,
71–73, 76–78, 83–86, 88, 90,
95, 99, 100–101, 103, 106,
143, 158–160, 177, 179–180,
184–185, 190, 198, 204, 220,
229, 251, 266, 285, 298
Michel Strogoff, film 48
Mitterand, François 261
Monflanquin, Lot-et-Garonne
10, 13, 14, 19, 44, 67, 71, 76,
78, 95–98, 101, 106, 109,
111, 159, 172, 180, 181, 198,
255, 257, 285
Moonies, sect 243
'Music in Guyenne', music
festival 14, 65, 88, 190, 192

## N

Nantes, Edict of 13
Napoleon Bonaparte 143

## O

OISE. *See* Oxford International
School of English
'Operation Bow Window' 245,
248
Oxford Garden Company 161,
162, 185
Oxford International School of
English 60

## P

Picotin, Maître Daniel, lawyer 2,
173, 189, 236, 237, 239, 242,
244, 246, 249, 303
Pouget de St-Victor, Robert 3,
5, 161–162, 164–165, 169,
171–174, 185, 303
Presswell, company owned by
Thierry Tilly 39, 41, 43, 85,
178
Procol Harum 51
Pyla, de Védrines property 25, 28,
33, 38, 83, 98, 100, 101, 251